The Origins of Human Social Relations

CENTRE FOR ADVANCED STUDY IN THE DEVELOPMENTAL SCIENCES

The Origins of Human Social Relations

Edited by

H. R. SCHAFFER

University of Strathclyde
Glasgow, Scotland

Proceedings of a C.A.S.D.S. Study Group on "The Origins of Human Social Relations" held jointly with the Ciba Foundation, London, July 1969, being the fifth study group in a C.A.S.D.S. programme on "The Origins of Human Behaviour"

ACADEMIC PRESS   1971   LONDON NEW YORK

ACADEMIC PRESS INC. (LONDON) LTD.
Berkeley Square House,
Berkeley Square,
London, W1X 6BA

U.S. Edition published by
ACADEMIC PRESS INC.
111 Fifth Avenue,
New York, New York 10003

Library of Congress Catalog Card Number: 71–170756
Standard Book Number: 0–12–622550–8

PRINTED IN GREAT BRITAIN BY
Adlard & Son Ltd., Bartholomew Press, Dorking.

Contents

Aspects of Early Social Behaviour

Comparative Perspectives

Social Perspectives

Basic Processes

Membership

Study Group on The Origins of Human Social Relations
held at the Ciba Foundation, London, July 21st–25th, 1969

M. D. S. AINSWORTH
Department of Psychology,
Johns Hopkins University,
Baltimore, U.S.A.

S. AXELRAD
City University,
New York, U.S.A.

J. BOWLBY
(Chairman I)
The Tavistock Clinic,
London, Britain

S. BRODY
City University,
New York, U.S.A.

G. W. BRONSON
Department of Psychology,
Mills College,
Oakland, California, U.S.A.

W. C. BRONSON
Institute of Human
Development, University of
California, Berkeley,
California, U.S.A.

B. M. FOSS
(Chairman II)
Department of Psychology,
Bedford College,
London, Britain

J. HIRSCH
Department of Psychology,
University of Illinois,
Urbana, Illinois, U.S.A.

J. KAGAN
Department of Social Relations,
Harvard University,
Cambridge, Mass., U.S.A.

J. V. LAWICK-GOODALL
Nairobi, Kenya

M. LEWIS
Educational Testing Service,
Princeton, New Jersey, U.S.A.

H. L. RHEINGOLD
Department of Psychology,
University of North Carolina,
Chapel Hill, U.S.A.

M. P. M. RICHARDS

   University of Cambridge,
Britain

L. A. ROSENBLUM

   Department of Psychiatry,
State University of New York,
New York, U.S.A.

H. R. SCHAFFER

   Department of Psychology,
University of Strathclyde,
Glasgow, Britain

J. P. SCOTT

   Center for Research on Social
Behaviour, Bowling Green
State University,
Ohio, U.S.A.

A. STEVENS

   Horton Hospital,
Epsom, Britain

J. TIZARD

   Department of Child
Development, Institute of
Education, London,
Britain

Developmental Sciences Trust

The study group reported in this volume was organized by the Centre for Advanced Study in the Developmental Sciences in collaboration with the Ciba Foundation which kindly accommodated the group. It was held during the period when preparations were actively in progress to establish the Centre in its own premises near Oxford. Since then, however, it has unfortunately become necessary to abandon the project to establish that Centre owing to failure to obtain sufficient financial support. The description of the proposed Centre included in previous volumes in the present series therefore no longer applies.

The organization which undertook the planning of the Centre is the Developmental Sciences Trust. The demise of the Centre in no way affects the existence of this Trust which will continue to carry out its purpose by other means. This purpose is to promote the growth of knowledge about the development of human behaviour and the factors that influence it. More specifically, the Trust aims, first, to stimulate and co-ordinate research in directions where it is most needed and to foster among scientists and teachers in these fields a developmental and multi-disciplinary perspective on human nature; second, to encourage the application of knowledge from the developmental sciences by those, in all sectors of society, engaged in coping with or preventing human problems.

The Trust is now being reorganized. In the meantime it will ensure that the proceedings of each of the five study groups already held as part of its initial programme will be published as planned.

Preface

The present volume is the result of a meeting, extending over several days, of a group of individuals all actively involved in the investigation of early social behaviour. This topic has for long been of interest to developmental scientists—partly because, according to some, the earliest relationship is thought in some way to form a prototype for all subsequent relationships, and partly because the lack of opportunity to form social bonds in early childhood is known to produce various more or less serious forms of behavioural pathology. Yet it is only comparatively recently that empirical data about the nature of the infant's social behaviour have become available; indeed, only in the last decade have systematic attempts been made to map out the developmental sequence of such behaviour and to isolate the variables which affect its course. Now an increasing number of investigators is becoming interested in this area, and it is therefore useful to bring together the efforts of some of these individuals in order to consider the direction which their research has taken, the data they have accumulated, and the theoretical assumptions on which their work is based.

At the study group a number of research reports and theoretical papers were presented and discussed, and in addition the group considered in several unscheduled sessions a variety of themes which the members wished to explore further. From these deliberations it will become apparent that the study of early social behaviour is currently undergoing a number of changes and that these involve, above all, a widening of the research worker's focus. This can be seen, for example, in the increasing attention paid to such individual difference factors as the sex variable and its influence on the infant's interpersonal relationships. It emerges also from the realization that striking variations may occur between social classes and cultural groups in the manifestation and shaping of early sociability. And in addition one may note that investigators are no longer exclusively preoccupied with the positive aspects of the infant's relationship with the mother but that consideration is also being given to such phenomena as infant aggression, maternal rejection, and the waning of attachments. The build-up of the relationship is still of interest, but so are the forces disruptive to the bond. Finally, a more cautious use is now beginning to be made of comparative material: the tendency automatically to take chicks or rhesus monkeys as models for man is being increasingly resisted as we are becoming aware of the influence of species differences as well as of species similarities. All these are signs of maturity, for they indicate a willingness to examine the individual's behaviour in the wider context of his specific biological equipment and particular social environment and thus to take into account a great many more variables and processes than had been considered previously.

The discussions of the study group were all recorded and subsequently transcribed in their original form. Inevitably, however, the editorial process has involved a great deal of abbreviation and re-arrangement. While so much loss both of material and of the original spontaneity of the discussions is to be regretted, it is clearly in the reader's interest to be given as concise and lucid an account of the group's deliberations as possible. It is worth stressing, therefore, that for the participants the meeting provided a most stimulating opportunity for the exchange of ideas. Much of the benefit of such a gathering lies in the diversity of professional disciplines, theoretical orientations, and empirical approaches represented among the members and in the discovery that new insights into a common problem may be provided by adopting diverse points of view. It is hoped that this stimulating effect can be translated into new research, for therein lies the ultimate benefit of such a meeting— both for the participants and for the readers of the proceedings.

The preparation of this volume was greatly helped by a number of people. In particular, I want to express my gratitude to Miss Rena Fenteman, whose conscientiousness and expertise made her the ideal sub-editor. Mrs. Anna Greenwood undertook most competently the arduous tasks of preparing the index and of proof reading. I am also grateful to the C.A.S.D.S. secretarial staff for transcribing the recorded sessions, and wish to express my special thanks to Mrs. Elizabeth Elder for the great care she took in preparing the typescript.

University of Strathclyde   H. R. SCHAFFER
Glasgow
January 1971

Aspects of Early Social Behaviour

Social Interaction in the First Days of Life[1]

M. P. M. RICHARDS and JUDITH F. BERNAL

University of Cambridge

INTRODUCTION

THE OBSERVATIONAL STUDY of mother–infant interaction which we are carrying out in Cambridge seems particularly relevant to a theme of close interest to this study group, namely the problem of reductionism. It has been argued that physiology provides a way round some of our behavioural problems and that physiological techniques will provide more objective and "truer" measures than our behavioural criteria. We strongly disagree with this viewpoint because we do not believe that description at the physiological level can ever explain phenomena at the behavioural level. This is perhaps best illustrated by an example. If a visually interesting object is presented to an alert 1-month old infant a number of behavioural changes follow fairly predictably. The infant turns his head towards the object and visually fixates it. At the same time his body movements are reduced and his arms, hands, and fingers may be orientated with respect to the object. Various physiological changes are also likely to be correlated with the presentation of the stimulus; and characteristic alterations in the EEG, heart rate, and respiration patterns may be recorded. These physiological changes do not, however, explain the observed behaviour, because knowledge of the physiology alone would not tell us what behaviour to expect from the infant. Knowledge and description at the behavioural level are essential for predicting behaviour. Ideally one would like to have description and analysis at both these levels as well as understanding of the transfer functions between them (see Hutt, Lenard, and Prechtl, 1969).

[1] We thank the Nuffield Foundation for the generous grant which supports our work. Our gratitude also goes to the mothers and midwives—without whose co-operation our research would be impossible—for their patience, assistance, and encouragement.

In our own work we are attempting to describe and analyse mother–infant interaction at many levels, from the sociological to the physiological, and to explore the transfer functions between each level. We shall illustrate this in more concrete terms by describing some of our preliminary results (see also Richards and Bernal, 1971).

METHODS

The plan of our study is to follow 150 infants and their mothers from the time of birth until the infants are 60 weeks old. The sample is selected to be medically and socially "normal" and excludes the extremes of the socio-economic distribution. All the infants are born at home (like almost half the population in Cambridge), and are first or second children.

The aim of our research is threefold. We want to describe some of the behaviour of an infant in his first year of life; we want to delineate some aspects of the environment in which the infant grows up; and we shall attempt to assess the influences of this environment, particularly the mother's behaviour, on the course of development. We assume a two-way behavioural interaction between the mother and her child; the behaviour of each will be influenced by, and will in turn partially determine, the behaviour of the other. Though it is not completely possible, either theoretically or practically, we would like to make independent assessments of both mother and infant at the beginning, then observe their interaction, and go on to describe the infant's development as a function of his individual characteristics seen at birth and his interaction with his mother. Independent assessment of mothers presents great problems as one cannot study maternal behaviour in the absence of an infant, and his particular behaviour may well colour his mother's maternal behaviour. We hope to obtain partially independent assessments by behavioural analysis of the interactions and, in addition, we are observing mothers with two successive infants.

Assessing the infant as an individual is perhaps rather easier, and to this end we have been using a variety of neurological and other procedures, mostly on the 8th day of life. However, our initial assumption that infants of this age are relatively uninfluenced by their mothers may have been unwise. A preliminary analysis of our results suggests that there may be behavioural differences related to maternal treatment as early as the 8th day and we are re-examining the question of an earlier assessment. The major difficulty with this is that, nearer birth, individual differences may be swamped by the effects of obstetric medication and other factors associated with delivery.

The procedures used in the study are given in detail elsewhere (Richards and Bernal, 1971), so these will be described briefly. Names of mothers who fulfil our criteria are provided by the midwives responsible for their deliveries. The mothers are interviewed about 2 to 6 weeks before their expected date of confinement. This interview covers social and medical topics and some of the mother's intentions about child care. We attend the delivery of about a third of the mothers in the sample to observe their initial reactions to their infants. When we are not present basic medical data are recorded by the midwife in charge. On the 2nd, 3rd, 8th, 9th, and 10th days we observe the infant being fed, and throughout the whole of this period the mothers keep a diary for us on a pre-coded form.

On the 8th day, the infant is neurologically examined by the Groningen method (Prechtl and Beintema, 1964) and other behavioural assessments are made. At all the visits the mother is asked a number of questions about her infant and her attitudes towards him. Follow-up visits are made at 8, 14, 20, 30, and 60 weeks, but in this chapter we shall be concerned with the first 10 days only.

METHODOLOGICAL ASSUMPTIONS

In the current atmosphere of methodological confusion and uncertainty in the social sciences, it seems desirable to state one's methodological assumptions explicitly.

Our primary aims are descriptive. We do not believe that we have sufficiently detailed knowledge of the interactions of mother and infant behaviour to begin research by formulating hypotheses for falsification. However, description is impossible without a theoretical framework which provides a basis for choosing the aspects of behaviour to be described and the categories to be used for their description. Our framework is biological and particularly reflects thought in population biology and ecology. Thus we are looking at variation within a single sample rather than comparing two or more groups in the more usual manner of work based on the neodarwinian paradigm of typological thought and the "ideal type". Our ecological background leads us to view the mother and child as part of a much wider social and environmental system. The interactions within such a system mean that it must be analysed as a whole: attempts to view the child independently of the world that surrounds him are bound to lead to distortion. It is for these reasons that we collect a good deal of sociological data.

Within this descriptive framework we do have some rather low-level hypotheses which have guided our work. For example, it seems likely that drugs given to a mother during labour will pass into the infant's blood stream and so influence his behaviour after birth. His changed behaviour will influence the maternal behaviour he receives and may set a drug-induced "style" of maternal interaction. These low-level hypotheses have led to concentration on particular aspects of behaviour and the environment. But the main work of setting up hypotheses will begin only as the study is completed. By then, we hope we shall be in a position to state firm and detailed hypotheses which may be falsified by future work. For these reasons we regard this project as a pilot study.

RESULTS AND DISCUSSION

To illustrate some of the points made earlier we present some preliminary results for the first 38 mothers recruited to our sample. As the number of mothers is very small we are forced to use the simplest kinds of analysis. We have divided the group by a number of major variables— parity, sex of infant, method of feeding, and obstetric medication—and compared measures of mother and infant behaviour in each subsample. We have found differences for all these variables and evidence of interaction between them. A more subtle behavioural analysis and a more sophisticated statistical treatment to parcel out variance between the relevant factors must await a larger sample. Meanwhile, we present a preliminary analysis of the behaviour of breast and bottle feeding mothers and their infants and of the influence of obstetric medication. We hope that, in particular, this will illustrate the importance of multilevel analysis.

Breast and Bottle Feeding

On the 8th day a test of non-nutritive sucking is carried out as part of the neurological examination. A sterile teat, plugged with cotton wool, is placed in the infant's mouth for 4 minutes. This is done just before a feed when all infants are awake and most are crying. The amount of sucking in the 4 minutes and the latency to cry on removal of the teat are recorded. The results indicate that breast-fed infants suck at higher rates and are more responsive to removal of the teat than bottle-fed infants (Table I). This is consistent with a previous finding that an anthropometric examination on day 3 or 4 produces higher levels of arousal in breast-fed than bottle-fed infants (Bell, 1966).

How may we explain the differences in response to the sucking test in the bottle- and breast-fed infants? There seem to be three main possibilities. Some aspects of the post-natal environment may differ in the two groups. Nutrition is the most obvious factor but there may be other differences in the treatment received by the infants. Second, there may be aspects of maternal behaviour apart from the actual feeding which co-vary with feeding method. The third possibility is that the infants in the two groups were different from the start. Perhaps the factors that lead a mother to choose a particular feeding method are associated with others that influence the pre- and post-natal behaviour of the infant.

TABLE I. NON-NUTRITIVE SUCKING IN BREAST- AND EBOTTL-
FED INFANTS ON DAY 8 OR 9

	Mean no. of sucks in 4 min	Median latency to cry after removal of teat (sec)	Mean crying totals for 90 sec after removal of teat (sec)
Breast-fed $N = 20$	213·0	15	24·0
Bottle-fed $N = 11$	171·4	38	16·8
Two-tailed Mann-Whitney U test	$p < 0·10$	$p < 0·02$	NS

We cannot test this directly as we lack enough data on the independent behaviour of the infant before the 8th day, but we can compare the two groups of mothers to see how similar they are. We have no direct information about nutritional factors but it should be remembered that formulas contain about twice as much protein as human milk and that bottle-fed infants are likely to receive larger volumes of food in the first few days before the breast feeders' milk has "come in". There will also be variation in the experience of objects sucked, and the bottle-fed infants will have had more experience sucking on a teat like the one used in the sucking test.

Our observations show that the breast-fed infants are fed for somewhat longer periods than the bottle-fed infants (Table II). These results are based on a 30-second recording grid; each behaviour category is noted as occurring or not occurring in each 30-second period. In addition, these observations suggest that breast-fed infants are touched, talked to, and smiled at more frequently. The mothers' diaries show that the breast infants spend less time in the cot and this seems to be true from the 1st day. Thus there is evidence for several differences in the postnatal environment of the two groups.

TABLE II. OBSERVATIONAL DATA ON DAYS 2, 3, 9, AND 10
FOR BREAST- AND BOTTLE-FEEDING MOTHERS

	Mean number of 30-sec periods		Significance level of difference*
	Breast-fed (N=17)	Bottle-fed (N=10)	
Length of feed	195·6	174·1	NS
Time nipple in mouth	107·9	79·7	<0·05
On nipple with interruption	20·0	17·6	NS
On nipple with interruption as percentage of time nipple in mouth	22·4%	21·6%	NS
Touch infant	23·6	8·7	<0·05
Stimulation to suck	18·8	15·0	NS
Smile at infant†	11·0	8·6	NS
Talk to infant	68·9	45·5	<0·10

* Based on 2-tailed Mann-Whitney test.
† N for breast-fed group = 13; for bottle-fed group = 8.

As an indirect test of the possibility that the infants in the two groups differed at birth, we have compared the mothers for a number of characteristics. Their birth histories (length of labour, maternal medication, etc.) are not significantly different. But we can also go back a little further and examine the reasons for choosing particular feeding methods. Sociological work (Newson and Newson, 1963) has found that there is a correlation between feeding methods and the husband's occupation. The Newsons suggest that this correlation is explained by increased modesty and a lack of privacy for working-class mothers who are the least likely to breast feed. We find the same social class relationship (Table III) and that bottle feeding mothers had received less education. We cannot test the modesty hypothesis directly though we do find that other people are more likely to be present during bottle feeds than breast feeds (mean time others are present during feeds: breast feeders, 44 per cent; bottle feeders, 75 per cent; $p = <0·02$). Privacy does not seem to be important for our Cambridge sample as we find no difference in the number of rooms per house for the two groups (mean number of rooms: breast feeders, 3·9; bottle feeders, 4·2, difference not significant).

TABLE III. ASSOCIATION BETWEEN FEEDING
METHOD AND HUSBAND'S OCCUPATION

| | *Registrar-General's classification of occupation* | |
	Classes I and II	*Classes III and IV*
Breast-fed	16	9
Bottle-fed	2	10
	Chi-square $= 5 \cdot 5$, $p < 0 \cdot 02$	

Some other variables do seem to distinguish the two groups. The breast feeding mothers were older at the birth of their second child (26·6 years against 24·3 years, $p = \; < 0 \cdot 05$) and had a shorter gap between the births of their first two children (24 months against 31·4 months, $p = \; < 0 \cdot 10$). These two differences are also found for the social class III and IV mothers alone. Our data on contraceptive practice suggest that the bottle feeders are using less efficient methods. This, coupled with the absence of a lactational suppression of ovulation, might be expected to lead to a shorter interval between successive births. From our results we may tentatively conclude that there is a fertility difference between the two groups, perhaps related to differences in the frequency of intercourse. The mothers in the two groups also intended to have a different family size before the birth of their second child (Table IV). However, this difference disappears if the social class I and II mothers are removed from the sample.

TABLE IV. INTENDED FAMILY SIZE FOR BREAST-
AND BOTTLE-FEEDING MOTHERS

	Two children or fewer	*More than two children*
Breast-fed	10	14
Bottle-fed	12	0
	Chi-square $= 9 \cdot 13$, $p < 0 \cdot 01$	

We may conclude that bottle and breast feeding mothers differ on a number of factors apart from their social class and therefore we feel it is unwise to assume that the two groups will produce infants that will behave in similar ways.

Maternal Medication in Labour

We have examined the preliminary data for possible correlations between the infants' and mothers' behaviour, and the drugs given to the mothers during labour. Of the 33 mothers in the group for this analysis, 23 received one or two intramuscular injections of 50 or 100 mg Pethilorfan (Roche Products, Pethidine to Levallorphan Tartrate 100 : 1·25) between 9 hours and 30 minutes before delivery. In addition, in the Pethilorfan group, four mothers were given Trichloryl (Mono-sodium Triclofos), seven Sparine (Promazine hydrochlor), one Welldorm (Dichloralphenazone), and one Trichloryl and Welldorm. Two mothers who did not receive Pethilorfan were given Trichloryl. Except for three mothers who had no Pethilorfan all mothers had a variable quantity of some form of inhalant anaesthetic (Trilene, nitrous oxide and air, or nitrous oxide and oxygen).

TABLE V. PRESENCE OF EYE SIGNS (NYSTAGMUS, STRABISMUS, AND SUNSET SIGNS) IN THE PETHILORFAN AND NO PETHILORFAN GROUPS

	No eye signs	Eye signs
Pethilorfan	9	13
No Pethilorfan	10	0
Chi-square $= 7.65$, $p < 0.01$		

Note: Two infants, not included in this table, both in the Pethilorfan group, did not open their eyes during the course of the examination.

We would have liked to compute a drug score for each infant based on the dose and time of administration of Pethilorfan to the mother. However, the kinetics of placental transfer of Pethidine has not been adequately studied (Moya and Thorndike, 1963; Moya and Smith, 1965; Beckett and Taylor, 1967) and no accurate data appear to be available for Pethilorfan. Thus we are forced to make the crudest comparison—that between the infants of mothers who were given Pethilorfan at any time during labour and those who did not receive the drug.

At birth all infants were rated on three-point scales for colour, reflex irritability, and muscle tone by the midwife in charge of the delivery. The time from birth to the first cry and to rhythmical breathing was also recorded. Infants in the Pethilorfan group tended to be given a higher rating at birth and to have longer latencies to the first cry and to rhythmical breathing.

As part of the neurological examination on day 8 or 9, the presence or absence of three eye conditions, namely strabismus, nystagmus and sunset signs, was noted. More than half the infants in the Pethilorfan group showed one or more of these signs but they were not seen in any infant in the other group (Table V). The sucking test, also administered at that time, did not give statistically significant differences between the two groups but the results suggest that the Pethilorfan infants have a reduced non-nutritive sucking rate and are less responsive to the removal of the teat (Table VI). If the Pethilorfan infants do show altered sucking behaviour it is likely that this will influence the interaction with the mother. The observational data indicate that the Pethilorfan infants tended to be fed for shorter periods, to have fewer 30-second periods with the nipple in their mouths, more periods in which feeding was interrupted, and received more stimulation to suck from their mothers (Table VII).

TABLE VI. NON-NUTRITIVE SUCKING TEST RESULTS FOR THE PETHILORFAN AND NON-PETHILORFAN GROUPS

		Mean no. of sucks in 4 min	Median latency to cry after removal of teat (sec)	Mean no. of cries in 90 sec after removal of teat
Breast fed: Pethilorfan	N = 13	208·2	15	26·5
No Pethilorfan	N = 6	233·2	11	21·3
Bottle fed: Pethilorfan	N = 6	169·5	44	11·0
No Pethilorfan	N = 4	192·3	31	23·3

TABLE VII. SOME MEASURES OF MOTHER–INFANT INTERACTION IN THE PETHILORFAN AND NO-PETHILORFAN GROUPS

		Feed duration	Nipple in mouth	Nipple in mouth with interruption	Maternal stimulation
Breast fed: Pethilorfan	N = 13	184·0	99·3	24·0*	21·6
No Pethilorfan	N = 6	226·7	123·3	16·3	12·0
Bottle fed: Pethilorfan	N = 5	146·2*	65·4	20·0*	17·0
No Pethilorfan	N = 4	186·3	96·5	12·5	12·5
Total Pethilorfan	N = 18	175·8	91·8	22·8*	21·2*
No Pethilorfan	N = 11†	207·0	108·6	15·5	12·0

* Indicates comparisons between the Pethilorfan and No-Pethilorfan groups significant at <0·05 (2-tailed) on a Mann-Whitney U test.
† One additional mother who both bottle and breast fed is added here.

We have tried to determine why particular mothers are given Pethilorfan. If one uses an argument analogous to that given for the bottle–breast issue, there may be other maternal factors associated with receiving Pethilorfan which might give rise to the differences in the infants, so we could not conclude that Pethilorfan had any direct effect on the infant. The criteria used by the midwives are that the mother should be "distressed" and that, where possible, the drug should not be given within 1½ hours of delivery. Though we found that Pethilorfan was not given to mothers who had brief labours, there was no significant association between the presence of eye signs and the length of labour. We also compared the two groups on a number of other factors and did not find differences with respect to parity, maternal age, maternal education, minor complications of pregnancy, the sex of the infant, birth weight, or the method of infant feeding. So we tentatively conclude that the Pethilorfan effect is a direct one and the differences in the mother–infant interactions are the result of the infant bringing altered behavioural characteristics to that interaction.

The number of subjects is very small for a definitive drug study and clearly the importance of these changes in the newborn period cannot be evaluated until the results of the follow-up visits are analysed. But the results are very suggestive and complement those found with barbiturates and other kinds of maternal medication (Brazelton, 1961; Stechler, 1964; Kron, Stein, and Goddard, 1966).

CONCLUSIONS

Our very preliminary results indicate that breast- and bottle-fed infants may differ at birth (as their mothers do) and have a different interaction with their mothers during the first 10 days of their lives. Either or both of these influences and, of course, the quantity or quality of the nutriment they receive, may contribute to the differences in their behaviour we find on the 8th day. Looking at any one factor or any one level might have led to the suggestion that the one factor investigated was the cause of the behavioural difference found. The situation is clearly much more complicated than that. An analysis of the mode of interaction in both the groups must await the collection of more data.

Using a similar kind of analysis we can show, at least tentatively, that Pethilorfan given to the mother during labour alters the infant's behaviour and so in turn changes the mother–infant interaction. The consequences of this may be profound because it is possible that the "style" of interaction is determined in this early phase. So, even if the direct effects of the drug on the infant's behaviour disappear soon after birth, an altered mode of interaction with the mother may continue and this could have developmental consequences for the infant. This is one of the possibilities that only longitudinal studies can investigate.

The Pethilorfan findings also illustrate the necessity for analysis at many levels. In a population where mothers are commonly medicated during labour it is necessary to consider the possible influences of the drugs on the mother and infant and on their interaction. To do this successfully, the analysis must include biochemical and physiological data about placental transfer and metabolism of the drug, and data about its effects on the mother's and infant's behaviour as well as the social reasons that lead to particular mothers receiving the drug. So far we can only sketch in a few of the relevant factors and merely acknowledge the existence of some of the others.

REFERENCES

BECKETT, A. H. and TAYLOR, J. F. 1967. Blood concentrations of Pethidine and pentazocine in mother and infant at time of birth. *J. Pharm. Pharmac.* **19,** suppl.

BELL, R. Q. 1966. Level of arousal in breast-fed and bottle-fed human newborns. *Psychosom. Med.* **28,** 177–180.

BRAZELTON, T. B. 1961. Psychophysiologic reactions in the neonate: II. Effects of maternal medication. *J. Pediat.* **58,** 513–518.

HUTT, S. J., LENARD, H. G. and PRECHTL, H. F. R. 1969. Psychophysiological studies in newborn infants. *Adv. Child Devl Behavior* **4,** 127–172.

KRON, R. E., STEIN, M. and GODDARD, K. E. 1966. Newborn sucking behaviour affected by obstetric sedation. *Pediatrics* **37,** 1012–1016.

MOYA, F. and SMITH, B. E. 1965. Uptake, distribution and placental transport of drugs and anesthetics. *Anesthesiol.* **26,** 465–476.

MOYA, F. and THORNDIKE, V. 1963. The effects of drugs used in labour on the fetus and newborn. *Clin. Pharmacol. Ther.* **4,** 628–653.

NEWSON, J. and NEWSON, E. 1963. *Infant care in an urban community.* Allen and Unwin, London.

PRECHTL, H. and BEINTEMA, D. 1964. *The neurological examination of the full term newborn infant.* Spastics Society/Heinemann Medical Books, London.

RICHARDS, M. P. M. and BERNAL, J. F. 1971. An observational study of mother-infant interaction. In N. Blurton Jones (Ed.), *Ethological studies of human behaviour.* Cambridge University Press.

STECHLER, G. 1964. Newborn attention as affected by medication during labour. *Science, N.Y.* **144,** 315–317.

Discussion

The Nature of Feeding in Breast- and Bottle-fed Infants

ROSENBLUM: How do you measure the number of sucks?

RICHARDS: We count indentations.

ROSENBLUM: May there not be a difference in the *mode* of sucking between breast- and bottle-fed babies? I wonder whether there is a difference in work done by the infant in sucking which is not reflected in your suck count.

RICHARDS: That is highly likely; indeed there is some evidence to support a difference in the mode of sucking. But it is possible to define a suck in terms which apply to both groups without excluding possible differences in mode.

BRODY: Were the bottle-fed babies always fed by the mother?

RICHARDS: Almost always. Only occasionally were they fed by their father or their grandmother.

FOSS: Are these infants on scheduled or demand feeds?

RICHARDS: Most of them are on a sort of flexible schedule; they are usually fed about every 4 hours, with up to an hour's variation either way. We have not yet looked for correlations between this and feeding method, but it is our impression that there are no marked differences.

LEWIS: Is there any difference in weight between the breast- and bottle-fed babies?

RICHARDS: We rely on weighings made by the midwives, and their scales are not particularly accurate. However, there are no gross differences between the two groups on the tenth day.

Sex Differences in Nursing

LEWIS: Some of our own data indicate that girl babies are more likely to be nursed than boy babies and that they tend to be nursed for longer periods. This draws attention to the fact that right from the beginning the interaction between mother and child may be influenced by the latter's sex. We have, for instance, found some rather striking differences in the mother's behaviour, specifically in amount of touching and holding, as a function of the sex of the infant, with mothers of girls showing more of this behaviour than mothers of boys. This seems to be important, because individual maternal differences in touch tend to be reflected in the degree and type of attachment behaviour found in the infant. We have found (S. Goldberg and M. Lewis. 1969. *Child Dev.* **40**, 21) that at 1 year of age girls show more attachment behaviour towards their mothers than do boys; and, moreover, that for both sexes the amount of touching the mother provides is correlated with the amount of attachment at this age. Do your data indicate that the sex of the infant influences the mother's decision to nurse or not?

RICHARDS: We ask the mothers at the first interview what they want, a boy or a girl, and why. We wish to match their preferences with what they get, to see if it makes any difference to the choice of feeding method. A lot more cases are required for such an analysis, but it is not our impression so far that the sex of the infant influences the decision to breast feed or not. However, this factor may affect the length of the period of breast feeding. All that has been discussed in this paper applies only to the mother's initial choice and does not refer to what happens after the tenth day. Many mothers give up nursing very soon after the tenth day, but others continue for several months; quite different factors may influence this choice.

The Multiple Determination of Early Behaviour

KAGAN: It seems to me that the differential effects produced by varied methods of feeding may be quite small in contrast to the influence of the attitudinal and personality variables that are operative. I believe it is essential to control these in order to produce matched samples. When we can do that, the differences between breast- and bottle-fed infants will be persuasive, but when so many major variables are free to influence the outcome it is hard to believe in effects produced by the method of feeding *per se*.

RICHARDS: As I said earlier, the present analysis of our data is a preliminary one. We have had to rely on simple group comparisons rather than on more sophisticated techniques. One of the points I have tried to make is that before attributing differences in infants to feeding method *per se* one should look at all the factors that are correlated with choice of feeding method, and among these there may well be attitudinal and personality variables. However, even if such variables are found to be important we still need to know how these are reflected in the treatment of the infant. When we have achieved a larger number of cases we shall attempt to analyse the role of different variables, using techniques such as principal component analysis. We feel that these sorts of techniques offer a better hope than trying to form matched groups of mothers— there are just too many variables that would have to be controlled to achieve successful matching.

TIZARD: There are some problems that are really better answered by large-scale epidemiological studies, which rely upon rather simple factual data collected uniformly from representative samples of the population, whereas other problems may require a much closer analysis of functional relationships for their elucidation. We have learned, for example, that there is an association between the duration of breast feeding on the one hand and sibship order and social class on the other hand (in "non-manual" households, and with first-born children, breast feeding is persisted with for a longer period). Such a relationship can be ascertained only from large-scale studies of representative samples. If you explore functional relationships in small and perhaps unrepresentative samples you run into the problems of analysis that are so familiar in case studies of clinic populations.

RICHARDS: I quite agree about the place of epidemiological studies. When I said that this project was intended to be a pilot study for the formulation of hypotheses I did not mean to imply that the methods we are now using were necessarily the best ones for falsification of hypotheses. For problems concerned with fertility, for instance, large-scale surveys are probably required; the same is true for the effects of maternal medication during labour. A colleague, Mrs. MacClure, has begun work on this subject, using records kept by the Cambridge Public Health Department. She hopes to match birth records with school medical examination reports to see if drugs given in labour are related to the results of the school medical examinations carried out when the children are 5 years old. But for certain other problems laboratory studies are required as the next step. The effects of maternal drugs on sucking in the newborn period is one such example.

Individual Differences in Strange-Situation Behaviour of One-year-olds[1]

MARY D. SALTER AINSWORTH, SILVIA M. V. BELL,
and DONELDA J. STAYTON

The Johns Hopkins University

INTRODUCTION

IN RECENT YEARS several studies of human development have used an unfamiliar or strange situation as a setting in which to observe systematically the effect of the presence and absence of a mother-figure on the response of infants or young children to strangeness or other fear-arousing stimuli (Cox and Campbell, 1968; Collard, 1968; Rosenthal, 1967a, 1967b; Schwarz, 1968; Rheingold, 1969). In the course of a naturalistic longitudinal study of the development of infant–mother attachment, we introduced our subjects to a novel situation which was designed specifically to highlight individual differences in infants' responses. We were interested especially in the extent to which an infant could use his mother as a secure base from which to explore, in his reaction to a stranger, and in his response to brief separation from his mother. Since our situation was intended as a test, a standard procedure was followed with all subjects. The situation was composed of eight

[1] The extended project which yielded the data herein reported was supported by grant 62-244 of the Foundations' Fund for Research in Psychiatry, and by USPHS grant RO1 HD 01712. That support is gratefully acknowledged. The present classification of individual differences in strange-situation behaviour and the system of scoring of interactive behaviour therein was devised while the senior author was a fellow of the Center for Advanced Study in the Behavioral Sciences, and also owes much to discussion with fellow participants in a seminar chaired by John Bowlby at the Department of Psychiatry, Stanford University, in 1968. We also appreciate help given by the following in various aspects of the collection or analysis of the data: George D. Allyn, Mary P. Blehar, John Conklin, Elizabeth A. Eikenberg, Edwin E. Ellis, William C. Hamilton, Andrea Jacobson, Mary B. Main, Robert S. Marvin II, Eleanor S. McCulloch, and Donna Murphy. Special acknowledgment is made to Barbara A. Wittig who helped in the original planning of the strange situation.

episodes, presented in fixed order, in which the baby faced an unfamiliar environment and also a stranger both when his mother was present and when she was absent.

The strange-situation procedure proved powerful in disclosing individual differences in regard to the three classes of behaviour for which it had been originally designed. Furthermore, it has emerged as a test situation well suited to a sensitive examination of the strength and quality of the attachment behaviour an infant directs towards his mother when under stress, as well as to an assessment of the balance between such attachment behaviour and exploratory behaviour.

For some time it has seemed useful to view an attachment figure as providing a secure base from which a child may venture forth to explore the world (Blatz, 1966; Salter, 1940; Ainsworth, 1963, 1967; Harlow, 1958). The more inclusive concept of a balance between exploratory and attachment behaviour followed from Bowlby's (1969) control-systems account of the dynamic equilibrium of mother–infant interaction and from several excellent accounts of mother–infant interaction in nonhuman primate species both in the field and in captive colonies (e.g. Hinde *et al.*, 1964; van Lawick-Goodall, 1968; DeVore, 1963). The model of an attachment–exploration balance focuses on two sets of behavioural systems, each with significant species-survival functions, which operate in dynamic equilibrium. Attachment behaviours, which constitute the first system, serve to promote the proximity of infant to mother, and are dovetailed into reciprocal maternal behaviours, such as retrieving. Attachment behaviour includes not only signalling behaviours, such as smiling, crying, and vocalizing, of which even a very young infant is capable, but also, later, more active behaviours such as approaching, following, reaching, grasping, and clinging. Exploratory behaviours, which constitute the second behavioural system, include locomotion, manipulation, visual exploration, and exploratory play, which promote acquisition of knowledge of the environment and adaptation to environmental variations. On some occasions, the infant ventures away from his mother in order to explore interesting features of his surroundings; on other occasions he seeks to be near his mother or in actual physical contact with her, so that, over time, his expeditions away from her alternate with, and are in some kind of balance with, his return to her. The balance is tipped towards exploration by complex, novel, and/or changing features of the environment, provided these are not so sudden, intense, or strange as to provoke alarm. The balance is tipped towards proximity-seeking by a number of conditions, both intraorganismic and environmental.

Important among the environmental conditions which heighten a child's attachment behaviour are alarm—including alarm at the merely strange—and threatened or actual separation from his mother.

In the first episodes of the strange-situation procedure used in this study the balance is tipped towards exploration. In subsequent episodes, which become successively more stressful, the balance is tipped away from exploration towards heightened attachment behaviour. Individual differences may be assessed partly in terms of how early in the situation and how intensely and actively attachment behaviour preponderates over exploratory behaviour, but also partly in terms of the balance between attachment behaviours and antithetical behaviours, such as resisting and avoiding—a balance which will be discussed more fully later.

In a previous publication (Ainsworth and Wittig, 1969) we reported the strange-situation findings for the first 14 subjects in our sample, and our impression that individual differences were related to differences in style of mother–infant interaction throughout the first year of life. In view of the expensive and very time-consuming nature of longitudinal research, it is an attractive notion that one might in a 20-minute procedure obtain a reasonably reliable and valid assessment of the nature of the relationship that has developed between an infant and his mother. Adequate validation of our strange-situation procedure as a test of infant–mother attachment will require a series of replicatory studies with different samples. Nevertheless, it is an obvious first step towards validation to appraise the degree of congruity between the strange-situation behaviour of our infant subjects and their behaviour at home in regard to the balance between exploratory and attachment behaviour, and to explore the relation between these two measures of infant behaviour and the quality of mother–infant interaction in the last quarter of the first year of life.

METHOD

A. Procedure

The room used for the strange situation contained office furniture on one side, leaving a 9×9 foot square of clear floor space. At one end of the room was a child's chair with toys on it and near it. Towards the other end of the room on one side was a chair for the mother, and opposite it a chair for a stranger. The baby was put down between the mother's and stranger's chairs, facing the toys, and left free to move as he wished.

The situation consisted of eight episodes which succeeded each other in a standard order.[2] To supplement the description which follows, Table I is provided for easy reference. The first three episodes were pre-separation episodes and relatively non-stressful. *Episode 1* was introductory. *Episode 2* was intended maximally to elicit exploratory behaviour. The mother put the baby down in the specified place, then

TABLE I. SUMMARY OF STRANGE-SITUATION PROCEDURE

Episodes	Participants	Duration	Behaviour highlighted by episode
1	Mother, baby, experimenter	30 sec approx.	(Introductory)
2	Mother, baby	3 min	Exploration of strange environment with mother present
3	Stranger, mother, baby	3 min	Response to stranger with mother present
4	Stranger, baby	3 min*	Response to separation with stranger present
5	Mother, baby	Variable	Response to reunion with the mother
6	Baby	3 min*	Response to separation when left alone
7	Stranger, baby	3 min*	Response to continuing separation, and to stranger after being left alone
8	Mother, baby	Variable	Response to second reunion with mother

* Episode was curtailed if the baby was highly distressed.

sat in her chair, playing a non-participant role. This and most subsequent episodes lasted 3 minutes. The first stress was introduced in *episode 3* with the entrance of a female stranger, who sat in her chair quietly for a minute, conversed with the mother for a minute, and then gradually approached the baby, inviting him to play with a toy which she offered him.

Episode 4, the first separation episode, began with the unobtrusive departure of the mother. If the baby continued his exploratory play,

[2] The following materials have been deposited with the National Auxiliary Publications Service: Instructions for conducting the strange-situation procedure, instructions to the mother, instructions for coding behaviours for frequency measures, and instructions for coding socially interactive behaviours. Order NAPS document 00762 from ASIS National Auxiliary Publications Service, c/o CMM Information Sciences, Inc., 22 West 34th Street, New York, New York 10001, remitting $3.00 for microfiche or $1.00 for photocopies.

the stranger did not participate; otherwise she tried to interest him in the toys, to see whether exploratory behaviour could be sustained in the mother's absence. If, however, the baby was much distressed, the stranger tried to distract him or to comfort him, but if she was entirely unsuccessful in this, the episode was curtailed. *Episode 5* was the first reunion episode. Having entered, the mother paused for a moment near the door to give the baby an opportunity to mobilize a spontaneous response, for it was expected that the separation experience would have heightened attachment behaviour and that the baby would seek proximity or contact with her. Meanwhile the stranger slipped out. The mother had been instructed to encourage the baby to play with the toys again, since we hoped to tip the balance towards exploratory behaviour again before further stress was introduced. When the baby had resumed play the mother left, pausing to say "bye-bye". In *episode 6* we wished to observe the baby's response to a second separation in which he was left entirely alone. *Episode 7* began with the entrance of the stranger, whose behaviour, as in *episode 4*, was contingent upon the baby's behaviour. Finally, in *episode 8*—the second reunion episode—the mother returned, and after the reunion had been observed the situation was terminated.

The behaviour of the participants was observed from an adjoining room through a one-way vision window. Two observers dictated independent narrative accounts into a multiple-channel tape-recorder, which also picked up the click of a timer every 15 seconds. These narrative reports were subsequently transcribed and coded, and constitute the raw data. Reliability checks were made of the observation and of the coding, and were highly satisfactory. (See Ainsworth and Bell, 1970.)

B. Subjects

The main sample consisted of 23 white, middle-class mother–infant pairs, who were originally contacted through paediatricians in private practice. They had been observed longitudinally from birth onwards at home, in the course of visits lasting approximately 4 hours occurring at least every 3 weeks. They were introduced to the strange situation when the infants were 51 weeks old. The last home visit was made at 54 weeks.

A second sample of 33 mother–infant pairs was observed in the strange situation by Bell (1970) when the infants were 49 weeks old. It was combined with the main sample in a normative account of strange-situation behaviour (Ainsworth and Bell, 1970), and in the present analysis insofar as strange-situation behaviour is concerned.

Since longitudinal data of infant–mother interaction in the natural home environment are not available for them, however, they cannot be included in the comparisons of strange-situation behaviour with behaviour at home.

C. Classification of Strange-situation Behaviour

The tentative classificatory system proposed by Ainsworth and Wittig (1969) for the first 14 subjects identified 3 groups—A, B, and C—which were distinguished chiefly by degree of distress in the separation episodes. An impressionistic review of the interaction characteristic of each mother–infant dyad suggested, however, that responses to the mother in the reunion episodes rather than separation distress would be a better basis for classification, the concurrent validity of which was to be assessed in terms of usual behaviour at home. Consequently a new classificatory system was devised. As before, three main groups were identified, *groups A, B,* and *C*. In addition subgroups were specified— eight in all.

Despite an awareness of possible criticisms (and of the statistical disadvantages) of applying a fine-grained classificatory system to a small sample, the provision of subgroups seemed justified on two interrelated counts: differences in configurational patterns of behaviour among the various subgroups, and internal consistency within the subgroup. Analysis of strange-situation protocols revealed clear-cut variations in the behavioural configuration exhibited by infants within each of the three main groups. In other words, specific types of behaviours in response to the cumulative stresses of the strange situation clearly identified clusters of infants within a main group. Internal consistency of the subgroups refers to the high degree of similarity in the strange-situation behaviour of the individual members of each subgroup. Subsequently we found that infants classified in a particular subgroup resembled one another more closely than they resembled infants in other subgroups, not only with respect to the criterion behaviours but also with respect to behaviours which were not used as a basis for classification. Indeed, the subgroups emerged in general as offering a much more significant basis of classification of individual differences than did the more broadly defined main groups—but these statements anticipate our findings and hence will not be discussed further here.

The criteria for classification of the strange-situation behaviour of family-reared, white, middle-class 1-year-olds are given in full in succeeding paragraphs. This classificatory system is based mainly, although not exclusively, upon behaviours in interaction with the mother during the reunion episodes.

1. *Group A*. These infants show little or no tendency to seek proximity, interaction, or contact with their mothers. If picked up they show little or no tendency to cling, or to resist being released. On the contrary, they tend either to avoid the mother by ignoring her when she returns, or to mingle a welcome with avoidance responses such as turning away, moving past or away, or averting the face.

Babies in *group A* show a tendency to treat the stranger much as they treat the mother, although perhaps with less avoidance. They are either not distressed during the separation episodes or distressed only when left alone.

The two *subgroups* of *group A* share the above-mentioned characteristics, but differ from each other in regard to the points listed below.

Subgroup A_1. (1) The baby either does not greet his mother upon reunion, or the greeting is limited to a mere look or smile. He either does not approach his mother at all, or the approach is abortive—i.e. he turns back or goes past her—or he comes only after much coaxing. He tends to ignore her throughout the reunion episodes, or, indeed, more actively to avoid her, by moving away from her or by averting his face. (2) If picked up, he does not cling; he does not resist being put down, and indeed he is likely to squirm to get down.

Subgroup A_2. (1) The baby shows a mixed response to his mother upon reunion, with some tendency to greet and to approach, intermingled with a marked tendency to turn away from, avert his face from, move past, or to ignore her. (2) If he is picked up he also shows a mixed response. He may cling momentarily, and if put down he may resist or protest momentarily, but he also tends to squirm to be put down, to turn away his face while being held, and to show other signs of mixed feelings.

2. *Group B*. The infants classified in *group B* respond to the mother's return in the reunion episodes with more than a casual greeting, although some may cry rather than smile. They show either a clear-cut desire for proximity or contact with the mother, or a wish for interaction with her, and they are active in seeking what they wish.

A *group B* infant may or may not be friendly with the stranger, but he is clearly more interested in interaction and/or contact with his mother than with the stranger. He may or may not be distressed during the separation episodes, but if he is distressed it is clearly attributable to his mother's absence and not merely to being alone. He may be somewhat comforted by the stranger, but it is clear that he wants his mother.

The four *subgroups* of *group B* share the above-mentioned characteristics but differ in regard to the points listed below.

Subgroup B_1. (1) When his mother returns, the baby greets her with a smile, and is interested in establishing interaction with her, although he does not especially seek proximity to her. (2) He does not especially seek contact with his mother, and if picked up he tends not to cling or resist release. (3) He shows little or no distress during the separation episodes.

Subgroup B_2. (1) When his mother returns, the baby not only greets her but he also tends to approach her and seems to want contact with her, but to a lesser extent than babies of *subgroup B_3*. On the other hand, he does not seek across-distance interaction with her to the extent that B_1 babies do. (2) If he is picked up by his mother he tends to accept contact, but he does not cling as strongly or resist release as conspicuously as do B_3 babies. (3) He shows little or no distress in the separation episodes.

Subgroup B_3. (1) The baby responds to his mother's return, although he may cry instead of smiling, and he tends actively to approach her. He clearly wants to be in proximity to her. (2) He actively seeks physical contact with his mother, and when contact has been achieved he tends to cling to her and strongly to resist release. (3) He may or may not be distressed in the separation episodes, but if he is not distressed when his mother is absent he is clearly more active in seeking contact and in resisting release than are babies of *subgroups B_1 and B_2*.

Subgroup B_4. (1) The baby obviously wants proximity to his mother not only in the reunion episodes but throughout. He differs from the other babies of *group B* by showing insecurity even in the pre-separation episodes. He is entirely preoccupied with his mother when she is present and explores little. (2) He actively seeks to maintain physical contact with his mother by clinging and by resisting release. (3) He is clearly disturbed in the separation episodes.

3. *Group C.* From the beginning *group C* was considered a heterogeneous group, distinguished from the other groups only by what was loosely specified as "maladaptive" behaviour. One aspect of this maladaptiveness was failure to use the mother as a secure base for exploration of the unfamiliar environment, even in *episode 2* before the stresses of the stranger and of separation were introduced. Some *group C* babies do not explore actively even in the pre-separation episodes; others are fairly active in exploration but do not seem to enjoy it.

Two subgroups of *group C* were distinguished, which share the above-stated general characteristics, but which differ as follows.

Subgroup C₁. (1) The baby tends to respond positively towards his mother when she returns, perhaps with reaching, perhaps with a more active approach. (2) He is interested in contact with her and seeks to maintain it through clinging and/or resisting release, but he is highly ambivalent towards her, mingling active contact behaviour with angry, contact-resisting behaviour such as pushing away from her, hitting or kicking her, and/or pushing away or throwing down the toys through which she may attempt to mediate interaction. (3) He is distressed during the separation episodes. (4) He may explore in the pre-separation episodes but he tends to do so less enthusiastically than babies of either *group A* or *group B*, and his exploration is coloured by either anxiety or anger or both.

Subgroup C₂. (1) The baby is unable to initiate active positive behaviour in achieving proximity or interaction with his mother, even in the pre-separation episodes. He may make some abortive attempts, but these are ineffective, and he is more likely to signal than actively to approach. (2) He shows no active seeking of contact with the mother and, if contact is instituted, he tends to be ineffective in maintaining it. (3) He may or may not be highly distressed during the separation episodes. (4) Because of passivity he shows striking inability to use his mother as a secure base from which to explore.

Once the infants had been classified into the various strange-situation groups and subgroups, several analyses were conducted. The purpose of these analyses is to explore further the differences implicit in the subgroups and to ascertain whether these distinctions represent stable and meaningful individual differences. We chose to examine here four main classes of evidence in relation to the strange-situation classification: (1) the interactive criterion behaviours upon which the classification was based; (2) other strange-situation behaviours, such as exploration, crying, and search; (3) infant behaviour at home, and particularly the balance between attachment and exploratory behaviours; and (4) maternal behaviour at home.

In regard to each of these classes of evidence there are additional special procedures which must be described. Rather than segregate all procedural matters into this section, it seems preferable henceforward to intersperse procedure and findings, in the interests of clear communication of a complex and detailed body of information.

FINDINGS

A. STRANGE-SITUATION BEHAVIOUR FINDINGS

1. Strange-situation Classification

Before comparing the strange-situation groups and subgroups in regard to the four sets of variables mentioned above, let us first consider the reliability of the classificatory procedure itself and the distribution of subjects among the subgroups.

The classificatory system was established on the basis of the strange situation responses exhibited by the 23 subjects of the main project. Later, it was applied to 33 subjects of Bell's (1970) sample. Classification of these latter subjects was undertaken independently by two judges, one of whom (MDSA) classified the strange-situation protocols with no other knowledge about the subjects. The two judges differed in regard to two infants only, and one of these was but a within-group discrepancy.

TABLE II. DISTRIBUTION OF CASES AMONG
STRANGE-SITUATION CLASSIFICATION

Subgroups	Main project sample	Bell's sample	Totals
A_1	3	4	7
A_2	2	2	4
B_1	1	3	4
B_2	3	4	7
B_3	9	14	23
B_4	0	3	3
C_1	2	2	4
C_2	2	2	4
Totals	23	33	56

Table II shows the distribution of both samples across groups and subgroups. *Group B* is the largest in both samples, and *subgroup B_3* is the largest subgroup. *Subgroup B_3* may therefore be considered "normative" in terms of frequency, but also (as will be shown in subsequent analyses) it best approximates to the "norm" of behaviour expected on theoretical grounds. Furthermore, it is apparent that even in these two small samples the proportion of cases classified in each subgroup is roughly comparable—except for the fact that *subgroup B_4* is represented only in Bell's sample.

2. *Analysis of Interactive Behaviour in the Strange Situation*

Classification of behaviour in the strange situation was based mainly upon a baby's response to his mother in the reunion episodes. Response to reunion may be viewed as involving four main systems of infant–mother interactive behaviours: proximity seeking, contact maintaining, proximity avoiding, and contact resisting. These systems comprehend behaviours that had been previously conceived as specific and discrete— namely approaching, greeting, clinging, and the like. For example, whereas the most clear-cut evidence of active proximity-seeking be- haviour is shown when a baby quickly crosses the room to establish contact with his mother, other behaviours such as signalling by reaching or crying can constitute less active attempts to gain proximity. Once it was appreciated that quite disparate behaviours could serve the same end, and that they could be ordered in terms of the "strength" of the behavioural system—that is, in terms of the degree of active initiative shown by the infant—it was possible to comprehend a large variety of behaviours within the scope of the above four variables.

An analysis of these four infant–mother interactive behaviours was undertaken in part to check that strange-situation subgroups, quanti- tatively assessed, were congruent with the original specifications for classification. First a detailed coding was undertaken, and then the codings were ordered into four seven-point scales (see page 20, note 2). Although the four behaviours in question were highlighted in the reunion episodes in particular, behaviour in the pre-separation episodes was also included in the coding and scaling. The resulting scores were used by Ainsworth and Bell (1970) to describe trends for the total sample. Here they are used to delineate the behaviours of the various subgroups, and as such, they provide a useful check on the objectivity of the classificatory procedure.

It may be seen in Fig. 1 that the weakest proximity-seeking and contact-maintaining behaviour, and the strongest proximity-avoiding behaviour, is shown by *subgroup A_1*, especially in the reunion episodes, *episodes 5* and *8*. In this it matched the specifications for classification.

Subgroup A_2, like *subgroup A_1*, showed strong proximity-avoiding behaviour. Unlike A_1 babies, however, A_2 babies mixed proximity avoiding with moderately strong proximity seeking. The A_2 subgroup also mixed contact-seeking with contact-resisting behaviours.

Subgroup B_1 resembles A_1 in that it is weak in proximity seeking and in contact maintaining. These babies were clearly different from A_1 babies, however, in their interest in maintaining interaction with the mother across a distance during the reunion episodes—an interest which was not shown consistently by any other subgroup, and which is not represented in the dimensions of interactive behaviour featured in Fig. 1. Our present analysis shows that they also have fairly strong proximity-avoiding behaviour in the reunion episodes, although this was somewhat weaker than that shown by either of the subgroups of *group A*.

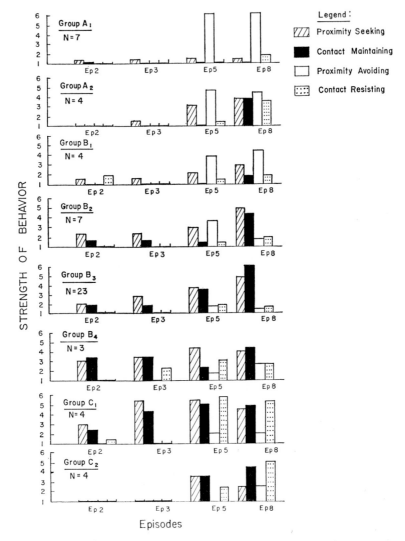

FIG. 1. Strength of interactive behaviours per episode for strange-situation subgroups.

Subgroup B₂ shows strong proximity-seeking behaviour in *episode 8*, and also fairly strong contact-maintaining behaviour. These behaviours are slightly stronger than those of *subgroup A₂*, although weaker than those shown by *subgroup B₃*. B_2 babies resemble B_3 babies in having weak proximity-avoiding and contact-resisting behaviour—and in these respects they differ from *subgroup A₂*.

Subgroup B₃ infants were strong in proximity seeking and strongest in contact maintaining in the reunion episodes, especially in *episode 8*. They were clearly distinguished from *group A* by weak proximity-avoiding behaviour, and from *group C* by weak contact-resisting behaviour.

Subgroup B₄ is intermediate between B_3 and the *group C* babies. It resembles *subgroup B₃* in showing relatively strong proximity-seeking and contact-maintaining behaviour in the reunion episodes, but these babies betrayed their insecurity by showing these behaviours to a greater extent in the pre-separation episodes as well. Unlike B_3 babies, their positive response to reunion is mixed with a degree of contact-resisting behaviour.

As implied in the specifications for classification, *subgroups C₁* and C_2 showed clear differences—and yet they showed one unsuspected similarity, which gives *group C* a point of real homogeneity. Very strong contact-resisting behaviour was shown not only by C_1 in both reunion episodes (as specified) but also by C_2 in *episode 8*. *Subgroup C₁* showed strong proximity-seeking behaviour in the reunion episodes but differed from B_3 and even from B_4 by showing it in *episode 3* as well. *Subgroup C₂*, which the specifications identified as passive, showed weaker proximity seeking than C_1. C_2 babies were, however, fairly strong in contact-maintaining behaviour in *episode 8*, as, indeed, were C_1 babies also. It was the mingling of contact-maintaining and contact-resisting behaviour, and also its angry quality, that made *group C* babies seem highly ambivalent in their relations with their mothers, and, indeed, distinguished them from other subgroups.

To summarize: *group A* was distinguished from *groups B* and *C* by less proximity seeking and contact maintaining, and especially by more proximity avoiding. *Group C* was distinguished from *group B* by more contact resisting. Although "adjacent" subgroups tended to resemble each other more closely than they did more "distant" ones, nevertheless the analysis supported the distinctions made between them.

3. *Exploratory Behaviour, Crying, and Search Behaviour*

Exploratory behaviour and crying played but a limited role in the specifications of the classification of strange-situation behaviour, and search behaviour in the separation episodes was not considered at all. Nevertheless, it is of value to examine group and subgroup differences in regard to these behaviours to ascertain the extent to which they are correlated with the classifications.

It was of particular interest to determine whether subgroups varied in the extent to which they displayed the expected shift from exploration to proximity seeking. In addition, since the subgroups exhibited different patterns of attachment behaviour upon reunion with the mother, it seemed of value to determine whether they differed also in the display of attachment behaviours during separation from the mother. Two forms of attachment behaviours likely to be evoked by the mother's departure were considered—crying, and search behaviour. Search behaviours, as defined in this study, include looking, approaching and/or remaining by the door or the mother's chair.

A frequency measure for two kinds of exploratory behaviours (exploratory locomotion and exploratory manipulation) and for crying was obtained by counting the number of 15-second time intervals in which the behaviour in question occurred, and by prorating for episodes which were longer or shorter than the standard 3-minute episode. Precise instructions for the identification and coding of these behaviours are given elsewhere (see page 20, note 2). Search behaviour, however, was coded and then assessed on a seven-point scale comparable to those devised for the interactive behaviours discussed in an earlier section.

It may be seen from Table III that search for the absent mother tends to be substantially stronger in *episode 6* when the baby was alone, than

TABLE III. MEAN STRENGTH OF SEARCH BEHAVIOUR
IN SEPARATION EPISODES FOR EACH STRANGE-
SITUATION SUBGROUP

Subgroups	Episodes		
	4	6	7
A_1	2·9	5·4	2·7
A_2	3·0	5·0	2·3
B_1	2·5	5·0	3·7
B_2	3·6	6·0	3·3
B_3	3·2	4·5	2·7
B_4	1·3	3·3	1·7
C_1	3·3	4·5	1·2
C_2	2·0	2·3	2·0

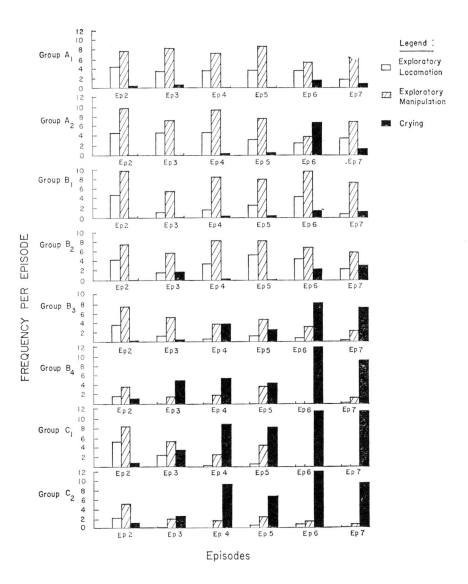

FIG. 2. Frequency of exploratory behaviour and crying per episode for strange-situation subgroups.

in *episodes 4* and *7*, when the baby may have been distracted by, or perhaps inhibited by, the presence of the stranger. Search behaviour was conspicuously weak throughout the separation episodes in the case of B_4, which had been specified as particularly helpless without the mother, and C_2 which had been specified as particularly passive. Otherwise all subgroups show roughly equal mean strength of search behaviour, although some small differences emerge in *episode 7*.

As shown in Fig. 2, crying was minimal in the pre-separation episodes; it occurred to an appreciable extent only in *subgroups B_4* and C_1 and in *episode 3* when the stranger was present. (Although we have largely omitted any account of response to the stranger in this report, it may be noted in passing that stranger anxiety occurred to any marked degree only in these two subgroups.) *Subgroups B_1* and B_2 cried minimally or not at all throughout the strange situation, and indeed absence of distress in the separation episodes had been included as a specification for the classification of these subgroups. *Subgroup A_1* also cried minimally or not at all. *Subgroup A_2* cried minimally except in *episode 6*, when they cried in response to being left entirely alone. *Group C* infants were most conspicuous for crying throughout the separation episodes, and for being difficult to comfort even in the reunion episodes. *Subgroup B_4* infants cried about as much as *group C* infants in *episodes 6* and *7*, but substantially less in the first separation episode, *episode 4*. Some of the babies in the largest, "normative" subgroup, B_3, cried in *episode 4*, but some did not; of those who did, some cried throughout and some only towards the end of the episode. On the occasion of a second separation (*episodes 6* and *7*) most of them cried, and those who had previously cried now cried sooner and harder. Thus, crying was a more typical response to separation for *group B* than for *group A*, and was most conspicuous in *group C*.

It is worth noting that search behaviour in the separation episodes, especially in *episode 6*, was strong in four subgroups (A_1, A_2, B_1, and B_2) in which crying was relatively infrequent. The implication is that attachment behaviour may be heightened by separation even in infants who show no signs of real separation distress. Thus, despite absence of separation distress, and despite relative infrequency of proximity-seeking and contact-maintaining behaviour upon reunion, it would be impossible to characterize even A_1 infants as lacking attachment to the mother.

The mean incidence of exploratory locomotion and exploratory manipulation is also shown in Fig. 2. It may be noted that the incidence of exploratory manipulation, whenever this behaviour appears at all, is always greater than the incidence of exploratory locomotion. It is not intended to compare these behaviours, however, but rather to take them together as indicative of exploratory activity.

It may be seen that the babies of all but two subgroups explored actively when they were alone with their mothers in *episode 2*, showing exploratory manipulation in from 8 to 10 of the 12 time intervals. The two exceptions were the babies in *subgroup B_4*, who had been so classified partly because they were too preoccupied with the mother to explore, and those of *subgroup C_2*, who had been so classified partly because they were too passive to be able to explore. Babies of *subgroups A_1, A_2, B_1* and *B_2* are conspicuous for maintaining exploratory activity at a fairly high level throughout all episodes of the strange situation. *Subgroups B_3* and *C_1*, who had explored a substantial amount in *episode 2* tended not only to be slowed by the presence of the stranger in *episode 3*, but also to explore very little from then on. This was especially the case with *C_1*. Finally, *subgroups B_4* and *C_2* explored very little throughout.

To summarize: for the "normative" subgroup, *B_3*, which constitutes about 40 per cent of the total sample, the balance was indeed tipped in favour of exploration of the unfamiliar situation at the outset. During *episode 3* they were preoccupied chiefly with visual exploration of the stranger. With the first separation episode, however, the balance was definitely tipped towards attachment behaviour—towards seeking to gain and to maintain contact and proximity with the mother. For the babies of *group A* and *subgroups B_1* and *B_2* the balance remained tipped towards exploration despite the potential stress of separation, and despite the fact that all showed some heightening of attachment behaviour, during the actual separation if not in response to reunion. For the babies of two small subgroups (*B_4* and *C_2*) the strange situation did not effectively evoke exploration: rather, attachment behaviour (which tended to be signalling behaviour instead of active proximity seeking) was preponderant from the beginning. The babies of *subgroup C_1* superficially resembled those of *subgroup B_3* in that they explored substantially at first and then shifted abruptly to attachment behaviour, but there were striking qualitative differences in the affective quality of both exploratory behaviour, which was mentioned above, and attachment behaviour, which was highly ambivalent in the case of *C_1*.

B. THE ATTACHMENT–EXPLORATION BALANCE IN HOME BEHAVIOUR

It has been shown that babies classified in different strange-situation subgroups show different configurations of attachment and exploratory behaviours. Broader significance can be attributed to strange-situation behaviour, however, only if it emerges as consistently related to characteristic behaviour in everyday life. Consequently, for those 23 subjects for whom detailed information was available, attention was directed towards analyses of infant behaviour at home in the last quarter of the first year.

The task of assessing infants' attachment–exploration balance in the home environment was extremely complex. Classification—rather than quantification—of separate behavioural dimensions again seemed best to represent the configurational quality of the behavioural phenomena. The basic concept is that a child who can use his mother as a secure base for exploration can move away from her freely, and yet tends to return to her on his own initiative from time to time, to play at her feet or to make brief contact before moving off again.

1. *The Classificatory System*

The classification was based on all visits in the last quarter of the first year considered together. Five main groups were identified[3]. The specifications of their classifications are summarized as follows:

Group I: The baby uses his mother as a secure base from which he can explore the world. There is a smooth balance between exploratory and attachment behaviour. (a) He can move away from his mother, even out of sight, busily interested in trying out locomotor skills or in exploring. (b) He is by no means oblivious to his mother while exploring, but keeps track of her whereabouts, even though he may not look at her frequently. He may occasionally interact with her across a distance; from time to time, he is likely to gravitate back to her. (c) He may seek to be picked up, but he does not necessarily want to be held more than a few moments before wanting to be put down again on the floor. Nevertheless, when held by his mother, regardless of which of them initiated the contact, he tends to show active, positive contact behaviour to her. (d) If the mother moves about from room to room he may follow her, but he tends not to be distressed by these minor everyday separations in his familiar home environment.

Group II: The baby can, on occasion, use his mother as a secure base from which he can explore, but at times the balance between exploration

---

[3] Complete specifications for this classification, as well as instructions for rating the maternal behaviour variables discussed below, may be obtained upon request from the authors, at the Department of Psychology, Johns Hopkins University, Baltimore, Maryland 21218.

and attachment behaviour shows clear disturbance of quality. The disturbance seems to be in reaction to maternal behaviour, for at times there is a mismatch between the infant's wishes for contact, proximity, and/or interaction and those of his mother. (a) When the mother is accessible and non-interfering, the baby can use her as a secure base. If the mother, wanting physical contact with the baby, interrupts his play he may resist, and subsequently ignore her and avoid proximity with her. (b) Sometimes he behaves as a *group I* baby in regard to keeping "visual tabs" on his mother, interacting with her across a distance, and occasionally gravitating back to her. Sometimes his proximity- and interaction-seeking behaviour is disturbed. If the mother fails to respond to the baby's attempts to initiate interaction or contact, he tends to respond to her rebuff with greatly heightened attachment behaviour. And yet, in some instances, he may eventually return to independent exploratory play, ignoring his mother as she ignores him. He is likely to substitute determined proximity-avoiding behaviour for intermittent proximity-seeking behaviour. (c) On occasions in which baby and mother seem attuned to each other the baby may not only seek physical contact with his mother much as a *group I* baby does, but also respond to it positively and actively. On other occasions in which mother's and infant's contact-seeking is mismatched the baby may actively resist contact with her instead of responding positively. (d) The response to everyday separations is variable for this group. Some react with more anxiety to the mother's leaving the room than does a *group I* baby, but when any *group II* baby is in a proximity-avoiding mood he tends to ignore her comings and goings.

Group III: The baby does not seem to use his mother as a secure base. He explores very actively, but displays relatively little proximity-seeking behaviour and does not seem much concerned with his mother's whereabouts. (a) This baby explores actively and "independently". He certainly can move away from his mother, including venturing out of sight. (b) He may to some extent keep "visual tabs" on his mother, but tends to have a take-it-or-leave-it attitude towards her presence. He is less interactive across a distance than a *group I* baby, and may not respond to his mother's attempts to interact with him. He may occasionally gravitate to his mother, but this is easily discouraged if his mother does not acknowledge him. (c) More than infants of other groups, he lacks interest in being picked up; he may well squirm to get down again after very brief holding; he lacks active contact behaviour even when he accepts contact; he tends not to protest when he is put down. (d) He seems to be able to adapt himself readily to his mother's absence from the room, or even from the house. He may or may not protest momentarily at her departure and he soon resumes his own activity.

Group IV: The baby does not seem to feel that his mother is a secure base. He explores actively, and he seeks contact and/or proximity on occasion, but the balance between these two sets of behaviour is disturbed, and to a greater extent than in the case of *group II.* (a) He may seem often as "independent" as a *group III* baby, but his periods of exploratory activity tend to be relatively brief. (b) More frequently than a *group III* baby, he seeks proximity and/or contact with his mother, and he also does so more actively. (c) Despite the fact that he actively initiates physical contact with his mother, he does not seem to find any great pleasure in it once it is achieved. He may, indeed, be markedly ambivalent to contact with his mother, both seeking contact and strongly resisting it. (d) More frequently than babies of other groups, he keeps track of his mother's whereabouts, and is distressed if he loses track of her or if she leaves. He tends to follow her about, and may become quite distressed if he is prevented from following.

Group V: The mother does not seem to function as a secure base for the baby. He tends to be passive either in seeking proximity/contact or in exploration or in both. He tends to engage in stereotyped, repetitive, autoerotic activities. Some babies in this group are passive only intermittently, while others are strikingly passive. (a) The most highly passive seem entirely unable to engage in sustained, independent, exploratory activity, but require the mother's participation to become active, and even then show little interest in exploring the properties of objects. The more intermittently passive may, on occasion, seem highly independent, going into forbidden areas and ignoring mother's prohibitions. This play, although seemingly independent, tends to be merely locomotor, however. Physical objects are more to be chewed or sucked than to be manipulated manually. (b) Proximity-seeking may occur intermittently, although some babies seem too passive to show active proximity-seeking behaviour. (c) If contact with the mother is achieved, the baby tends to accept it passively, and does not resist release when put down. Indeed the more consistently passive of the *group V* babies show little or no active contact seeking, merely waiting until the mother initiates contact. (d) More than infants in *groups I, II,* and *III,* the *group V* baby is concerned with his mother's whereabouts, although he may not display his concern either through clear signalling or through a definitely active following. (e) He engages in frequent autoerotic activity.

2. Attachment–Exploration Balance at Home and Strange-situation Classification

Table IV shows the distribution of the 23 infants in our longitudinal sample in regard to both the classification of attachment–exploration balance at home and the classification of strange-situation behaviour.

TABLE IV. CLASSIFICATION OF STRANGE-SITUATION BEHAVIOUR AND CLASSIFICATION OF ATTACHMENT–EXPLORATION BALANCE IN BEHAVIOUR AT HOME

Attachment–exploration balance at home: Groups	Strange-situation behaviour classification						
	B_3	$B_1 + B_2$	A_2	A_1	C_1	C_2	Totals
I	8	–	–	–	–	–	8
II	1	3	–	–	–	–	4
III	–	1	2	–	–	–	3
IV	–	–	–	3	1	–	4
V	–	–	–	1	1	2	4
Totals	9	4	2	4	2	2	23

Let us consider the match between these two classifications, gearing ourselves primarily to the classification in terms of home behaviour.

Group I. Eight infants were classified in *group I*, and *all* of these had been classified in *subgroup B_3* in regard to strange-situation behaviour. This implies that 1-year-olds who can at home consistently use the mother as a secure base for exploration do so also initially in the strange situation. It also implies that babies who display a smooth balance between attachment and exploratory behaviour at home are readily tipped in the strange situation from exploration to proximity- and contact-seeking.

Group II. Four infants were classified in *group II*. Of these, three were classified in either *subgroup B_1 or B_2* in regard to strange-situation behaviour,[4] and one in B_3. This implies that babies who experienced some mismatch with their mothers in regard to the attachment–exploration balance at home, but who nevertheless could on occasion use their mothers as a secure base, tended in the strange situation to emphasize exploration somewhat at the expense of attachment behaviour, even after the stress of two minor separations from their

---

[4] Since only one infant in the main-project sample was classified as B_1, *subgroups* B_1 and B_2 are combined in this and further analyses.

mothers. Fig. 1 showed that the B_1 and B_2 infants also showed more proximity-avoiding behaviour in the reunion episodes than did the babies of the "normative" group, B_3. This emphasis on continuing exploration and ignoring the mother, or even rebuffing her overtures, was also apparent at home on the occasions of mismatch between the baby's wishes and his mother's.

Group III: Three infants were classified in *group III*; of these, two were classified in A_2 and one in B_2 in regard to strange-situation behaviour. This implies that infants who are conspicuously "independent" at home, concerned with exploratory activity substantially more than with seeking proximity and contact with the mother, behave similarly in the strange situation. In neither situation is attachment behaviour absent, but in both situations the baby can occupy himself without conspicuous distress when the mother is absent or inattentive. The strange situation did heighten attachment behaviour in the last reunion episode, and in this sense these infants responded to stress as predicted. A disturbance in the quality of their response, however, is reflected by the fact that proximity-avoiding and contact-resisting behaviours (clearly evident also at home) are mingled with proximity and contact seeking in the strange situation. This generalized statement applies equally well to the two A_2 infants and to the B_2 infant, although the latter exhibited proximity-avoiding behaviour less consistently.

Group IV: Four infants were classified in *group IV*. Three of these babies were classified in *subgroup A_1* in regard to strange situation behaviour, and one in C_1.

The behaviour of the C_1 baby in the strange situation was entirely consistent with her behaviour at home. In both settings she was capable of exploratory play, ambivalent in interaction with her mother, and prone to acute distress in separation situations.

The three A_1 infants presented a different picture. For them the strange situation heightened the "independent" component of their characteristic home behaviour. They explored actively in the strange situation, ignored the mother strikingly, and thus showed a "snubbing" kind of rejection. A possible explanation of their behaviour under stress will be offered in the discussion section of this chapter. It is sufficient here to point out that the strange situation, although it did not intensify all components of the behavioural configuration observed at home, highlighted a considerable degree of disturbance in the dynamics underlying the attachment–exploration balance.

Group V: Four infants were classified in *group V*. Of these, two were classified as C_2 in strange-situation behaviour, one as C_1, and one as A_1.

Passivity, whether thoroughgoing or intermittent, was the distinguishing feature of *group V*. The two C_2 infants were strikingly passive both at home and in the strange situation; neither showed any substantial degree of initiative either in exploration or in proximity-seeking in either environment. They also showed a substantial amount of stereotyped, "autoerotic" behaviour in both settings—sucking in one case and rocking in the other—and, indeed this was one reason for classing their behaviour as "maladaptive" in the strange situation.

The C_1 infant was intermittently passive at home—she chewed and sucked objects when left in the playpen for long periods, but was very active in locomotion on the rare occasions when she was free to move about. This behaviour was quite consistent with her strange-situation behaviour. It might be added that she was anxious about her mother's whereabouts and exceptionally fearful of strangers—both at home and in the strange situation.

Finally, the infant classified in *subgroup A_1* in regard to strange-situation behaviour was particularly conspicuous for autoerotic behaviour at home—sucking, rocking, rubbing parts of his body: and even his seemingly exploratory behaviour was so stereotyped, repetitive, and compulsive that it seemed more like rocking than it did like exploration of the properties of objects. In the strange situation his "exploratory" behaviour was maintained throughout, but it was a precise replication of the stereotyped behaviour he showed at home. On the other hand the separation anxiety he showed at home was not displayed in the strange situation.

Thus, the stresses of the strange situation highlighted certain behavioural characteristics of *group V* infants which were manifested in their home behaviour. Moreover, these stresses intensified, in three of the four infants, a component of the dynamics of infant–mother interaction which was not in all of them so readily detected at home— namely anger and ambivalence in response to contact.

In summary, there is an impressive degree of congruence between a baby's response to his mother in the strange situation and the quality of the attachment–exploration balance at home. It is clear that babies who have the smoothest attachment–exploration balance at home and the most positive attachment behaviour (compare the specifications for classification in *group I*), show clear-cut and unambivalent attachment behaviour towards the mother after two stressful although brief separations from her in a strange environment. In cases in which there is some disruption in the smoothness of the attachment–exploration balance at home, due to a mismatch between mother and baby—as in *group II*—the tendency is to show less proximity- and contact-seeking with the mother after the stress of separation.

Babies who are independent at home—i.e. *group III*— show some heightening of proximity and contact-seeking under strange-situation stress, but also show proximity-avoiding behaviour. Those who at home alternate anxious proximity-seeking with independent behaviour—i.e. *group IV*—respond either with heightened ambivalence towards the mother (C_1) or with heightened "independence" defined by striking proximity-avoiding behaviour (A_1).

Finally, babies such as those of *group V* who are passive, autoerotic, and/or incompetent in their behaviour at home tend to show a disturbance in the quality of their exploratory behaviour in the strange situation, and heightened ambivalent reactions towards the mother.

C. MATERNAL BEHAVIOUR

An underlying hypothesis of this study is that infants who differ in regard to attachment–exploration balance have experienced different kinds of mother–infant interaction. Ainsworth and Wittig (1969) reported, on the basis of an impressionistic analysis, that *group B* infants (according to their tentative strange-situation classification) differed from *group A* and *group C* infants in regard to several features of mother–infant interaction. Ainsworth and Bell (1969) showed that the present strange-situation classifications were significantly related to mother–infant interaction in the feeding situation during the first 3 months, and also to ratings of maternal behaviour in dimensions not specifically related to feeding. The common factor in all of these assessments seemed to be the degree of sensitivity the mother showed to the baby's signals, in noticing them, interpreting them accurately, and in responding to them promptly and appropriately. It was clear that the mothers of *group B* were significantly more sensitive than the mothers of *group A* and *group C* babies, but *A* and *C* mothers did not seem to be distinguished effectively by any of the assessments used.

In an attempt to identify aspects of maternal behaviour that might distinguish between *A* and *C* mothers, new rating scales were devised for the assessment of maternal behaviour during the last quarter of the first year. The dimensions which will be reported here are: acceptance–rejection, co-operation–interference, accessibility–ignoring, and, in addition, sensitivity–insensitivity—which had seemed to be the common factor in the previous analyses.

These dimensions were rated on nine-point scales, each with five anchor points clearly specified (see page 34, note 3).

Sensitivity–insensitivity: This scale deals with the mother's response to the infant's signals and communications. The sensitive mother is able to see things from her baby's point of view. She is tuned-in to receive her baby's signals: she interprets them correctly, and she responds to them promptly and appropriately. Although she nearly always gives the baby what he seems to want, when she does not she is tactful in acknowledging his communication and in offering an acceptable alternative. She makes her responses temporally contingent upon the baby's signals and communications. The sensitive mother, by definition, cannot be rejecting, interfering, or ignoring.

The insensitive mother, on the other hand, gears her interventions and initiations of interactions almost exclusively in terms of her own wishes, moods, and activities. She tends either to distort the implications of her baby's communications, interpreting them in the light of her own wishes or defences, or not to respond to them at all.

Acceptance–rejection: This dimension refers to the balance between the mother's positive and negative feelings about her baby, and to the extent to which she has been able to integrate these conflicting feelings or to resolve the conflict between them. A highly rejecting mother frequently experiences resentful, angry, rejecting feelings which over-whelm her positive feelings towards her baby. She may openly voice her rejection, saying that he is a nuisance and interferes substantially in her life, or she may manifest her rejection by constantly opposing his wishes, or by a generally pervasive atmosphere of irritation and scolding. At the opposite pole, the accepting mother accepts infant behaviour which other mothers might find hurtful or irritating, such as angry behaviour or disregard of her overtures. She may occasionally feel irritated by his behaviour, but she does not make an opponent of him, and she cheerfully accepts the responsibility of caring for him despite the temporary limitation this places on her other activities.

Co-operation–interference: The highly interfering mother lacks respect for her baby as a separate person. She tries to impose her will on his, or to shape him to her standards, or merely follows her own whims without regard for his moods, wishes or activity-in-progress. At the positive pole is the co-operative, "co-determining" mother who respects the baby's autonomy, and plans to avoid situations in which she might have to interrupt his activity or to exert direct control over him. She interferes abruptly or forcefully only in rare emergencies.

Otherwise, when she intervenes on her own initiative she is skilful in "mood-setting" and in other techniques which help her baby to feel that what she wishes is also congenial to him.

Accessibility–ignoring: The accessible mother's attention is nearly always tuned-in to the baby, so that she can perceive his signals and communications both when he is near and when he is in another room by himself. This mother can attend to his communications despite distraction by other demands, activities, and interests. At the negative pole, the mother is often so preoccupied with her own thoughts and activities that she does not even notice the baby, let alone acknowledge his signals. When he is elsewhere she seems to forget that he exists, and his sounds do not seem to filter through to her. She seems to notice him only when she deliberately turns her attention to do something to or for him, making a project of it.

These four dimensions were rated separately for each visit during the last quarter of the first year. Five judges participated, three of them working without knowledge of any other assessments. Precautions were taken to avoid halo effects across variables. The final rating was decided upon in conference, and was almost invariably the median rating for all visits rated. Reliability coefficients between pairs of judges were determined. The mean coefficients for all pairings for each of the scales are as follows: sensitivity–insensitivity 0·89, acceptance–rejection 0·88, co-operation–interference 0·86, and accessibility–ignoring 0·87.

As expected, the sensitivity–insensitivity scale was highly correlated with the other three scales (see Table V). Acceptance–rejection was highly correlated with co-operation–interference and also, to a somewhat lower degree, with accessibility–ignoring. The lowest correlation was between co-operation–interference and accessibility–ignoring, and even that was moderately and significantly positive. An examination of scatter diagrams made it clear that all four variables were closely related at the positive end, while the scatter of scores fanned out to a greater or lesser extent at the negative end. Thus, for example, co-operative mothers are accessible, but interfering mothers are not necessarily ignoring, and vice versa.

The means of each of the strange-situation subgroups on each of the four maternal behaviour measures are shown in Fig. 3. On each scale the mothers of B_3 babies receive the highest mean rating, and on each the mothers of the B_1 and B_2 infants come next. This consistency is reflected by a coefficient of concordance significant at beyond the 0·01 level.

TABLE V. INTERCORRELATIONS AMONG RATINGS OF MATERNAL BEHAVIOUR

	Acceptance–rejection	Co-operation–interference	Accessibility–ignoring
Sensitivity–insensitivity	0·89	0·86	0·82
Acceptance–rejection		0·89	0·70
Co-operation–interference			0·57

As anticipated, the sensitivity–insensitivity dimension yielded no differentiation between the mothers of *group A* and *group C* babies. In regard to the other scales, we were successful in obtaining some differentiation between the *A* and *C* subgroups. *Group A* mothers—and especially A_1 mothers—are more rejecting than are *group C* mothers. A_1 and C_1 mothers are the most interfering, and A_2 and C_2 mothers are the most inaccessible and ignoring. Thus the various strange-situation subgroups differ in regard to maternal behaviour and, consequently, in regard to characteristic mother–infant interaction.

The mothers of B_3 babies are clearly the most sensitive: responsive to the baby's signals and capable of perceiving things from his point of view. They are also accessible, accepting, and non-interfering. The B_3 mother respects her baby as a separate person; she also respects his activity-in-progress and thus avoids interrupting him. She accepts his exploratory behaviour, which leads him away from her just as she accepts his desire for contact and interaction which leads him to her.

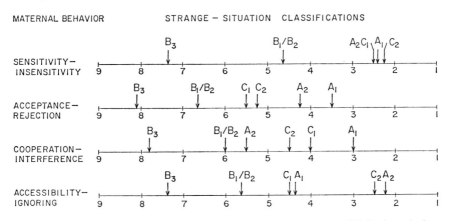

FIG. 3. Mean ratings of strange-situation groups regarding maternal behaviour during last quarter.

The mothers of B_1 and B_2 babies are, in regard to each of the four dimensions of behaviour, intermediate between the B_3 mothers and the mothers of *groups A* and *C*. They may be described as inconsistently sensitive. For reasons which differed in each case they were also inconsistently accessible to the baby; there were distinct periods during which he was given much attention. During the periods of attention three of the four mothers were somewhat interfering, tending to interrupt exploratory play. Indeed, in two cases there was clear mismatch in regard to desire for physical contact; the mothers sometimes interrupted the baby to give him cuddling when he did not wish it, only to be rejecting or perfunctory at other times when the baby himself sought contact.

The mothers of A_1 babies were not only highly insensitive but also more rejecting and interfering than the mothers of any other subgroup. They were quite unable to see things from the baby's point of view or to be guided by the baby's display of initiative. They did not so much ignore the baby's communications as discount them as relevant guidelines, and thus were very arbitrary in their interventions.

The mothers of A_2 babies were not only highly insensitive but also inaccessible for prolonged periods. They were impatient with the role of housewife and mother, and found other activities to occupy them both at home and away from home. When at home they could go in and out of a room, preoccupied with other thoughts, and not even acknowledge the baby's existence. Only if the baby's signals were strong and persistent enough would they finally respond. Because of their inattentiveness to the baby they were infrequently interfering, although they were not co-operative and co-determining. They were somewhat rejecting, however, in the sense that the baby tended to be rejected along with the maternal role.

The mothers of C_2 babies were also highly inaccessible and ignoring. They differed from the A_2 mothers in that they had a strong emotional investment in the maternal role. They were severely disturbed women, very fragmented in their behaviour, and although they gloried in being mothers, they found a baby's demands anxiety-provoking. In order to hold themselves together and to carry on their routine activities they had to ignore the baby, and to "tune-out" his crying. This ignoring was even more extreme during the first quarter-year than it was in the last quarter-year when these ratings were made. They left the baby in a crib, alone in a room, to cry for prolonged periods. When the C_2 mother finally did intervene, the intervention was absolutely non-contingent upon the infant's signals. It is this arbitrary quality of response that distinguishes the inaccessible C_2 mothers from the inaccessible A_2 mothers. It is thus not surprising that the C_2 babies behaved extremely passively and "maladaptively" both in the strange situation and at home, whereas A_2 babies, whose strong, persistent signals finally brought a response, developed active, although "defensive" behaviours to cope with the mother and with the environment.

The mothers of C_1 babies were disparate except for the fact that both were highly insensitive. One was highly interfering but differed from the A_1 mothers in that she was not rejecting. She was well-meaning but continually interrupted her daughter to train her, to show off her accomplishments, and to gratify her own desires to be playful and affectionate. She was "at" the baby so much of the time that she was in fact highly controlling. The other C_1 mother was compulsive, much preoccupied, and quite unresponsive to any signals from the baby that she did not interpret as emergency signals. Consequently she obtained a low rating on accessibility. Although both little girls behaved similarly in the strange situation, the background of mother–infant interaction differed, and to a much greater extent than in the case of any other subgroup.

CONCLUSIONS

Let us recapitulate these complex findings, and venture some hypotheses about the dynamics which may account for the fact that there is a notable degree of clustering of maternal and infant behaviours common to the several assessment procedures used.

First, mothers who are sensitive to their babies' signals tend to be also accessible, co-operative, and accepting. At home their babies engage in secure-base behaviour and tend not to be disturbed by minor everyday separations. In the strange situation these babies behave at first as they do at home, using the mother as a secure base from which to explore. The successive stresses of the strange situations, however, reduce their exploratory play and heighten attachment behaviour, and most (but not all) of them evince distress in the separation episodes. This pattern of mother–infant interaction associated with maternal sensitivity is considered to be the normal, healthy pattern of infants towards the end of the first year of life; it was displayed by about one-third of the sample.

To the extent that infants and their mothers depart from the above-described normative behaviour, individual differences become more conspicuous, the classificatory groups become smaller, and it becomes somewhat more difficult to generalize. Nevertheless there is a second group of mother–infant pairs who approximate to the normative pattern in many ways and whose deviations therefrom show a fair degree of homogeneity. The mothers may be described as inconsistently sensitive to their babies' signals and communications. All of them tend to have lacunae in their accessibility to their babies; and most of them tend on occasion to be interfering. The baby may respond to his mother's inconsistency by behaviour geared situationally to the variations in her behaviour—sometimes using her as a secure base from which to explore, at other times exploring independently and avoiding his mother. At still other times especially in response to maternal rebuff, his attachment behaviour is importunate. In the strange situation, these babies use the mother as a secure base at first, but differ from the normative group in that they maintain exploration at a fairly high level throughout all episodes, as though the independence they sometimes showed at home is used defensively to meet the stresses of the strange situation, and they respond to reunion with less heightening of attachment behaviour. These infant–mother pairs seem clearly intermediate between the normative group and the rest of the sample.

The remainder of the sample is characterized by insensitive mothering. Despite the fact that there is much more variation in patterns of inter-action in these infant–mother pairs than among those with more sensitive mothering there are nevertheless some consistent clusters which suggest hypotheses about their underlying dynamics.

This set of hypotheses stems from the observation that babies who show both minimal distress in the separation episodes of the strange situation and striking proximity-avoiding behaviour in the reunion episodes—*group A*—have the most rejecting mothers. In contrast, babies who are both highly distressed in the separation episodes and markedly ambivalent to their mothers upon reunion—*group C*—are not conspicuously rejected by their mothers, although the mother–infant relationship is clearly unharmonious. This suggests that a baby who has been rejected by his mother has readily available to him defensive reactions against the kind of stresses he encounters in the strange situation—defences which are not available to other infants. Specifically, our findings lead us to two interrelated hypotheses: (1) that a dis-harmonious or unsatisfactory relationship with his mother evokes insecurity in the infant—an insecurity which generally manifests itself in heightened proximity and contact seeking as well as a low threshold to separation distress; such insecurity is commonly labelled separation anxiety; (2) that, since rejection entails a history of painful experiences associated with contact and with contact-seeking, an infant who is conspicuously rejected not only experiences the insecurity evoked by a disharmonious relationship with his mother but also experiences conflict between heightened proximity and contact-seeking and a desire to avoid proximity and contact—a conflict which engenders the development of defensive reactions. These defensive reactions channel the baby's activity towards independent play, which absorbs him and allays his insecurity and at the same time blocks his proximity-seeking behaviour.

These hypotheses seem to account for the complex relationship between infant behaviour at home and in the strange situation. Let us examine first the findings which support the second hypothesis. Mothers who both rejected and ignored their infants, but who were not conspicuously interfering—such as those of *subgroup A_2*—had infants who seemed to have learned to turn away from the mother and to absorb themselves in independent activity. They seemed to use exploratory play as a substitute for maternal attention both at home and in the strange situation. At home they were absorbed in play to the point of entirely ignoring the mother for prolonged periods when she was unresponsive. In the strange situation, they were minimally distressed by her absence and maintained their exploration throughout. Although the cumulative stress of the separation episodes heightened attachment behaviour in some measure, it also exacerbated defensive independence as manifested in proximity-avoiding and contact-resisting behaviours directed towards the mother upon reunion. Thus, when introduced to a situation which increased insecurity, these infants relied largely on their own activities and avoided turning to the mother. To be so readily available to a baby in the strange situation, this defence must have already developed as a way of coping with insecure feelings aroused by a mother who ignored and rejected him at home.

There was another group of highly rejecting mothers—those of *subgroup A_1* babies. In contrast to those of *subgroup A_2* they were not conspicuously ignoring, but they were highly interfering. It was characteristic of them constantly to interrupt the baby's exploratory activity. Their own initiation of physical contact was therefore unpleasantly intrusive, and they tended to respond perfunctorily or even punitively to the baby's initiations of contact. At home their babies tended to play independently at times and to ignore the mother—much like A_2 infants—but at other times they sought proximity actively and somewhat anxiously, especially if the mother left the room. In the strange situation, however, when the mother was constrained to a non-interventive role, the A_1 infant maintained his exploration throughout, showing no distress upon separation and markedly ignoring his mother upon reunion. At home it seems likely that his independent activity was so frequently disrupted that he could use defensive exploration and proximity avoiding in only a fragmentary way. The defence became fully operative, however, when he was introduced to an insecurity-provoking situation in which his mother was non-interfering.

Elsewhere (Ainsworth and Bell, 1970) we interpreted proximity-avoiding behaviour as a primitive form of defence, that resembles the repressive defence Bowlby (e.g. 1960) has termed "detachment" that occurs in the course of longer separations and is conspicuous in many children when first reunited with their mothers. It was hypothesized that this defence is homologous to a response shown by infants during the extinction period of experiments on the conditioning of attachment behaviour, in which the infant looks away from, instead of responding to, a stimulus object that had previously been rewarding (cf. Brackbill, 1958; Rheingold et al., 1959). Here we further maintain that proximity-avoiding behaviour is a defensive reaction against the insecurity inherent in a disharmonious mother–infant relationship. Such a response may be viewed as an active behaviour, incompatible with and blocking attachment behaviour, which develops as a result of a history of unsatisfactory proximity- and contact-seeking experiences with a rejecting mother.

Further support for our hypothesis is provided by the behaviour of those babies who experienced a disharmonious relationship with the mother, but who were not conspicuously rejected—namely *group C*. Mothers of *group C* babies were insensitive, and either grossly ignoring or interfering. All interacted playfully and affectionately with the baby on occasion, however, and tended neither to react punitively towards him nor to rebuff him actively. The infants were especially vulnerable to the stresses of the strange situation, and showed a conspicuous lack of defensive proximity-avoiding behaviour and of sustained independent exploration.

Non-rejecting mothers who were highly interfering in the baby's exploration—those of *subgroup C_1*—(one of whom was intermittently ignoring as well) had babies who displayed greater insecurity both at home and in the strange situation than any other infants in the sample. They were fussy at home, in fact by 1 year of age they had the highest incidence of crying in the sample and in the strange situation they were clearly ambivalent towards contact with the mother.

Non-rejecting mothers who were grossly ignoring—those of *subgroup C_2*—had infants who were extremely passive and easily distressed both at home and in the strange environment. Infants in this subgroup experienced no consistent feedback to their signals and were given little opportunity to explore and to gain feedback by learning to control inanimate objects. Consequently, they were strikingly passive and tended to engage in excessive autoerotic behaviour. They were highly distressed in the strange situation and could cope neither with the opportunity to explore nor with the successive stresses. Upon reunion with the mother, they showed fairly strong attachment behaviour, limited somewhat by their pervasive passivity, but, like the C_1 babies, they also displayed angry contact-resisting behaviours more conspicuously than at home.

Thus infants who had a disharmonious relationship with a mother who is not openly rejecting show signs of acute insecurity. In addition, they react to stress with heightened ambivalence to the mother. It seems that these infants, lacking the defensive reactions of rejected babies, still turn to the mother under stress. Frustrated in their expectation of finding solace and security in the attachment relationship, however, they attack the mother angrily in a futile expression of their distress.

Let us summarize our hypotheses about the relation between strange-situation behaviour and the dynamics of mother–infant interaction. To the extent that the mother has been sensitively responsive to the baby's communications and mother–infant interaction has been characteristically harmonious, the baby is able to use his mother as a secure base from which to explore even an unfamiliar situation, but responds to the stress introduced by the separation episodes with heightened attachment behaviour, relatively uncomplicated by ambivalence and not blocked by competing, defensive, proximity-avoiding behaviour. To the extent that a baby's interaction with his mother has been characteristically disturbed by her rejection of him, he responds to the stresses of the strange situation with defensive proximity-avoiding behaviour, which competes with and tends to block off attachment behaviour. To the extent that mother–infant interaction has been made disharmonious through maternal interference or ignoring, but in which maternal rejection is either moderate or very well masked, a baby seems unable to defend himself, reacting with great distress in the separation episodes and with ambivalence to his mother in the reunion episodes. This corpus of hypotheses, although derived from a small sample, promises breadth of applicability to other samples despite the fact that they may well include constellations of mother–infant interaction not comprehended here.

Insofar as there is a single quantifiable dimension of mother–infant interaction implicit in our hypotheses, this is a crude one of harmony–disharmony, with the implication that towards the disharmonious pole qualitative differences are so great that it is difficult to order them magnitudinally, let alone quantify them.

The considerations raised in this discussion should clarify our reasons for opposing the use of a dimension of strength or intensity of infant–mother attachment (e.g. Ainsworth, 1969, and in press) at least in the present state of our knowledge. Attachment behaviour, to be sure, may be perceived as stronger or weaker, and the degree of strength may be seen to vary situationally. It tends to be heightened by the stresses of the strange situation, but different attachment behaviours seem to be affected differentially according to the constellations of interaction characteristic of an infant–mother pair. If proximity-seeking and contact-maintaining behaviour are taken as criteria of the strength of attachment, then the infants of *subgroups* C_1, B_2, B_3, and B_4 would be judged strongly attached and *subgroups* A_1 and B_1 very weakly attached. In terms of crying and separation distress, the infants of *subgroups* C_1, C_2, and B_4 would be judged strongly attached, and those of *subgroup* B_2 as well as A_1 and B_1 very weakly attached. In terms of active search during the separation episodes the babies of A_1, A_2, B_1, and B_2 would be judged strongly attached, and those of C_2 and B_4 weakly attached. Judgements in terms of home behaviour would arrange the infants in different orders again. According to no single criterion, whether applied to strange-situation behaviour or home behaviour, would the eight infants classified in *group I* and *subgroup B_3* be distinguished as the normative, healthy group which we are convinced they are. Our conclusion is that the infants of no subgroup may be assumed to be either more strongly attached or more weakly attached than the infants of other subgroups. On the contrary, the evidence suggests that the infants of each subgroup are attached to their mothers in their own fashion, and that the qualitative flavour of the attachment relationship overrides in significance the notion of "strength of attachment".

We believe that the strange situation holds great promise as a kind of test situation from which inferences may be made about the quality of the infant–mother attachment relationship and about the characteristic harmony or disharmony of mother–infant interaction. One of us (Bell, 1970) has already used it successfully in this way. Much more research is obviously required both to replicate and confirm our findings. It is not known, for instance, how much resemblance our data might bear to the findings for other age groups, or groups from other cultures, nor how applicable our hypotheses might be to these other groups. It might turn out, for example, that a normative group of 3-year-olds should be classed in *subgroups B_1* or B_2 rather than in B_3, and that at that age such strange-situation behaviour might well reflect an optimum attachment–exploration balance rather than the "mismatch" implied by B_1 or B_2 behaviour in 1-year-olds.

In regard to replication studies, care must be taken not to assume that behaviour variables which have similar or identical labels are in fact the same. Thus, for example, proximity-seeking behaviour has been here defined in terms of the active initiative taken by the child in approaching his mother and making contact with her, and not, as in other studies, in terms of the mean distance maintained between infant and mother, or by the proportion of time spent near the mother or further away. Conclusions may differ from one study to another merely because of differences in procedural details. Obviously, if our classificatory system or behavioural dimensions are to be of use to others as indices and criteria, the procedural details upon which our findings are based should be replicated.

REFERENCES

AINSWORTH, M. D. S. 1963. The development of infant–mother interaction among the Ganda. In B. M. Foss (Ed.), *Determinants of infant behaviour, II.* Methuen, London.

AINSWORTH, M. D. S. 1967. *Infancy in Uganda: infant care and the growth of love.* Johns Hopkins University Press, Baltimore, Md.

AINSWORTH, M. D. S. 1969. Object relations, dependency, and attachment: a theoretical review of the infant–mother relationship. *Child Dev.* **40,** 969–1025.

AINSWORTH, M. D. S. The development of infant–mother attachment. In B. M. Caldwell and H. N. Ricciuti (Eds.), *Review of child development research,* Vol. 3. University of Chicago Press, in press.

AINSWORTH, M. D. S. and BELL, S. M. 1969. Some contemporary patterns of mother–infant interaction in the feeding situation. In A. Ambrose (Ed.), *Stimulation in early infancy.* Academic Press, London.

AINSWORTH, M. D. S. and BELL, S. M. 1970. Attachment, exploration, and separation: illustrated by the behavior of one-year-olds in a strange situation. *Child Dev.* **41,** 49–67.

AINSWORTH, M. D. S. and WITTIG, B. A. 1969. Attachment and exploratory behavior of one-year-olds in a strange situation. In B. M. Foss (Ed.), *Determinants of infant behaviour IV.* Methuen, London.

BELL, S. M. 1970. The development of the concept of object as related to infant–mother attachment. *Child Dev.* **41,** 291–311.

BLATZ, W. E. 1966. *Human security: some reflections.* University of Toronto Press.

BOWLBY, J. 1960. Grief and mourning in infancy and early childhood. *Psychoanalytic study of the child* **15,** 9–52.

BOWLBY, J. 1969. *Attachment and loss.* Vol. I: *Attachment.* Hogarth Press, London; Basic Books, New York.

BRACKBILL, Y. 1958. Extinction of the smiling response in infants as a function of reinforcement schedule. *Child Dev.* **29,** 115–124.

COLLARD, R. R. 1968. Social and play responses of first-born and later-born infants in an unfamiliar situation. *Child Dev.* **39,** 325–334.

COX, F. N. and CAMPBELL, D. 1968. Young children in a new situation with and without their mothers. *Child Dev.* **39,** 123–131.

DEVORE, I. 1963. Mother–infant relations in free-ranging baboons. In H. L. Rheingold (Ed.), *Maternal behavior in mammals.* Wiley, New York. Pp. 305–335.

HARLOW, H. F. 1958. The nature of love. *Am. Psychol.* **13,** 673–685.

HINDE, R. A., ROWELL, T. E. and SPENCER-BOOTH, Y. 1964. Behavior of socially living rhesus monkeys in their first six months. *Proc. zool. Soc. Lond.* **143,** 609–649.

RHEINGOLD, H. L. 1969. The effect of a strange environment on the behavior of infants. In B. M. Foss (Ed.), *Determinants of infant behaviour IV.* Methuen, London. Pp. 137–188.

RHEINGOLD, H. L., GEWIRTZ, J. L. and ROSS, H. W. 1959. Social conditioning of vocalizations in the infant. *J. comp. physiol. Psychol.* **52,** 68–73.

ROSENTHAL, M. K. 1967a. Effects of a novel situation and of anxiety on two groups of dependency behaviours. *Brit. J. Psychol.* **58,** 3 and 4. Pp. 357–364.

ROSENTHAL, M. K. 1967b. The generalization of dependency from mother to stranger. *J. Child Psychol. Psychiat.* **8,** 117–134.

SALTER, M. D. 1940. *An evaluation of adjustment based upon the concept of security.* University of Toronto Press. (University of Toronto Studies, Child Development Series, No. 18.)

SCHWARZ, J. C. 1968. Fear and attachment in young children. *Merrill-Palmer Q.* **14,** 313–322.

VAN LAWICK-GOODALL, J. 1968. The behaviour of free-living chimpanzees in the Gombe Stream Reserve. *Anim. Behav. Monogr.* **1,** no. 3.

Discussion

Methodological Considerations

SCOTT: In the strange situation you described there are three possible sets of relationships, namely those between mother and child, stranger and child, and mother and stranger. You have said nothing about the third; yet, presumably, the nature of the mother's interaction with the stranger must also affect her behaviour to the child.

AINSWORTH: We tried as far as possible to control the behaviour of the adults in the strange situation. The only interaction between mother and stranger was confined to the middle minute of episode 3, when the stranger was told to start a conversation with the mother. So there was nothing more than a very formal interaction between them at this particular point.

SCOTT: The mother's behaviour is an important variable in considering individual differences in child response in this situation. Were all the mothers instructed to act alike, even towards the infant?

AINSWORTH: We attempted to control the behaviour of the mother by telling her to play a non-participant role in *episode 2*, and we told her when to go and when to come back. We did not tell her whether to pick up the baby or not when she returned, and some did and others did not do so. Also, not all were able to play the non-participant role very effectively, and some mothers interfered quite a lot.

FOSS: There are considerable problems in being rigorous at all in this kind of experiment; they result not only from maternal variables but also from such factors as variation in infant state and the response to being filmed. Yet since useful correlations are produced a measure of reliability must be present. Have you done any reliability studies?

AINSWORTH: Not yet. One of the problems is the length of time that ought to be left between two sets of tests. I have no doubt that, having been upset in the strange situation once, an effect will be found the second time, but just which way it would go for which babies I do not know.

FOSS: Harriet Rheingold, did you get cumulative effects in your studies of the strange situation?

RHEINGOLD: Yes. We placed the child repeatedly in the same situation, with and without his mother, and got definite changes over time. It is one of the problems inherent in the use of this technique: once an infant has been exposed to a strange situation it is no longer strange.

RICHARDS: One consideration affecting reliability arises from the general problem of interpretation of observations. For instance, your home visitor observed the mother and child and then wrote an account of what she had seen; on the basis of this a number of people made judgements. It is highly probable that these accounts contained loaded language reflecting the observers' own interpretations. This could give quite spurious reliabilities between raters. What is wanted, therefore, are independent accounts by different observers witnessing the same behaviour in the first place.

AINSWORTH: We have that for the strange situation. Two independent observers dictated into a duo-channel tape recorder, so that we could then code different kinds of behaviour in both accounts. The degree of reliability obtained in this way was generally very high. With regard to home visits, I made joint visits to each family with each of the visitors, and in nearly every case concluded that their judgements had been well founded. It was easy for a rater, when reading the narrative reports of a visit, to distinguish observation from interpretation, although he might nevertheless be influenced by the observer's interpretation. As it happened, the regular visitor's report was usually assigned for rating rather than mine in the case of joint visits, and the rater therefore could not be aware of any discrepancy of interpretation. That such discrepancies were of little moment was shown, however, by the high reliability coefficients between ratings. I had intended to make a proper assessment of reliability of observation by separate codings of behaviours reported by the two observers in a joint visit. Unfortunately, when I joined a visit the regular visitor often used her relative freedom from the constraint to observe in order to administer a developmental test, to take still or movie photographs, or to play a more than usually relaxed participant role. The upshot was that my narrative reports were very much fuller than those of the regular visitors on that occasion—a fact which made the comparison of codings less than maximally useful.

Foss: There is also the problem of judges sharing the same general interests and theoretical orientation; this, however, is a problem common to many studies in psychology.

Lewis: A further problem arises from attempts to measure attachment behaviour. Attachment can be viewed as an underlying structure, and the way we usually measure it is to look at the behaviour in the service of that structure, i.e. proximity to the mother, touching the mother, or the response of the infant to the mother's departure. When an infant shows a large amount of that particular behaviour we assume he has a large amount of that structure. Moreover, when there is a nonsignificant correlation between the particular behaviour, measured at two different points in time, we usually assume that the phenomenon is variable and unstable over time. There is, however, another view, namely that there are multiple responses in the service of any particular structure which are alternatives to one another, and that, furthermore, there is no reason to assume that a particular overt behaviour pattern will remain constant in the service of that structure. Crying, for instance, varies as a function of age, although the basic structure remains relatively constant. It is clear that multiple responses at any given time or over time are needed in order to map both individual differences and changes over time.

Schaffer: One may think of these differences in terms of styles of proximity seeking, likely to be greatest about the age of 1 year when variability in motor ability tends to be more marked than at any other age. There are some highly mobile infants who can run after the mother and climb all over her, others who can merely crawl or slide in order to keep up with her, and still others who are as yet immobile and who have to resort to visual contact or crying. It is therefore necessary to take into account the functional equivalence of a number of behaviour patterns that overtly are quite different.

AINSWORTH: We did try to record not only physical but also visual contact in the strange situation. The passive infants (*group C₂*) had a very characteristic style, for they just sat and looked at the mother. However, the others who explored tended to look at her very little; they were absorbed in their surroundings or in the stranger. But this material needs breaking down according to groups in a more precise manner, and this should answer your question.

Unresponsiveness, Defensiveness, and Proximity Avoidance

AINSWORTH: Two behaviour patterns emerge from the analysis of the strange situation which, as far as I know, have not been reported elsewhere and to which I attach particular significance. These are the ambivalent contact-resisting pattern and the defensive proximity-avoidance pattern. They are both crucial to our classification system, relate to behaviour at home, and are meaningfully associated with maternal variables.

G. BRONSON: I agree that an infant may sometimes appear unresponsive to his mother because he is angry or ambivalent. But are there not instances when the ignoring is more a statement of "I am more interested in doing something else, please don't interfere" than a defensive pattern? After all, sooner or later a quality of independence marks a child's behaviour and then, however strongly attached he may be, there will be times when he just does not want to interact with the mother. How can one differentiate these instances from the ambivalent or defensive pattern?

AINSWORTH: Very often, I believe, a baby's "secure-base" behaviour implies just this kind of interest in outside happenings. If the mother does interfere, the infant's exploration may become tinged with a defensive attitude and difficult to discriminate from proximity-avoiding behaviour. This seemed the case of the babies we classified in *group II* in regard to attachment–exploration balance at home. With these infants the chief basis for discriminating defensive episodes from a more genuine independence in exploration was through a careful analysis of interaction over a whole visit, and indeed over several visits. Interestingly enough, the strange situation discriminates these infants from others; they tended to show B_1 or B_2 behaviour. Finally, let me emphasize that I have been speaking of babies nearly 1 year old. I strongly suspect that "independence" would be more often genuine and less often defensive in 3- and 4-year-olds and probably also in 2-year-olds.

As for looking-away behaviour, I was not geared to note it when we began to observe infants in a strange situation. It first became obvious in its most conspicuous form where a child would start towards the mother, stop, turn and walk away, refusing to come back despite the mother's entreaties. I then began to notice that some babies, on reunion with the mother in the strange situation, merely ignored her whereas others showed this much more distinct looking-away behaviour. It was not until a careful examination of the home-visit data that we were able to make hypotheses about what the baby might be defending against.

BOWLBY: I am not at all sure that the concept "defence" is justified here. It carries with it a lot of theoretical overtones in psychoanalysis, and I am not convinced that the behaviour you described conforms to these. A more parsimonious description would be proximity avoidance, as that does not imply the same theoretical assumptions.

AINSWORTH: One reason for calling it defensive was that the behaviour pattern reminded me of the kind of response that one finds after longer separations and that you labelled "detachment behaviour". It involves a looking away and blankness that can be seen when the child is reunited with the mother after prolonged periods away from her. Now I do not think that a 3-minute separation is long enough to evoke this behaviour if it were not already part of the child's repertoire at home. It is, in other words, a response that the child acquires as a result of his normal interaction with the mother and hence shows variation according to the type of mother–child relationship.

Pathology in Infant Behaviour

SCHAFFER: One of the overriding impressions I receive from this material is of the high incidence of pathology. I use the word advisedly, for if one considers the B_3 group as one's stereotype of the normal, then the deviations from it are really quite considerable in number. I appreciate, of course, that the sample is small and by no means representative, but the range of mother–infant behaviour patterns that most of us would consider as undesirable or at the very least not optimal is quite alarming if generalized to the population as a whole. It would be most interesting to know what implications these data have for the future development of these children.

BOWLBY: It all depends on one's expectations in this respect. After all, the B_3 group represents about 40 per cent of the sample, and the really deviant cases represent about 20 per cent. Now these percentages are not far off the usual estimates of mental health and illness in the population generally, so they do not seem to me to be out of line.

AINSWORTH: But this does highlight the fact that the percentage even of infant disturbance is really much higher than most people think. As to the future implications of these observations, we lack the data to answer this question.

LAWICK-GOODALL: Later pathology is certainly not the inevitable result of early deviance. I observed a chimpanzee infant with an almost incredibly careless mother, who treated her in the most inappropriate way. She was shoved into the dorsal position at 2 months, when the norm is 6 months; and as soon as she broke contact at 5 months the mother would just walk off and leave her, instead of waiting to take her up. Whenever the little one was anywhere near the mother she was whimpering, because the mother was always walking away. At 7 months, when the infant is normally leaving the mother and exploring and playing with others, this infant just would not leave. She hung on continuously and became most distressed if she accidentally let go. This went on until the age of one-and-a-half, and then suddenly she became one of the most independent infants we know. Seeing her now, at the age of 4, one would never guess that she had had such a strange infancy, for she appears completely normal.

STEVENS: She might be normal now, but it would be interesting to see what sort of a mother she would make.

Fear of the Unfamiliar in Human Infants

G. W. BRONSON

Mills College, Oakland

THE APPEARANCE OF wariness as a reaction to the visually unfamiliar is a unbiquitous phenomenon of early development. The material I shall present concerns individual differences in this reaction, including variations in age of first appearance, and some of the antecedents and consequences found to be related to a relatively earlier or later onset.

The data come from two longitudinal studies: the Berkeley Growth Study and Mary Ainsworth's longitudinal study of the first year of life.[1] Subjects of the Berkeley Growth Study were examined at the research centre every month from birth to age 14 months, and then at progressively longer intervals up into adulthood; the material which I present covers the first $8\frac{1}{2}$ years of life. Mary Ainsworth's infants were observed in their homes at 3-week intervals throughout the first year of life, and then in an experimentally controlled "strange situation" at age 1 year.

Figure 1 presents the distributions of age at first appearance of fearfulness as inferred from the data of the two studies. Fear was presumed to be present in infants of the Berkeley Growth Study when a subject cried in response to the novelty inherent in the monthly developmental examinations (for details of the examining procedure see Bayley, 1932). To determine the age of onset of fear in Mary Ainsworth's study, home-visit protocols were rated for behaviours indicative of fear in response to the presence of the observer, namely a long delay before smiling, inhibition of movement, and crying (see Bronson, 1969). Despite the

[1] The Berkeley Growth Study was supported by NIMH grant MH 08135 to the University of California Institute of Human Development. Dr. Mary Ainsworth's study was supported by the Foundation's Fund for Research in Psychiatry grant 62-244, and by UPSHS grant HD 01712. I am indebted to Mary Ainsworth for permission to examine data from the latter research programme, and to Nancy Bayley for access to material of the Berkeley Growth Study.

considerable differences between the two studies both in the circumstances of observation and the criteria of fearfulness, the age distributions proved to be almost identical. Fear seemed present in a few infants
at least as early as the fourth month, but for other infants it was not
observed until about the end of the first year. Although fear of strangers
is sometimes called "eight-months anxiety", it seems clear that many
infants begin to show the response considerably before this age. Note
also that these data provide no evidence of sex differences in the age of
onset of fearfulness.

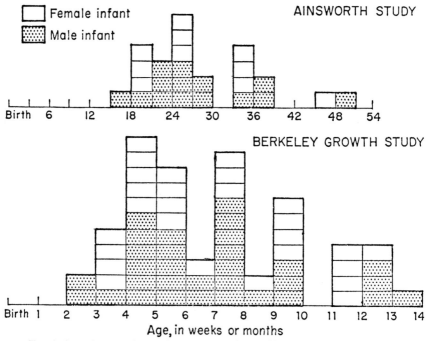

Fig. 1. Age of onset of fear of strangers as observed in two longitudinal studies.

Later correlates of an early or late onset of fearfulness have been
examined in both studies. In the Berkeley Growth Study a rating of
"degree of shyness" was introduced when subjects were 10 months of
age and continued through the $8\frac{1}{2}$-year examinations. Comparisons
of the average shyness scores of those subjects who had first evidenced
fear by age 6 months with the scores of infants who developed such
reactions only after 6 months showed that: (1) male infants characterized by a relatively early onset of fear were significantly more shy

at about the end of the first year, as assessed by the six ratings of shyness averaged across monthly observations at ages 10 to 15 months; (2) in the age period 2 to $3\frac{1}{2}$ years, males who had been precocious in the onset of fear were again found to be significantly more shy; (3) at older ages, i.e. 4 to $8\frac{1}{2}$ years, the trend remained but the relationships fell short of statistical significance. In marked contrast to the male subjects, the female sample not only failed to show any of these relationships, but the trend was slightly in the opposite direction. In brief, for males—but not for females—a relatively early onset of fear predicted a greater degree of shyness from infancy into the preschool years (Bronson, 1970).

It might be suggested that the continuities observed in the development of males, and their absence in females, reflect a tendency for mothers of boys to be more consistently extreme, one way or another, in attitudes that affect their infants' reactions towards strangers. However, a careful analysis of the patterns of male and female development (including some findings not included in this review) makes this interpretation unlikely (see Bronson, 1970). An alternative and, to me, more plausible hypothesis is that infant males are more permanently affected than females by events of early infancy. If that is the case, the developmental continuities observed in the male sample represent relatively enduring infant orientations, and not simply a reflection of stable characteristics present in their home environments.

There is a further piece of evidence from the Berkeley Growth Study relating to sex differences in the continuity of development in this area. In a previous article (Bronson, 1968) it was argued that extreme early fearfulness constitutes a predisposition towards pathological development. Although the Berkeley Growth Study made no systematic ratings of subjects' pathology, in conducting the adult interviews Nancy Bayley was informed by four of the subjects (two men and two women) that they had suffered from schizophrenic episodes as adults. The two men were found to have been, as infants, significantly different from other male subjects in being rated as extremely shy in the 10- to 15-month observations; the two females, in contrast, were near the group mean in these early shyness ratings (Bronson, 1970).

In so far as the data allowed, similar sex differences in developmental continuity were observed in Mary Ainsworth's study. In Ainsworth's study the measure equivalent to degree of shyness at the end of the first year was the intensity of fear when subjects were confronted by a stranger in the experimentally controlled strange situation. Episode 3 of this procedure, in which both the mother and stranger were present, was selected for these ratings; in other episodes in which the stranger was present the mother was either absent, or returning from an absence, and hence fear behaviours were confounded with separation anxiety (see previous chapter for a summary of the various episodes). Raters coded the protocols describing infant reactions to the entrance and the subsequent approach of the strange person on scales designed to assess the degree of fear (these scales combined various signs of wariness, including a failure to smile, disruption of play, crying, return to the mother, etc.; for details see Bronson, 1969).

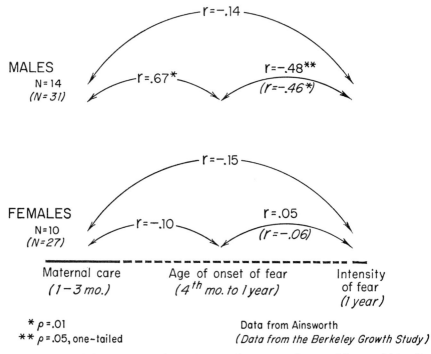

FIG. 2. Correlations among ratings of maternal care, age of onset of fear, and intensity of fear at age 1 year.

The correlations between the age of onset of fear and the intensity of fear of the strange person at age 1 year are shown in Fig. 2. As in the Berkeley Growth Study, for males—but not for females—an early onset of fear was significantly related to more intense fearfulness at age 1 year. For comparison, the correlations between the onset of fear and shyness at age 10 to 15 months computed for subjects of the Berkeley

Growth Study are also given in Fig. 2; these can be seen to be almost identical to those found for Mary Ainsworth's data.

One of the strengths of Ainsworth's study is the carefully collected data on the quality of maternal care. At the time of writing the mothers' behaviours towards their infants had been codified for only the first 3 months of life. As the six maternal care scales published by Ainsworth and Bell (1969) proved to be highly intercorrelated I have averaged them to provide a single index of a mother's sensitivity and concern towards her infant. Figure 2 shows this index to be highly related to the age of onset of fear for males, with infants of the more responsive mothers showing a relatively later onset. Among the female subjects, however, no such relationship appeared. Over a longer time span the effects of variations in early maternal care appeared to be minimal for both sexes: Fig. 2 shows only trivial relationships between ratings of maternal care during the first 3 months and the intensity of fear at age 1 year.

Two major issues arise from the material I have reviewed: (1) what factors contribute to individual differences in the age of onset and subsequent intensity of fearfulness? and (2) how can one explain the repeated findings of sex differences in the developmental continuity? Let me conclude by briefly noting my thoughts on these issues.

That the quality of maternal care in the early months affected the age of onset of fear in males is a plausible finding, indicating that mothers can provide a security which reduces fearfulness. However, both the failure of this measure to predict the onset of fearfulness in females, and its minimal relationship, in either sex, to the intensity of fear in the strange situation at age 1 year, argue for the operation of other variables; the different developmental patterns observed in the male and female samples suggest that genetically based constitutional differences may be interacting with experiential factors to produce the observed variations in the development of fear reactions.

The initial finding of a sex difference in developmental continuity emerged quite unexpectedly from my analysis of data from the Berkeley Growth Study; its replication in Mary Ainsworth's data tends to convince me of its validity, but I have, as yet, found no adequate explanation for the phenomenon. As I noted earlier, explanations based upon presumed differences in maternal behaviours towards infant males and females seem insufficient. My present leaning is towards hypotheses that assume young males to be more permanently affected than females by the quality of early experiences, but the exact nature and timing of these events, and why this should be so, I find hard to specify.

REFERENCES

AINSWORTH, M. D. S. and BELL, S. M. 1969. Some contemporary patterns of mother–infant interaction in the feeding situation. In A. Ambrose (Ed.), *Stimulation in early infancy*. Academic Press, London.

BAYLEY, N. 1932. A study of the crying of infants during mental and physical tests. *J. Genet. Psychol.* **40**, 306–329.

BRONSON, G. W. 1968. The development of fear in man and other animals. *Child Dev.* **39**, 409–431.

BRONSON, G. W. 1969. Sex differences in the development of fearfulness: a replication. *Psychon. Sci.* **17**, 367–368.

BRONSON, G. W. 1970. Fear of visual novelty: developmental patterns in males and females. *Devl. Psychol.* **2**, 33–40.

Discussion

Constitutional Determinants of Fear

SCHAFFER: If, as Bronson suggests, there is indeed a constitutional basis to fearfulness, it might be worth looking for related variables in early development—variables, that is, that are functionally related to fear rather than phenomenologically similar. I have in mind such things as the inherent perceptual sensitivities which Bergman and Escalona (1949. *Psychoanal. Study Child*, **3**, 333) once described, or even something like three-months colic.

SCOTT: Genetically one does not need correlates with other forms of behaviour; on the other hand one would expect correlations between parents and offspring. This being true, one might also expect that the infant would not only inherit fearfulness but also learn to be afraid by observing his mother. Experience certainly does play a part: our own work with dogs has shown that one can produce a very timid animal by rearing him in a restricted environment and later bringing him into a varied and, to him, most bewildering world. However, there are large breed and individual differences between animals that have been reared in an identical manner. Moreover, it is worth stressing that some data suggest that there is no general trait of timidity or fear, but that there are specific kinds of fearfulness. Our animal experiments have shown that different sorts of fear have different genetic bases and are not correlated with one another. Basenjis, for example, tend to be afraid of strange objects (and therefore difficult to test in a strange apparatus), yet they are not at all afraid of other dogs. There are also temporal differences: when young these dogs show strong fear of human beings, but this soon disappears and never returns.

G. BRONSON: Might it not be that fear and anger can inhibit one another? In other words, if an animal is angry it appears less fearful, and if fearful it shows less aggression. It would seem adaptive for an animal to be mainly oriented one way or another in a provoking situation.

SCOTT: I doubt whether fear and aggression can be considered as the ends of the same continuum. They appear to be independent variables, i.e. the same animal may be both highly fearful and highly aggressive, although, of course, the behaviours appropriate to fear and anger may conflict in any one situation.

The Manifestation of Fear

BRODY: I am worried about the use of the word fear, because it can mean so many things in different organisms and have many different manifestations. You may have a baby who is fearful at 6 months yet not at all at 9 months, but who has developed severe inhibition or rocking or anger instead. If one looks hard enough at the anger one may find some underlying anxiety, yet the overt manifestation is utterly different from that of fear.

SCHAFFER: It is obviously important to be clear as to what, operationally speaking, we mean by fear, and I wonder whether Bronson's criteria do not refer to differential behaviour rather than to fear as such. Take as an example latency of smiling, i.e. the absence of positive responsiveness or a prolonged delay in its appearance. I would question whether this can be taken as an indication of negative responsiveness: in one of our studies, for instance (H. R. Schaffer. 1966. *J. Child Psychol. Psychiat.* 7, 95), we found that mere staring at the stranger, without any sign of either positive or negative responsiveness, was a characteristic stage that preceded the onset of fear but did not coincide with it.

G. BRONSON: We assumed that when an infant had failed to show any sign of friendliness after a long period of interaction with the stranger he could be judged as being afraid. Moreover, there was a high correlation between this measure and more direct indices of wariness such as inhibition of activity or crying. Nevertheless, I agree with you about the need for a more precise definition of what we mean by fear. The present criteria were adopted as an expedient to deal with data collected for other purposes.

SCHAFFER: The trouble is that fear of strangers is by no means an on-off phenomenon which the infant either has or does not have. On the contrary, it appears to be highly sensitive to all sorts of conditions both within the child and in the situation, and particularly so to the appearance and behaviour of the stranger. In consequence, it becomes extremely important to specify the various conditions of observation and the measures used if one is to compare data from different studies. Otherwise one gets apparent disagreement on things like age at onset, incidence, and developmental course which are simply a function of procedural differences.

Sex Differences in Fearfulness

KAGAN: I would like to suggest another interpretation with regard to your sex differences. In our longitudinal study (J. Kagan. *Continuity and Change in Infancy*. John Wiley, New York, in press) we found that girls showed more distress when they were brought to the laboratory and placed in a strange crib than boys. Also Leslie Cohen (personal communication) found that girls, at 8 weeks of age, reacted differently to a mobile when they were placed in a novel bassinet in order to view it than when they were placed in a familiar bassinet; boys, on the other hand, showed no differential behaviour. Nancy Bayley, in the Berkeley Growth Study, was not able to judge whether it was the person or the situation that was causing anxiety, so it may be that the lack of continuity for fearfulness among girls in her study was due to different forces bringing about fear at different ages, with the situation more important in the first half-year of life and people thereafter. We found that 4-month old girls who were irritable in the experimental situation showed the most creative play at 2 years; whereas for boys this relationship was absent. So it may be that sex differences in predictability involve cognitive rather than affective variables; at any rate we need to bear in mind that the pattern of continuity of the two sexes for these two kinds of variables may be quite different.

Sex Differences in Early Behaviour

GENERAL DISCUSSION

Genotypes, Phenotypes, and Predictability

ROSENBLUM: I am always surprised when sex differences are reported for early behaviour. Obviously there are some different biological tasks, but by and large it seems to me that early in life the two sexes have more tasks in common than otherwise. They have to eat and drink, seek shelter and warmth, and in general interact with their environment in certain basic ways that should show more overlap than distinction. Why should one believe that for most basic capacities there is differential genetic selection for males and females?

HIRSCH: If you start at the level of the genotype you would expect differences. Because of their chromosome content the male and female are different from the moment of fertilization, so I am almost surprised when their behaviour is *not* different. There need not, of course, be a perfect relationship between genotype and phenotype; environmental pressures, for example, affect the behavioural outcome. Just as the same genotype will present a range of phenotypes as one studies it in different environments, so it is misleading to think there can be laws of environmental influence which are general across genotypes. It is therefore possible for a given external event to produce quite different effects on the sexes.

RICHARDS: There is every reason why boys and girls should develop in different ways, for not only does each sex have its own genotype but they also grow up in different environments. The mother is a different person to her son and to her daughter. There is even an asymmetry in the intra-uterine environment because there is greater genetic similarity between a mother and a female foetus than between her and a male foetus. So right from the beginning conditions are different, and a sex difference in almost any kind of behaviour does not surprise me. The real problem is the difference in developmental predictability—why should girls be more predictable than boys? A consideration that may be relevant is that throughout childhood girls spend more time in the presence of someone of their own sex.

TIZARD: Another possibility is that males are simply more excitable than females, and that this affects the reliability of their test scores. Is there any evidence to bear out such an interpretation?

KAGAN: As far as I am aware there are no sex differences in immediate test–retest correlations.

G. BRONSON: Sex differences in individual consistency over time must depend very much on what is measured. In my studies of fearfulness the boys were more predictable; and in Schaefer and Bayley's (1963. *Monogr. Soc. Res. Child Dev.* **28**) extensive survey of relationships between patterns of mothering and subsequent behaviour, the males also showed far more instances of continuity in various measures of social behaviour.

RICHARDS: I was thinking more of cognitive functions, such as vocalization and language.

SCOTT: In our experiments with dogs we found differences in the extent to which various traits are subject to genetically determined variation; but the differences were much more evident in emotional and motivational characteristics than in cognitive characteristics. For example, we found breed differences in a large number of performance tests. Although at first glance this looked like a factor of general intelligence, further analysis showed that the factor was actually based on the tendency of basenjis to be wary of strange objects. These animals, therefore, showed poor performance in any test which involved strange apparatus. The only difference that appeared to be a reflection of purely cognitive capacities was the tendency of beagles to vary their behaviour and delay habit formation. In a maze test this caused them to do rather poorly on the first trial, but to reach a greater degree of perfection on the last trials.

HIRSCH: I have doubts about this distinction between emotional and cognitive traits. I suspect that the distinction we ought to make is between gross aspects and fine-grained aspects of behaviour. It has been estimated that there are something like 100,000 genes in the human being, so if we study gross characteristics it will be difficult to trace genetic effects. The more fine-grained things we study—such as colour blindness or taste sensitivity—the better our chances of relating them to heredity.

Genetic and Environmental Explanations of Sex Differences

G. BRONSON: One of the main issues is whether the observed continuity in individual behaviour is due to the relatively stable characteristics of the individual or whether over the relevant time span the environment remains relatively more stable for one sex than the other and hence evokes more consistent reactions. The latter would appear to make prediction possible, but it would not, of course, mean that early experience has established relatively inflexible orientations in the individual.

KAGAN: But must that be true? Isn't that statement just another paraphrase of the heredity–environment issue? The trait would not be stable unless the environment supported it.

G. BRONSON: To some extent this becomes a question of degree. I believe that some domains of behaviour tend to be relatively firmly set by early experience and therefore remain fairly consistent even if the environment subsequently changes. I consider degrees of fearfulness to fall into this category for males, in that constitutional factors interacting with experience during the first half-year seem to determine the degree of fearfulness at later age periods. But females appear to remain labile and at each successive age are likely to show more or less fearfulness according to the concurrent environment.

KAGAN: In *Birth to Maturity* (Kagan and Moss. 1962. Wiley, New York) we found that correlations over age for dependency were greater for girls than for boys. But for aggressiveness the boys showed greater predictability, and we regarded that as indicative of the effect of sex role standards on continuity of behaviour. That is a psychodynamic interpretation, but there are other relations that may involve biological dimensions. For instance, several people (J. Cameron *et al.*, 1967. *Science* **157**, 331; T. Moore. 1967. *Human Development* **10**, 88) have established that vocalization is more predictive of later cognitive development in girls than in boys, and we have also found greater stability of vocalization in infancy for girls than for boys. This pattern may be mediated by biological forces. It is possible that the typical dominance of the left cerebral hemisphere over the right emerges earlier ontogenetically and is more clear cut in the female than in the male. One could then expect a closer functional relation between information processing and expressive vocal sounds among girls than boys.

Support for this hypothesis comes from a developmental study of dichotic listening (D. Kimura. 1967. *Cortex* **3**, 163). A series of independent studies has affirmed that when pairs of different digits are presented simultaneously to the two ears through earphones, more digits are accurately reported from the right ear than from the left. Since the auditory receiving area of the temporal cortex receives more fibres from the contralateral than from the ipsilateral ear, the right ear advantage indicates that the left hemisphere, typically the speech hemisphere, is preferentially processing the information. Kimura administered the dichotic task to boys and girls aged 5, 6, 7, and 8 years. Both sexes showed left hemisphere (right ear) dominance at the three older ages, but at age 5 only the girls showed a significant superiority of right over left ear. In the boys no clear dominance was indicated at this age—a finding interpreted by Kimura as indicating that boys may lag behind girls in the development of left hemisphere dominance for speech.

Additional support for the notion that language competence is more elaborated in the left hemisphere for females comes from a study in which right or left temporal cortex was removed from male and female adult epileptic patients (H. Lansdell. 1968. *Cortex* **4**, 257). The patients were tested 1 year after surgery on the Wechsler-Bellevue Intelligence Test. Removal of left temporal cortex had a more serious detrimental effect on verbal functioning among females than among male patients. Removal of right cortex had a more detrimental effect on quality of functioning on the non-verbal tasks for males than for females.

The data thus suggest that left hemisphere dominance and accompanying language elaboration are less equivocal for females than for males, and that consequently verbal functioning is more elaborated in the left hemisphere for girls than for boys. Although the data base may be thin and the hypothesis a little too bold, it is not completely bizarre to suggest that the sex differences in the significance of vocalization during the first year reflect subtle differences in cerebral dominance. The data are consistent, statistically reliable, and invite theoretical attention.

ROSENBLUM: I am puzzled why, from an evolutionary point of view, the human race should have evolved a more rapid or more complete differentiation of the left temporal cortex in females.

RHEINGOLD: An admittedly far-fetched suggestion is that at one time the female infant was sacrificed and that those most able to endear themselves to others by means of smiling and vocalizing were most likely to survive. So there was pressure to develop these functions as early as possible.

SCOTT: To understand sex differences from an evolutionary point of view one must take into account not only the individual but also the evolution of social organization with its tendency towards differentiation of sex roles. The sex difference in vocalization is possibly related to different methods of social control, males using aggressive methods and females non-harmful vocal methods. This is highly adaptive in the case of offspring and so might lead to better verbal ability in girls.

ROSENBLUM: Oh, there are other possible suggestions, such as that females are more valuable biologically and that it is therefore more important that they should develop quickly and that they should receive more parental attention. But all this is sheer speculation.

SCOTT: Some of the animal experiments have come up with interesting facts about sex differences. One finding refers to the reaction of the female nervous system to the male hormone with respect to aggressiveness. Most male and female nervous systems react identically to the male hormone with respect to sexual excitation, but not to aggression. Castrating a female mouse and injecting it with a male hormone will not produce an aggressive mouse, but by pre-treating it with male hormone a day or two after birth you can produce a female that will as an adult respond like a male with increased aggressiveness. So the male and female nervous systems are really basically different. Another example comes from our work with dogs. Tests for dominance in a male group or a mixed male–female group of animals shows that it is usually the heaviest animal that comes out on top, but this is not the case in an exclusively female group, where a small female is just as likely to be dominant as a large one. Amongst the males, dominance is nearly always settled by fighting, and of course weight is then decisive. With females, however, dominance is settled by means of threats and vocalizations and rarely by physical means.

RICHARDS: It may well be that we shall end up with two different kinds of descriptions for the development of certain aspects of behaviour, one for boys and another for girls. We already have this for psychodynamics, and maybe we shall also have to have it for cognitive functions.

Departures from the Mother[1]

H. L. RHEINGOLD AND C. O. ECKERMAN

University of North Carolina at Chapel Hill

AT SOME POINT in his life the mammalian infant leaves his mother's side. The first excursion is typically small in distance and brief in time. In many species the first excursions are met by prompt retrieval but are not thereby suppressed; they occur again and again. With time and experience the infant leaves more often, goes farther, and stays away longer.

The infant's separating himself from his mother constitutes a fact of biological importance. It is of consequence for the preservation of both the individual and the species: of the individual, since it confers the advantage of greater familiarity with the environment and thus increases the likelihood of adaptation to the environment; for the preservation of the species, since it allows the mother to care for the next offspring, and leads eventually to the formation of breeding pairs.

The infant's separating himself from his mother is also of psychological importance, for it enormously increases his opportunities to interact with the environment and thus to learn its nature. He touches an increasing variety of objects; he fingers, grasps, pushes, pulls and thus discovers the changes in stimulation that some objects provide. He moves from place to place within a room and from one room to another and thereby learns the position of objects relative to other objects and the invariant nature of many sources of stimulation. In a word, he learns the properties of the physical world.

Despite the significance of the infant's separating himself, the behaviour has not often been precisely documented, even for the human infant,[2] and seldom has it been the primary subject of study. Here we

[1] This investigation was supported by Public Health Service research career programme award HD-23620 and research grant HD-01107. The paper refers to material presented elsewhere (Rheingold and Eckerman, 1970).

[2] Ainsworth in several papers (e.g. 1961, 1964) has recorded the behaviour as a stage in the infant's attachment to his mother; Mahler (1968) has also noted the behaviour as critical for mental health.

wish to call attention to this behaviour in man and animal, to summarize the data available for the nonhuman primate infant, and to outline some procedures for the experimental analysis of the behaviour in the human infant based upon recent work in our laboratory.

Nonhuman primate studies of the interaction between mother and infant supply information on the frequency, distance, and duration of the infant's separations as well as on the mother's responses to his first departures. The data show that as the primate infant matures he leaves his mother more frequently (Kaufman and Rosenblum, 1969); goes farther from her (Kaufmann, 1966; Vessey, 1968; Jay, 1963; DeVore, 1963; Schaller, 1963); and stays away longer at one time (Altmann, 1959; Kaufman and Rosenblum, 1969).

As the primate infant leaves the mother, she is not passive. The data show, first, that these nonhuman primate mothers restrain their infants from leaving and retrieve them once they have left; and, second, that the frequency of this behaviour increases over the early days of the infant's life and then decreases (Doyle et al., 1969; Harlow et al., 1963; Hinde and Spencer-Booth, 1967; Rosenblum and Kaufman, 1967; Jensen et al., 1968). It is clear that the mother's behaviour reflects the increasing frequency of the infant's attempts to leave—the topic of central concern here—and that over time he wins his way.

In the past couple of years we have studied children in the process of separating themselves from their mothers. Two studies are reviewed to show that the behaviour can be subjected to experimental analysis. The first was carried out in a semi-naturalistic setting with children between 1 and 5 years of age, the other in the laboratory with 10-month-old infants.

To measure the relationship between a child's age and the distance he will travel from his mother, 48 children were studied, three boys and three girls at each half year of age between 12 and 60 months. We placed a mother and child at one end of an unfenced lawn, the mother sitting in a chair, and the child at her knee but free to roam at will for the 15 minutes of the study. Neither mother nor child had been in this place before. The mean farthest distance travelled from the mother by 1-year-olds was 6·9 metres; by 2-year-olds, 15·1 metres; by 3-year-olds, 17·3 metres; and 20·6 metres by 4-year-olds. Variability after the second year of life was considerable. Nevertheless, a linear regression of distance on age was significant at p less than 0·01. The equation for the estimated regression line was

$$\hat{Y} = 2·43 + 0·35X$$

which suggests that for each added month of age the child went about a third of a metre farther.

In the laboratory we investigated some of the properties of the environment that lead the 10-month-old human infant away from his mother (Rheingold and Eckerman, 1969). A simple situation composed of mother, infant, two adjacent rooms, and a few toys provided the laboratory setting. The mother placed the infant beside her in one of the rooms and the door stood open to the second room; neither room had been seen by the mother or infant prior to the test. The properties of the environment were altered by varying the number and location of toys within the second room and by having toys present from the start or added later.

The results showed that infants left their mothers and with no distress entered a new environment, whether or not it contained a toy. When toys were added to the environment, infants who previously had no toy entered faster, stayed there longer, and played with the toys more than infants who previously had a toy. Furthermore, when the new environment contained three toys rather than one, the infants travelled farther from their mothers and stayed away longer, playing with the toys.

That infants crept into the experimental environment of this study and moved about freely, with no distress, contrasted sharply with the marked distress and almost complete inhibition of locomotion shown by infants *placed* alone in the same environment in a previous study (Rheingold, 1969).

At this point it is appropriate to consider the relations between the infant's separating himself from his mother and some other classes of behaviour.

The first is the class labelled the infant's attachment to his mother, and of course for some species this also includes attachment to the nest and littermates. Mammals of necessity stay with their mothers for some time. It is clear that early they distinguish mothers from other organisms, that often they accord mothers and familiar organisms more positive responses than they accord others less familiar, and that they are upset by the departure of these familiar social objects. Attachment, furthermore, persists throughout the life of some species, although the form of the behaviour changes.

The term "detachment" for the behaviour of interest can be used for balance with attachment and for contrast. But detachment does not signal the end of attachment, nor is it simply the opposite of attachment. Attachment and detachment should be viewed as an interplay of classes of behaviour, both developing side by side and coexisting for the life of the individual.

The kind of separation we are talking about, moreover, should not be confused with the separation of "separation anxiety". Observation and laboratory studies have shown us that the infant who *separates himself* does so without anxiety.

The infant's leaving the mother is also related to the class of behaviour called exploratory. The psychological advantages which, it is proposed, result from the child's leaving his mother's side are those very products assumed to result from exploratory behaviour: an increase in a store of perceptions; new opportunities to learn what can be done with an object and what results from manipulating it; an increase thereby in techniques for controlling external events. Furthermore, in our studies of the infant's departures from his mother, some of his behaviour appears to be under the control of those same factors that control exploratory behaviour—among them, novelty, complexity, and change.

Many questions about the process by which the infant separates himself from his mother still await investigation. Questions about the role of environmental stimuli in effecting his departure lend themselves most easily to experimental analysis. The visual properties of social and nonsocial objects, it is proposed, control the infant's departures and contacts. As we have shown, they also determine how long it takes him to leave his mother, how far he goes, and whether he is willing to lose sight of his mother. The feedback properties of objects, furthermore, will determine the duration of contact, the nature and extent of manipulation, and hence the time away from the mother; they may also control the child's subsequent return to the objects.

Naturalistic studies in the child's own home can supply complementary information. As in the nonhuman primate studies, the frequency of contacts, approaches, and departures by both infant and mother can be charted at different ages and in the same child over a span of time. Which behaviours of the infant evoke maternal restraining and retrieving?

In summary, we have described a class of behaviour which has not often been the subject of formal study. Its universality among infants of all species is not recommendation enough for it to engage scientific attention. Far more important are its biological and psychological consequences; it has been proposed that among these are the increased opportunities for learning on the part of the infant. Primarily by his own physical contacts with objects, near and distant, he learns the structural arrangements of objects in space, and the tactual and feedback properties of objects, both social and nonsocial.

The behaviour is patent, it can be measured, it need not be inferred, and, as we have demonstrated, it can be experimentally manipulated. Further, it lends itself nicely to comparisons among species.

The infant's detachment from his mother is not proposed as a negation of attachment to her, but current preoccupation with the attachment of the young to its mother should not obscure the importance of detachment. Its study can present the same challenge that the infant seems to find in going forth on his own.

REFERENCES

AINSWORTH, M. D. 1961. The development of infant–mother interaction among the Ganda. In B. M. Foss (Ed.), *Determinants of infant behaviour II*. Methuen, London. Pp. 67–112.

AINSWORTH, M. D. 1964. Patterns of attachment behaviour shown by the infant in interaction with his mother. *Merrill-Palmer Q*. **10**, 51–58.

ALTMANN, S. A. 1959. Field observations on a howling monkey society. *J. Mammal*. **40**, 317–330.

DEVORE, I. 1963. Mother–infant relations in free-ranging baboons. In H. L. Rheingold (Ed.), *Maternal behavior in mammals*. Wiley, New York. Pp. 305–335.

DOYLE, G. A., ANDERSSON, A., and BEARDER, S. K. 1969. Maternal behaviour in the lesser bushbaby (*Galago senegalensis moholi*) under semi-natural conditions. *Folia primatol*. **11**, 215–238.

HARLOW, H. F., HARLOW, M. K., and HANSEN, E. W. 1963. The maternal affectional system of rhesus monkeys. In H. L. Rheingold (Ed.), *Maternal behavior in mammals*. Wiley, New York. Pp. 254–281.

HINDE, R. A. and SPENCER-BOOTH, Y. 1967. The behaviour of socially living rhesus monkeys in their first two and a half years. *Anim. Behav*. **15**, 169–196.

JAY, P. 1963. Mother–infant relations in langurs. In H. L. Rheingold (Ed.), *Maternal behavior in mammals*. Wiley, New York. Pp. 282–304.

JENSEN, G. D., BOBBITT, R. A., and GORDON, B. N. 1968. Sex differences in the development of independence of infant monkeys. *Behaviour* **30**, 1–14.

KAUFMAN, I. C. and ROSENBLUM, L. A. 1969. The waning of the mother–infant bond in two species of macaque. In B. M. Foss (Ed.), *Determinants of infant behaviour IV*. Methuen, London. Pp. 41–59.

KAUFMANN, J. H. 1966. Behavior of infant rhesus monkeys and their mothers in a free-ranging band. *Zoologica, N.Y.* **51**, 17–27.

MAHLER, M. S. 1968. *On human symbiosis and the vicissitudes of individuation*. Vol. 1. International Universities Press, New York.

RHEINGOLD, H. L. 1969. The effect of a strange environment on the behavior of infants. In B. M. Foss (Ed.), *Determinants of infant behaviour IV*. Methuen, London. Pp. 137–166.

RHEINGOLD, H. L. and ECKERMAN, C. O. 1969. The infant's free entry into a new environment. *J. exp. Child Psychol*. **8**, 271–283.

RHEINGOLD, H. L. and ECKERMAN, C. O. 1970. The infant separates himself from his mother. *Science, N.Y.* **168**, 78–83.

ROSENBLUM, L. A. and KAUFMAN, I. C. 1967. Laboratory observations of early mother–infant relations in pigtail and bonnet macaques. In S. A. Altmann (Ed.), *Social communication among primates*. Univ. of Chicago Press, Chicago, Ill. Pp. 33–41.

SCHALLER, G. B. 1963. *The mountain gorilla, ecology and behavior*. Univ. of Chicago Press, Chicago, Ill. Pp. 265–266.

VESSEY, S. H. 1968. Behavior of free-ranging rhesus monkeys in the first year of life. *Am. Zool.* **8**, 740; and personal communication.

Discussion

Initiative in Maintaining Proximity

SCOTT: The onus for maintaining contact between mother and child seems to shift with age. In most animals the separations take place initially on the volition of the mother—it is she who wanders off and the offspring who maintains contact. To what extent are human mothers different in this respect?

RHEINGOLD: The human mother leaves her infant often, right from the beginning of its life. The infant cannot, of course, by himself effect contact for many months. The question that remains is whether his first movements are towards his mother, to maintain contact, or away from her, to explore the environment. A ready answer does not lie at hand. But in other mammals, except those like the nonhuman primates (who maintain contact by clinging) and the ungulates, precocial infants do not follow the mother very early in life. The mother often leaves the nest to feed and for excretory purposes, and the young stay in the nest even though the infants of many of these species are capable of loco-motion. Are their first departures from the nest, which occur some time later, a following of the mother or a leaving of the mother? I have been impressed by the leaving I have seen in hamsters and kittens in our laboratory. The mothers respond to these first departures by endless retrieving, which stops after a few days. Such frequent retrieving I have not seen in the human case. Surely human mothers retrieve if the infant is in danger, but generally the environment of the home, the first setting of his excursions, has been made safe for him.

AINSWORTH: I am not at all sure that we should judge human maternal retrieval behaviour entirely according to the standards of Western cultures. In Uganda, for example, it seemed to me that mothers do more necessary retrieving than do mothers in Baltimore. The Ganda infant is placed on the floor beside his mother as soon as he is able to sit. When locomotion emerges—and it comes early among the Ganda—a baby is free either to stay close to his mother, or to clamber up on her lap (which is easy because she also sits on the floor), or to move away to explore. He often chooses to explore. Although dangerous or fragile objects are usually kept out of his reach, there are some unavoidable hazards from which he has to be retrieved. The door is kept open for light and air, and when a baby heads outside and out of sight he is promptly retrieved. Although a mother may leave him alone in a room very briefly, she usually takes him with her when she moves from place to place. If there is no one to look after him while she is cooking or serving hot foods or liquids she has to watch him constantly and to pull him back from the fire or the teapot, which are typically at ground level and easily accessible.

In Baltimore, mothers typically make much use of cribs, playpens, and other devices in which a baby may be confined. The outside doors are kept closed. Even though a baby is free to move about on the floor, his mother leaves him behind if she goes to another room. He may follow her with or without a delay, but she tends not to retrieve him promptly if he does not follow. There is less need to retrieve him since there is less danger.

Of course, some mothers in both societies retrieve unnecessarily, and even to a degree that is grossly interfering—because they fail to prevent a baby's access to hazardous objects or areas, or simply because they are over-anxious or over-controlling. And in both societies, soon after a baby achieves locomotion, mothers begin to supplement or supplant physical intervention with control through verbal commands and prohibitions. Nevertheless, there are cultural differences: the Ganda mother typically and for a relatively longer period takes more responsibility for maintaining proximity and hence for retrieving her baby than does the Baltimore mother.

ROSENBLUM: What appears to be involved here is a sort of mentally carried equilibrium distance that is appropriate for a mother-and-infant pair at any given age, and this is carried by both the mother and the infant. And the important thing, in the naturalistic setting, is to appreciate the reciprocal nature of this equilibrium, so that, if an infant is unable to establish or maintain the characteristic distance for that age the mother will maintain it. Infant monkeys, for example, are normally responsible for setting the distance between themselves and the mother, but when one anaesthetizes an infant the distance remains virtually the same as when he is active, because the mother takes over the responsibility.

Determinants of Proximity Range

AMBROSE: I am interested in what determines the maximum distance that can be tolerated at any given age. Is it the possibility of visual perception being maintained between the two partners? Or the time it might take for the two to come together again? To what extent are sensory modalities other than the visual involved? For example, in your laboratory setting the infant was at one point out of visual contact with the mother. Would you predict that, if the mother were emitting auditory stimuli, such as singing, the infant would go further away?

RHEINGOLD: He might; but alternately such stimuli might call him back to her side. One of the limitations of the work in the laboratory is that the room is fairly small so I do not really know how far he would go. At younger ages he might actually go further away. Casual observations in stores and even in our psychology building, outside the laboratory space, have shown that some infants, still under 1 year of age, creep away 20 or 30 feet and then have to be retrieved by the parent.

BOWLBY: I feel that the conditions in which you are studying these children are somewhat atypical. James Anderson (1971. In N. Blurton-Jones (Ed.), *Ethological Studies of Human Behaviour*. Cambridge University Press) has been investigating this problem in a naturalistic setting, namely a London park, where mothers are sitting while their toddlers are running about. Of a sample of 35 children aged between 15 and 30 months approximately two-thirds remained within a maximum distance of about 200 feet from the mother, travelling away from her and back again without her taking any action to ensure proximity. Anderson was impressed by the ability of these children to remain mother-oriented while establishing a distance that took them out of her immediate control. The remaining children moved off farther and the mother had to go after them. Most had been attracted by something of special interest. It seems therefore that proximity is a function of such factors as the nature of the physical setting, its scope for exploration, and where on a fear-assurance continuum one may place the conditions under which the study takes place.

AINSWORTH: The extent to which a child separates himself from the mother is also to some degree a function of the preceding situation. A child who has been in his cot all morning and is then put on the floor will explore away from the mother far more than a child who has been on the floor for quite a long time. Presumably when children are brought to the laboratory they have been held for some time before they are eventually put down, and exploration will accordingly be more marked.

RHEINGOLD: I have no doubt that, up to a point, we can manipulate the duration of time that an infant spends away by attending to variables such as you mention. He returns for many reasons, but I would like to suggest that one of the main reasons may be that he has exhausted the other possibilities of the environment and so has nothing else to do. The variables I would most like to work with are the characteristics of environmental stimuli. It seems fairly clear that we can decrease the duration of time the infant spends away by providing little of interest in the environment or by introducing alarming stimuli. But I wonder how far we can increase the duration by just adding more stimulation—more toys—or by increasing the amount of feedback objects provide when manipulated.

Attachment and Detachment

SCHAFFER: These data raise the question of the relationship between attachment and detachment, and I wonder how we might best conceptualize this relation. It seems to me that there are two general possibilities. One is to consider it as a reciprocal relationship and to maintain that attachment decreases as detachment increases. This involves thinking of attachment purely in terms of physical proximity, of feet and inches, and it is really in this sense that people like Harlow have discussed this phenomenon, attributing its decline to the onset of other systems such as exploration. According to the other view, however, physical distance alone may not be an index for attachment at all, at any rate once a child is of an age to internalize the mother. In other words, an infant at first requires almost continuous perceptual confirmation of the mother's presence, but once he has formed a central representation of her which he can spontaneously retrieve he can leave her, because, so to speak, he carries her with him. It would be useful if one could operationally separate these two different conceptions.

KAGAN: Do not complex constructs like attachment need conjunctive definitions? When the child wanders away we cannot tell whether he is interested in something in his surroundings and not concerned about his mother, or whether he is, as you say, carrying her with him. A good definition of a secure attachment would note not only that the child can wander away but also that, when faced by a discrepant event, he returns to the mother. The conjoint occurrence of these two responses seems a wiser operational definition than either response alone.

RHEINGOLD: The danger is that we tend to talk about attachment as though it is a thing, so that we reify it just as we did with intelligence. Attachment is indexed by multiple behaviours, and these change with the age of the child and with various preceding conditions. Far more work is still needed to find out how these separate behaviours go together at different ages. At the moment attachment is still too global a concept, with a lot of sentimental appeal, and we shall be doing the concept a disservice if we do not refine it and tie it more closely to empirical operations. Furthermore, let us not be so engrossed in the contact that the baby indubitably makes with the mother that we fail to notice that he also separates himself from her and leaves her.

Comparative Perspectives

Infant Attachment in Monkeys[1]

LEONARD A. ROSENBLUM

State University of New York

SOMEWHAT PARALLEL TO the growing body of material on the development of attachment processes in human infants, there are data on a similar dimension in the behavioural development of nonhuman primates. Harlow has been perhaps most prominent in this field (e.g. Harlow *et al.*, 1963) in his studies of "affectional responses" in both the natural and surrogate mother situation. Similarly, Jensen and Bobbitt (e.g. 1967) in their concept of "dependence" have encompassed an array of behavioural responses which seem congruent with those identified as reflecting attachment in human infants. The patterns that have been studied in primates all incorporate strong adient responses of the infant towards the mother. In particular, they include sustained attempts to seek and maintain close proximity and physical or visual contact with the mother. In addition these attachments in monkeys have included the appearance of marked protest and emotional disturbance upon forced or accidental separation from the mother or artificial surrogate, and rapid, strenuous movements towards her and emotional recovery following her return (Seay *et al.*, 1962; Hinde *et al.*, 1966; Rosenblum and Kaufman, 1967).

Since it is feasible to manipulate early experiences with the mother in nonhuman primates, various attempts have been made to distinguish factors which may influence the intensity of developing attachments. These studies have included comparisons of real and artificial mothers as the attachment object (Hansen, 1966), the impact of "enriched" and "privation" environments on the mother–infant relationship (Jensen *et al.*, 1968), as well as the impact of repeated separations and rotation of mothers throughout the early period of life (Mitchell *et al.*, 1967). The research at the Primate Behavior Laboratory of the Downstate Medical Center, conducted initially in collaboration with I. C. Kaufman, has as

[1] This research was supported by USPHS Grant No. MH-15965 and Research Scientist Development Award No. K5, MH-23685.

its present focus the study of naturally occurring and experimentally influenced species variations in maternal behaviour as these influence the development of infant attachment. The current paper will present a series of data drawn from a number of related comparative studies. Each study bears upon several hypotheses derived from the child literature regarding factors which may influence the level and endurance of infant–mother attachment patterns.

Variables Influencing Attachment

One major factor which has received attention in the discussion of infant attachment in humans is the role of the quality and/or intensity of mother–infant interactions in distinction to the mere quantity of time the dyad spends together. In theoretical terms, whether with respect to postulated increases in reinforcement contingencies (Gewirtz, 1961) or in terms of heightening stimulus saliency of the mother (Cairns, 1966), it has been suggested that a more intensive quality of interaction between mother and infant will result in greater attachment to the mother. Schaffer and Emerson (1964), after their study of social attachments in infancy, note " . . . the mother's constant presence is apparently no sufficient guarantee that the infant will develop a very close attachment to her. What is required is a more active impinging of mother on child so that somewhat more limited availability may make a close tie feasible when combined with a high degree of responsiveness and a considerable amount of interaction." It is worth noting here that rhesus monkey infants exposed to a periodically rejecting mother-surrogate spent greater time in contact with her than controls raised on non-responsive but equally available surrogates (Rosenblum and Harlow, 1963). In an early, classic study, Tinklepaugh and Hartman (1932) presented observations on variations in maternal behaviour and the subsequent independence of offspring. These observations also seem to support the contention that more intensive interaction and impingement of the mother on the infant may mediate the development of more intense and long-lasting attachment patterns to her.

One additional area of concern in the recent child literature on the development of infant attachments has particular pertinence to studies of nonhuman primate development, especially those carried out in relatively complex social settings. I refer here to the role of single versus multiple caregiving figures as the infant develops ("aunts"; Hinde, 1965), or what Caldwell and her colleagues (1963) have termed for children "monomatric" and "polymatric" family settings. In various human cultures, both primitive (Mead, 1962; Ainsworth, 1963) and modern (Gewirtz and Gewirtz, 1965), infants may be exposed to a number of caretakers or may be the exclusive responsibility of one individual, usually the biological mother. Within western cultures, both Caldwell and associates and Schaffer and Emerson among others have lent support to the hypothesis that the specificity and intensity of dependence upon the mother tends to relate negatively to the number of mothering figures with whom the infant interacted during early development. It is the specific purpose of this paper to present observations on several species of nonhuman primates pertinent to the impact of these two major variables on the development and maintenance of infant attachment, i.e. the impact of caretaking from single as against multiple affiliative figures and the congruent role of variations in the intensity of mother–infant interactions on the development of this attachment.

Normative Developmental Studies

The initial data stem from a long series of observations on two species of macaque, the pigtail (*Macaca nemestrina*) and the bonnet (*Macaca radiata*). Two major features of the general social behaviour of these species in the laboratory immediately strike the observer. Notation of these distinctions between the species helps to provide the context within which the subsequent maternal behaviour and infant developments are most reasonably understood. It is generally the case that both upon initial formation and for very long periods thereafter, though to a lessening degree over time, destructive aggressive encounters are observed in groupings of adult pigtails brought in from the wild. Indeed, over the last 8 years more than a dozen adult females have been lost in such encounters; and numerous others, including infants and juveniles, have been severely wounded or killed. Violent aggressive encounters resulting in injury may appear even in well established groups, in which general tranquillity seems to have been achieved. Fighting is common in response to disruptions in laboratory routine and occurs occasionally even after everyday events such as feeding or cleaning. On the other hand, in wild born bonnet subjects observed in identically structured groups and physical settings such hostile encounters are exceedingly rare even at the beginning of group formation. Indeed it is only in the presence of severe disruption of a group, such as that following the introduction of several new animals to an already established group, that any sustained destructive interactions are seen in bonnets.

In apparent congruence with this species difference in the levels of aggressive interaction, within hours of the formation of such groups and continuing quite indefinitely thereafter, one observes an enormous difference between the two species in the basic social dimension of individual distance (Rosenblum *et al.*, 1964). Pigtail adults do not in general make physical contact with one another nor spend appreciable time in close proximity even when aggression has subsided, except when engaging in other dynamic social interactions such as grooming or mating. On the other hand virtually all bonnets, including the adult

FIG. 1. A huddle of three bonnet females, the centre one of which holds a newborn infant.

males, spend long periods of the day in closely formed group or sub-group contact huddles (see Fig. 1). This species difference in individual distance patterning is quite stable over a variety of changes in environmental conditions (Rosenblum *et al.*, 1969). What is of the greatest importance, of course, is the fact that these species differences remain characteristic even after the birth of offspring, and thus are integrated into the differential early experiences to which infants of the two species are exposed.

It is characteristic of many group-living species, and this includes the primates, that the appearance of a new infant in the group evokes great interest on the part of other group members. In pigtails and bonnets there are differences in maternal reaction to this group interest which appear in the first moments of the infant's life and lay the basis for marked differences in the infant's early social experience. Bonnet mothers, within moments of delivering their young, often even prior to expulsion and consumption of the placenta, reunite in contact with one or more of their group members. These associates of the mother are allowed to touch, explore, and even handle her newborn. Unlike some langurs (Jay, 1963) the bonnet mother will not allow another animal to carry away her infant, but she will nonetheless allow considerable access to it. The pigtail mother, on the other hand, remains separated from the group, and often will attack vigorously those group members who approach her, particularly if they are subordinate. Should the curious partner be dominant over the new mother, the latter may merely turn her back to prevent access to the infant and swiftly move away when the dominant partner is in any way distracted.

This initial difference in maternal reaction in the two species follows a consistent line of development for the next several months of the infant's life. By the second or third week of life, when the infant macaque makes its first regular attempts to leave the mother, mothers of both species show some apprehension at these efforts to break contact. The pigtail mothers, however, consistently show more frequent attempts to restrain the attempted departures of their young infants. In the course of the next several weeks, as the infant's increasing strength and dexterity expand its capacity to break free of the mother, it is also the pigtail mother who more frequently guards her freely locomoting infant by shuffling along next to it, one hand at its side, or by hovering over the slowly moving infant like a protective canopy. As we see in Fig. 2, although these restrictive protective behaviours occur in both species, considerably higher levels are manifested in pigtail mothers than in bonnets throughout the early period of their infants' life. Throughout this period the mother terminates the excursions and activities of her infant by the rapid retrieval of the young back to her ventrum. After the end of the second month of life prolonged visual watching or brief visual checking of the infant serves as the primary protective tie of mother to infant, with rapid retrieval the most frequent overtly protective maternal behaviour. Again it is the pigtail mothers that more frequently engage in retrieval behaviour. In general, pigtail mothers protectively restrict the behaviour of their infants with consistently greater frequency than that of bonnets throughout the first 6 months of life (see Figs. 3a, b).

Consistent with these differences in maternal protective behaviour it is not surprising that from the first days of life onwards, bonnet infants

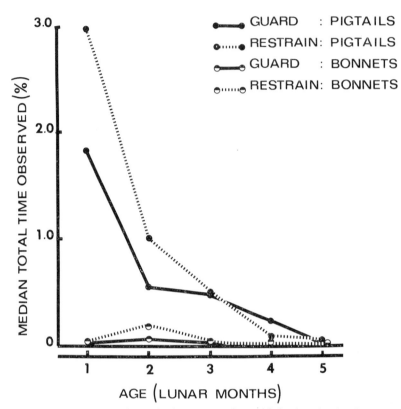

FIG. 2. The appearance of restrain-departure and guard behaviour in pigtail and bonnet mothers during the first 5 months of the infant's life.

engage in consistently higher levels of positive interaction with other adult members of the group (see Fig. 4). These interactions included social explorations, grooming of the infant, clasping of one another, non-threatening facial gestures by the adult, and occurrences of the infant climbing on the body of another adult. As a consequence of the individual distance pattern of their species, in addition to this difference in active affiliative interactions between infant bonnets and adults other than their mother, bonnets receive considerably higher levels of passive contact with other adults during the neonatal period. As a result, in bonnets the total experience of positive social relations with other members of their group is overwhelmingly greater than in pigtail infants of the same age.

This early difference in infant affiliative interactions with adults other than the mother is apparently complemented by a greater extent of

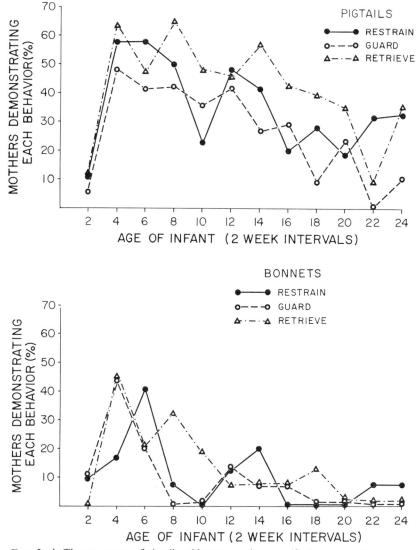

FIGS. 3a, b. The percentage of pigtail and bonnet mothers manifesting each of the maternal protective behaviours during the first 24 weeks of the infant's life.

social interaction with peers in bonnets. In terms of social play inter-actions, the most prominent type of social behaviour observed in bonnet infants during the first year is that they almost continuously engage in more social play than do their pigtail counterparts of the same age.

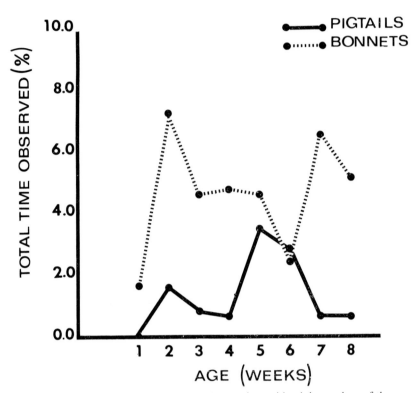

FIG. 4. The development of active affiliative interactions with adult members of the group other than the mother during the first 8 weeks of life.

In no small measure this is due to the fact that bonnet infants have very frequent access to peers almost immediately following birth as a result of the continuing contact patterns of the mothers within the group. Indeed it is not unusual to see bonnet infants engage in play bouts, with each partner maintaining some degree of ventral- and occasionally nipple-contact with their respective mothers. It is of interest, however, that when all forms of play, both social and nonsocial, become extremely prominent in both species, i.e. after the first 4 months of life, total engagement in all forms of play does not differ substantially in the two species. Each is observed in play during approximately 10–11 per cent of the observation periods. Thus it is not the propensity to engage in playful activities which distinguishes the infants of the two species.

Rather, it seems to be the case that in bonnets play tends to become primarily socially directed, whereas in pigtail infants of the same age, for whom dispersal and related dominance patterns may interfere with the free expression of close social interactions, infants primarily engage in non-social, "exercise" play activities.

Let us return now to the unfolding mother–infant relationship. During the same period that play behaviour develops most prominently, mothers of both species begin engagement in a series of abdyadic behaviours, i.e. those which serve temporarily at least to drive the dyad apart (Kaufman and Rosenblum, 1966). These behaviours include:

FIG. 5. A pigtail female forcibly breaking contact with her 5-month-old infant.

preventing the infant from making or maintaining contact with the mother (infant removal, see Fig. 5); preventing the infant from attaining or maintaining oral contact with the nipple (weaning); and finally, physical punishment of the infant, which includes restrained biting of the infant's shoulder, neck, and head when the latter fails to respond to the mother's weaning or removal attempts. It is striking that it is the pigtail mothers who continue their relatively coercive maternal pattern by more actively and more frequently rejecting, weaning, and punishing their infants than do bonnets with infants of the same age. Thus, for example, whereas more than half the pigtail mothers engaged in high levels of rejection (at least one rejection per 5 minutes of observation) during the fifth to the end of the eighth month of their infants' life, only about 6 per cent of the bonnet mothers engaged in such frequent rejections. Similarly, the 1,601 punishments recorded for nine pigtail mothers observed during the first year of their infants' life averaged 6·2 seconds each whereas the 846 punishments recorded for eight bonnet mothers averaged only 4·1 seconds in duration. Thus, by this measure at least, the intensity of rejection episodes in addition to their frequency was greater in pigtail than in bonnet mothers.

TABLE I. COMPARISON OF BONNET AND PIGTAIL NORMATIVE DEVELOPMENT AND MANIFESTATIONS OF INFANT ATTACHMENT

Behaviour	Bonnets	Pigtails
Gregariousness	High	Low
Maternal protection	Low	High
Infant interaction with adults	High	Low
Peer-play	High	Low
Maternal rejection	Low	High
Response to birth of sibling	Minimal	Disturbance
Cohesiveness of family units	Low	High
Response to maternal loss	Brief agitation (adoption)	Depression

As summarized in Table I, we see that a differential pattern of mother–infant relations emerges in these two species when observed under normative group conditions in the laboratory. In relative terms, a pigtail mother isolates herself with her infant from anything more than minimal forms of interaction with other group members. She heightens her relationship with the infant by the intensity of her interactive patterns with him. She often coerces his behaviour, at first by thwarting his attempts to move freely into the environment and subsequently by intermixing her support and care with frequent, often intense, punitive patterns. The bonnet mother on the other hand allows her infant considerable positive interaction with other group members, both adults and peers, and remains relatively more passive and permissive with regard to the infant's association with her. In the light of suggestions from the child development literature one may expect that dissimilar levels of attachment can be found in bonnet and pigtail infants. If these patterns have been interpreted correctly, one might anticipate that, in comparison to bonnets, pigtails would manifest more intense and enduring attachments to their mothers. Several sets of data tend to confirm this hypothesis.

Response to the Birth of a Sibling

The first dramatic indication one observes of differential attachment to the mother in infants of the two species occurs when an infant's mother gives birth to her next offspring. Although precise quantitative data are not yet available on this phenomenon, qualitative observations on the birth of a number of second offspring in both species indicate some striking differences. Pigtail infants often show a sharp disturbance in their ongoing behaviour when a sibling is born (see Fig. 6). Often

Fig. 6. A pigtail infant whose mother, in the foreground, has recently delivered her second infant. Note the thumbsucking and curled hind feet, reflecting the infant's distress following the birth of the sibling.

there is a prominent onset of self-orality in the form of thumb-sucking and, in several of the males, penis-sucking. Marked decreases in play and general activity also have been observed in several cases. On the other hand bonnet infants evince only brief disruptions in behaviour in apparent response to their sudden inability to reach the mother's ventrum. However, no sustained or pronounced emotional reaction to the birth of a sibling has ever been observed in a bonnet infant. The depressive responses of pigtail infants to the birth of a sibling occur in some cases at even 18 months of age, but are generally transient. Nonetheless they seem to reflect far greater general disturbance at this partial psychological "loss" of the mother than is true of bonnets. As such these responses are taken as a reflection of the infant pigtail's more intense attachment to the mother at the time such siblings are born.

Cohesiveness of Family Units

It is by no means the case, however, that the birth of a sibling represents a termination in the bond between an infant and its mother. Particularly in the case of pigtails quite the opposite appears to be the case. Pigtail infants continue to move towards the mother after a sibling is born, and even after the major signs of emotional disturbance have abated, i.e. after 2 to 3 weeks, the mother remains the primary focus of their activity. At night these older infants generally sleep huddled at, or clinging to, the side or back of their mother, while she holds the newborn offspring at her ventrum.

In order to assess the enduring bond of infant to mother in the two species, systematic observations were carried out on two long-term multi-generational groups, one in each species. The groups were formed in the laboratory 6 years prior to the beginning of these observations. When observations began, the pigtail group contained 18 subjects, including a breeding male, 4 mothers, their 12 offspring and 1 attached 5-year-old male. The groupings of uterine-kin or "family clans" each contained one to four infants and their mother. The mean age of these pigtail clan infants was 31·8 months (range: 3–60 months). The bonnet group contained 19 subjects, including a male, 5 females, their 12 offspring, and also a 5-year-old unattached male. The size of the bonnet family clans ranged from 2–4 and the mean age of bonnet clan infants was 30·3 months (range: 8–59 months). There were no statistically significant differences in the ages of infants in the two groups and each species group contained 3 subjects under 1 year of age, 4 subjects from 12 to 36 months of age, and 5 subjects over 36 months of age.

Observations of these animals over a 3-month period indicated a striking difference between the species in the relative cohesiveness of family-clan units. Pigtails were significantly greater than their bonnet counterparts in the percentage of their total interactions which involved other clan members in terms of each of the major social categories of physical contact, grooming and social play (see Fig. 7). As one might expect, as infants grew older their involvement with the mother and their siblings in each species tended to decrease; however, in every age range the preference for involvement within the clan was greater in pigtails

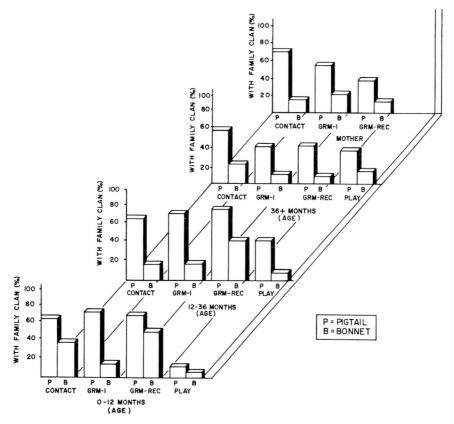

FIG. 7. The relative involvement with family-clan members in bonnets and pigtails as a function of age. The four behaviours depicted are physical contact, groom-initiate, groom-receive, and social play.

than in bonnets. These findings support the hypothesis that pigtails establish a more enduring and selective relationship with the mother than do bonnets. It seems likely that as an outgrowth of attachment to the mother there is a mutual orientation of pigtail siblings towards the mother over long periods which facilitates and fosters the growth of related attachments and interactional preferences for siblings, both older and younger (see Fig. 8). An additional fact emerges from this material that is of some general significance in considerations of the evolution of the family structure and the pertinence of research in primate social behaviour. Within these extremely cohesive pigtail family units (which ultimately represent semi-autonomous segments of the larger troop to which they belong) behaviours which occur only rarely between non-clan members can occur quite frequently. Thus, as indicated above, passive physical contact occurs relatively infrequently between unrelated pigtail adults placed into artificially constituted groups in the laboratory; however, contact between pigtail clan members was just as frequent as had previously been seen only in bonnets.

FIG. 8. A pigtail family-clan. The mother on the left with her yearling, her 2½-year-old son in the middle, and her 4½-year-old daughter on the right holding an 8-month-old grandchild.

Separation Studies

As in studies of children (e.g. Schaffer and Emerson, 1964; Heinicke and Westheimer, 1966; Ainsworth and Bell, 1970) the response of an infant monkey to temporary separation from its mother may serve as a dramatic reflection of his attachment to her. We have carried out a number of mother–infant separations in both bonnets and pigtails during the first half-year of life. These infants were raised under the same form of group rearing conditions described earlier.

Thus far, 13 bonnet infants, ranging in age from 2–6 months, have been observed with their mothers prior to separation, during a 2–8 week separation period, and following reunion with the mother. All infants remained in their group rearing pens during separations. In general, quite similar responses to separation were observed in each of these bonnet infants: the infants initially were somewhat agitated, cooing frequently, and moving about the pen in apparent searching behaviour; however, quite rapidly, often in the first minutes after separation, the infants moved towards and established contact with available bonnet adults. These usually were other females, but occasionally even the adult male became engaged in sustained contact with separated infants. Contact, following, and orientation towards this adult was then maintained in a manner quite comparable to that previously observed in relation to the biological mother. In general this transfer of "filialadience" by the infant to a substitute figure was quite successful in establishing what might appropriately be labelled an "adoption" by the adult (Rosenblum and Kaufman, 1967). The infant in turn passed through the period of separation from the biological mother with only minor disruptions in the ongoing levels of its behaviour, showing no sustained affective responses to the loss. In one of our separation studies with bonnets, for example, five infants 2–5 months of age were separated for 2–4 weeks. All infants maintained prolonged periods of ventral–ventral contact with other adults during the separation. Both of the younger and two of the three older infants achieved full adoptions by other females of the group. These four subjects spent an average of 56·4 per cent of the total observation time in close ventral–ventral contact with a foster mother during the separation (see Fig. 9). These scores compared quite favourably with the 53·9 per cent of the day that the same infants had spent with their own mothers in the month prior to separation. Even the "unadopted" infant in this study spent about 8 per cent of the day in contact with other group adults. None of these infants showed any detectable depression nor pronounced disruption in behaviour during separation. Engagement in play generally seems to be a sensitive indicator of emotional state in young monkeys. Frightened, disoriented, or disturbed animals will rarely engage in play bouts of any duration. In the older bonnet infants of this separation study, in whom social play had already developed, play was engaged in during 3·4, 2·9, 8·7 and 5·9 per cent of the observation periods during 4 successive weeks of separation. These levels represented an insignificant change from the 4·6 per cent score of the pre-separation period. Non-social play similarly decreased only slightly to 4 per cent during separation from a pre-separation median of 4·4 per cent.

Furthermore, so intense were the adoptive relationships established by these four infants, that in the first week following reunion with their biological mothers they still spent 60·3 per cent of the day in ventral–

ventral contact with the foster mothers. Moreover, one of the 2-month olds failed to achieve any ventral–ventral contact with its biological mother during the first week of reunion and one adopted 4-month old never re-established ventral–ventral contact with the real mother following the separation experience.

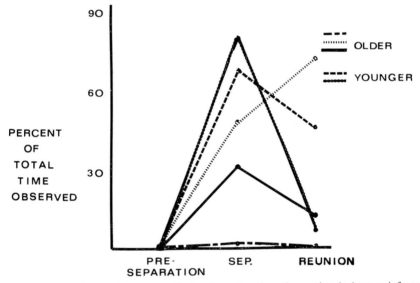

FIG. 9. Ventral–ventral contact with females other than the mother in bonnet infants, before, during, and following mother–infant separation. The younger infants were 8–10 weeks, the older 18–24 weeks at separation.

The response to the loss of the mother in pigtail infants differs dramatically from that observed in bonnets. In the course of various studies 14 pigtails in the 4–6 months age range have been separated from the mother for 2–8 weeks. The following three-stage pattern, with some variation in intensity, has been observed in nine of these cases: (1) The immediate response to separation involves loud screams and cooing, rapid pacing and searching movements and sporadic, brief, and rather distracted exploratory and play behaviours. This agitation phase continues somewhat abated throughout the first day, and often is prominent in the first evening of the separation. (2) By the second day, a marked change in behaviour occurs. The infant sits immobile, hunched into a tight ball, head down, eyes closed (see Fig. 10). Male infants are often seen holding the penis in their mouth. Spontaneous movements and exploration are virtually absent. Play of all types

FIG. 10. A depressed pigtail infant after 1 week of separation.

disappears. The infants can best be described behaviourally as pro-foundly depressed (Kaufman and Rosenblum, 1967). Although most of these infants eat and drink adequately, two have required some brief fluid support, and one additional infant died during this depressive stage, despite our efforts. (3) After about a week, the depression, as reflected in its behavioural indices, gradually lifts, posture becomes normally upright, and brief movements and explorations gradually reappear. Finally, as recovery ensues, social responsiveness emerges and even play is seen. Towards the end of a month of separation, these infants appear generally alert, active and relatively normal. However, they are still deficient in several developing behaviours, such as play, when compared to unseparated infants. It should be noted that the remaining five infants studied thus far, although measurably affected by the loss of the mother, failed to show any pronounced or sustained depression and passed more quickly from a period of agitation towards recovery.

In further distinction to their bonnet counterparts, all pigtail infants show a tremendous reassertion of filial adience upon reunion with the mother, even after 8 weeks of separation. Ventral–ventral contact is achieved almost immediately and sustained at unusually high levels for as long as 3 months after reunion. Even when contact is broken, infants rarely move far from the mother. These sustained manifestations of heightened attachment after reunion are particularly striking in view of the fact that non-separated infants evidenced continued decreases in such behaviour during these age periods.

Repeated Depression in Separated Infants

At present the precise nature of the depression observed in separated pigtail infants is not entirely clear. However, recent work in my laboratory, although not completely analysed, indicates that the depression is a psychological response to a disruption in the relationship with the mother. That is, the syndrome is not merely the physiological consequence of a disruption of a more general nature, such as might be involved in disturbed sleeping or eating patterns. This fact has been ascertained in the following manner. Five pigtail infants were separated in the usual fashion, at 4–6 months of age. Regular observations were made each day to ascertain the course of the spontaneous separation reaction in each infant. Three of these infants exhibited marked depression patterns of the type described above, one a transient depression, and the fifth no sustained affective disturbance. These responses followed the usual time course and the marked depression that occurred began gradually to lift after about a week of separation and was replaced by relatively more normal infant behaviours.

In addition to the usual observations of the separated infants, however, special observations were made 3–4 days each week during the 8 weeks of separation instituted in this study. For these special periods each of the mothers of these separated infants, restrained in an open-wire chamber, was individually introduced into the pen for 30 minutes. As observers have often noted regarding the responses of children to brief encounters with the mother during separation, our separated monkey infants responded quite strikingly to the appearance of their mother in the pen. For a varying number of weeks, each of the previously depressed infants, even when behaviour had recovered to quite normal levels during the usual observation periods (no mother present), responded to the brief reappearance of their mother by the rapid and dramatic manifestations of the full depression pattern. Characteristically these animals, playing or moving more freely about the pen when the mother was absent, would stop immediately upon her introduction, move to an upper bar or corner, begin cooing, change their posture into the rolled-up ball described above, and would soon show the closed or droopy eyelids so characteristic of the depression pattern (see Fig. 11).

FIG. 11. Two separated pigtail infants, 6 weeks after mothers had been removed. The infant on the right, although quite recovered when the mother was absent, shows a repetition of his depression in response to the brief reappearance of his mother within the pen.

In general, during the time their mother was present, these infants remained withdrawn and motionless, only periodically looking at the mother, then cooing briefly and closing their eyes once again. The repeated appearance of the depression in response to the brief return of the mother lasted for approximately 3, 5, and 8 weeks in the three depressed infants respectively. This repeated depression pattern appeared only as a response to the infant's own mother, as the presentation of mothers of the other infants failed to produce anything remotely resembling the pattern described. Moreover, when elicited in the weeks after the original depression had lifted, the depression in response to the mother's return disappeared immediately upon her removal from the pen.

This repetitive depression in response to the mother certainly argues against any simplistic hypothesis suggesting that the depression pattern we have observed is merely the result of metabolic disturbances in the young, separated infant. Although such physiological disorders may come to play a role, these data leave little doubt that the basis of the pattern lies in the infant's psychological response to the loss of the mother.

A final point is worth noting with regard to this study. Although the restraint of the mother complicated matters, the fact that separated infants often failed to move towards the returned mother, either avoiding contact or lapsing instead into the depression pattern, suggests the possibility of some form of the proximity- and interaction-avoiding behaviour shown by some separated children after reunion. As Ainsworth and Bell (1970) report, this avoidance has not yet been demonstrated in nonhuman primates, and the approach of the current study may provide an opportunity to examine the unfolding of such a pattern in relation to the impact and duration of the separation experience.

These monkey studies lend support to the several hypotheses outlined above derived from the child literature. As summarized in Table I, bonnet adult spacing patterns involve prolonged periods of contact and close association with other group members. Perhaps as a concomitant of this relatively more gregarious pattern, bonnet females restrict and protect their young infants less often than do pigtails. Infant bonnets in consequence, from the first days of life onwards, are involved in rather high levels of positive, affiliative interaction with other members of the group, including adults and peers. Finally, towards the end of the first half-year, when macaque mothers increasingly turn their attention away from the young and rejection of the infant appears, bonnet mothers maintain a more passive relationship to the young than do pigtails, by relatively infrequent engagement in such rejection activities. Thus in total, in a comparison of the ontogeny of mother–infant relations in these two species throughout the first year the following characterizations emerge: the bonnet mother is seen as one of many positive figures involved in the development of her infant and as a relatively non-coercive and non-intrusive maternal figure; the pigtail female, on the other hand, is viewed as a more distinct, exclusive attachment figure, who underlines her singularity to her infant throughout development by a series of highly intense interactions with her young, including both early restriction and protection as well as later punishment and rejection. In keeping with the hypotheses concerning the development of attachment in children, these normative data would suggest that pigtail infants should develop more intense and enduring attachments to the mother. In terms of more pronounced disturbance following the birth of siblings in pigtails, the sustained cohesiveness of pigtail family units over many years, and the dramatic debilitation and depression observed in pigtails in response to the loss of the mother, strong support is offered for the validity of these hypotheses, and their application to nonhuman primates.

Monomatric vs. Polymatric Rearing in Squirrel Monkeys

One added dimension of support for the hypothesis that "polymatric" rearing conditions foster less intense and exclusive attachment to the biological mother is offered in some of our recent work on mother–infant relations in squirrel monkeys (Fig. 12). Developmental problems have only recently been studied in this small South American species (Rosenblum, 1968). However, it is now well established that squirrel monkey infants often develop close and relatively enduring relationships with one or more other female members of their group; these females act quite maternally towards the infant and in general assume a caretaking role which has been labelled that of an "aunt" (Hinde, 1965). This occurs with the apparent full acceptance and equanimity of the mother. Often beginning in the first week or so of life, prospective aunts explore, handle, vocalize towards, and ultimately retrieve young infants from the backs of their mothers and carry them about on their own back for considerable periods. Unfortunately, under some conditions not yet well understood, squirrel monkey mothers not only allow their infants to be taken by aunts, but are either unwilling or unable to take back their infants for periodic nursing. To date six infants have actually died as a result of biologically inappropriate aunting experiences.

Nonetheless, by the appropriate formation of a series of groups, some

FIG. 12. Squirrel monkey mothers and their young infants. The infant spends most of the day clinging to the mother's back, as shown on the left. The infant periodically swings his head to the ventral surface for nursing, as seen in the dyad at the right.

of which contain only mothers and their infants and others of which contain in addition a number of non-mothers to serve as prospective aunts, we can examine experimentally the impact of what appropriately may be termed monomatric or polymatric rearing conditions. Several such groups have now been studied both in terms of normative development in the presence or absence of aunting, and in terms of the response of aunted (polymatric) and non-aunted (monomatric) infants to separation from the biological mother. As indicated in Fig. 13, the development of filial attachment to an aunt does not compete with the normally unfolding relationship with the biological mother. That is, close filial contact with the biological mother decreases at approximately the same rate in infants receiving aunting and those which do not. This fact lends support to the hypothesis that infants maintain the capacity to develop a number of non-competitive close attachments. That such attachments do, however, reduce selective dependence upon the biological mother and the linkage of emotional stability and normal behavioural development in her presence is indicated by the response of aunted infants to separation from the mother. In the most general terms, when the mother is removed such infants simply climb onto the back of the aunt and pass through a separation period relatively undisturbed. As indicated in Fig. 14, even vocalization—reported as the

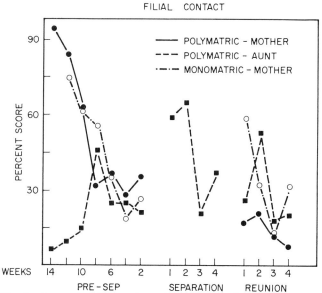

FIG. 13. The development of filial contact with mothers and aunts. Separations occurred at 18–21 weeks. Note the similarity in the decline of filial contact with the mother in the monomatric and polymatric groups.

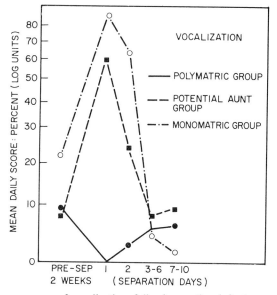

FIG. 14. The appearance of vocalization, following mother–infant separation in squirrel monkeys. The "potential aunt" group contained females which failed to act as aunts. Note the virtual lack of vocalization in the polymatric group infants whose aunts were available during separation.

initial response to separation in all species that have been studied—is virtually absent in squirrel monkey infants whose mothers have been removed but whose aunts continue to be available.

In conclusion then these studies on a number of nonhuman primate forms lend support to the hypothesis that phenomena relating to human infant attachment rest upon a meaningful biological base. Moreover, the pertinent evolutionary antecedents of childhood attachment are evident and available for study in nonhuman primates in ways often difficult or ethically impossible to carry out at the human level.

REFERENCES

Ainsworth, M. D. The development of infant–mother interaction among the Ganda. 1963. In B. M. Foss (Ed.), *Determinants of infant behaviour II.* Pp. 67–104. John Wiley, New York.

Ainsworth, M. D. S. and Bell, S. M. 1970. Attachment, exploration and separation; illustrated by the behavior of one-year-olds in a strange situation. *Child Dev.* **41,** 49–67.

Cairns, R. B. 1966. Attachment behavior of mammals. *Psychol. Rev.* **73,** 409–426.

Caldwell, B. M., Hersher, L., Lipton, E., Richmond, J. B., Stern, G. A., Eddy, E., Drachman, R. and Rothman, A. 1963. Mother–infant interaction in monomatric and polymatric families. *Am. J. Orthopsychiat.* **33,** 653–664.

Gewirtz, J. L. 1961. A learning analysis of the effects of normal stimulation, privation and deprivation on the acquisition of social motivation and attachment. In B. M. Foss (Ed.), *Determinants of infant behaviour.* Methuen, London. Pp. 213–299.

Gewirtz, J. L. and Gewirtz, H. B. 1965. Stimulus conditions, infant behaviors, and social learning in four Israeli child-rearing environments. In B. M. Foss (Ed.), *Determinants of infant behaviour III.* John Wiley, New York. Pp. 161–179.

Hansen, E. W. 1966. The development of maternal and infant behavior in the rhesus monkey. *Behaviour* **27,** 107–149.

Harlow, H. F., Harlow, Margaret K. and Hansen, E. W. 1963. The maternal affectional system of rhesus monkeys. In H. L. Rheingold (Ed.), *Maternal behavior in mammals.* John Wiley, New York.

Heinicke, C. M. and Westheimer, Ilse. 1966. *Brief Separations.* International Universities Press, New York.

Hinde, R. A. 1965. Rhesus monkey aunts. In B. M. Foss (Ed.), *Determinants of infant behaviour III.* John Wiley, New York.

Hinde, R. A., Spencer-Booth, Y. and Bruce, M. 1966. Effects of 6-day maternal deprivation on rhesus monkey infants. *Nature, Lond.* **210,** 1021–1023.

Jay, P. Mother–infant relations in langurs. 1963. In H. L. Rheingold (Ed.), *Maternal behavior in mammals.* John Wiley, New York. Pp. 282–304.

Jensen, G. D. and Bobbitt, Ruth A. 1967. Changing parturition time in monkeys (*Macaca nemestrina*) from night to day. *Lab. Anim. Care* **17,** 379–381.

Jensen, G. D., Bobbitt, Ruth A., and Gordon, Betty N. 1968. Effects of environment on the relationship between mother and infant pigtail monkeys (*Macaca nemestrina*). *J. Comp. Physiol. Psychol.* **66,** 259–263.

KAUFMAN, I. C. and ROSENBLUM, L. A. 1966. A behavioral taxonomy for *M. nemestrina* and *M. radiata*; based on longitudinal observations of family groups in the laboratory. *Primates* **7**, 205–258.

KAUFMAN, I. C. and ROSENBLUM, L. A. 1967. The reaction to separation in infant monkeys: anaclitic depression and conservation-withdrawal. *Psychosom. Med.* **29**, 648–675.

MEAD, M. 1962. A cultural anthropologist's approach to maternal deprivation. In *Deprivation of maternal care*. World Health Organization Monograph Series, No. 14, pp. 45–62.

MITCHELL, G. D., HARLOW, H. F., GRIFFEN, G. A. and MOLLER, G. W. 1967. Repeated maternal separation in the monkey. *Psychon. Sci.* **8**, 197–198.

ROSENBLUM, L. A. 1968. Mother–infant relations and early behavioral development in the squirrel monkey. In L. A. Rosenblum and R. W. Cooper (Eds.), *The squirrel monkey*. Academic Press, New York. Pp. 207–233.

ROSENBLUM, L. A. and HARLOW, H. F. 1963. Approach-avoidance conflict in the mother-surrogate situation. *Psychol. Rep.* **12**, 83–85.

ROSENBLUM, L. A. and KAUFMAN, I. C. 1967. Variations in infant development and response to maternal loss in monkeys. *Am. J. Orthopsychiat.* **38**, 418–426.

ROSENBLUM, L. A., KAUFMAN, I. C. and STYNES, A. J. 1964. Individual distance in two species of macaque. *Anim. Behav.* **12**, 338–342.

ROSENBLUM, L. A., KAUFMAN, I. C. and STYNES, A. J. 1969. Interspecific variations in the effects of hunger diurnally varying behavior elements in macaques. *Brain, Behaviour and Evolution* **2**, 119–131.

SCHAFFER, H. R. and EMERSON, P. E. 1964. The development of social attachments in infancy. *Monogr. Soc. Res. Child Dev.* **29**, 3, Serial No. 94.

SEAY, B., HANSEN, E., and HARLOW, H. F. 1962. Mother–infant separation in monkeys. *J. Child Psychol. Psychiat.* **3**, 123.

TINKLEPAUGH, O. L. and HARTMAN, K. G. 1932. Behaviour and maternal care of the newborn monkey (*Macaca mulatta*). *J. Genet. Psychol.* **40**, 257–286.

Discussion

RICHARDS: Could you describe the methods of observation which you used in these studies?

ROSENBLUM: The data are mostly based on a complex tape recording system. The material was dictated into a continuously running tape recorder, which acted as the time record that was fed into a computer. The material was then printed out in terms of absolute duration for each of the approximately 140 behaviour patterns that we recorded each week for every infant and was expressed as a percentage of the total time we observed the infants. So the data derive from many thousands of minutes of observations on each bonnet and pigtail infant.

Causes and Implications of Species Differences

KAGAN: What are the natural ecologies of bonnet and pigtail monkeys that might account for their behavioural differences?

ROSENBLUM: Bonnets are found in southern India and Ceylon and pigtails in Malaya; their ecologies do not appear to differ in ways which might account for the sort of differences we see in the laboratory. In fact we do not know much about the reasons for the behavioural differences between the two species. The clumping, for instance, appears to have little to do with heat loss—for that matter, you would probably not see much difference in contact patterns in the wild, in that both species are likely to sit in clumps. The crucial difference lies in the likelihood that bonnets sit with friends and neighbours while pigtails sit primarily with brothers and cousins.

KAGAN: The opportunity to form polymatric relationships clearly reduces the probability of separation depression. I wonder, however, to what extent genetic factors can be eliminated. Is there any evidence to suggest species differences in the susceptibility to depression?

ROSENBLUM: I have just begun one or two studies on this problem. Cross-fostering, for example, should help to provide an answer. We shall raise a bonnet with a pigtail mother in a pigtail group and then see if it becomes depressed upon loss of that mother. Also I am removing bonnets from the group and putting them into complete isolation, and although I have done this so far in only a very few cases it does seem that they do not become depressed under such circumstances either. My general impression of the bonnet is that it is a much "cooler" animal; in other words, that there is a personality difference between the two species. Bonnets are able to size up a situation more quickly, they adapt much more readily to a learning situation, they persevere less in frustration tasks. Their dominance relations are much less severe than those of pigtails, and this is one of the factors we shall investigate for its relevance to mother–infant interaction. We have already made one such study: into a mixed group of two bonnet mothers and their babies and two pigtail mothers and their babies we introduced either a pigtail male or a bonnet male, and found there was an immediate and dramatic change in the dominance of the male's conspecifics. If, for instance, a pigtail male is brought in, the pigtail mothers move to the upper levels of the pen and let their infants go more freely, and as a result there is a marked increase in infant play. So far we have done this experiment only cross-sectionally, but I am planning longitudinal studies to see whether, for instance, there are differences in the response to the loss of a dominant, free mother as opposed to the loss of a subordinate, restrictive mother.

Infant and Maternal Responses to Separation

KAGAN: Your data on the pigtail infants' separation responses remind me of the work on "helplessness" in animals. When animals are put into an insoluble problem situation (such as shock that cannot be avoided) they give up trying to escape after a while; and even when the problem has been made soluble they remain passive and helpless. One might argue that when your monkey is separated from his mother he has a representation of her which cannot be realized. This experience may induce the same kind of helplessness seen in other species and which behaviourally resembles depression.

RICHARDS: Is anything known about such aspects of monkeys' cognitive development as object permanence and the ability to remain oriented to an absent object?

ROSENBLUM: One can only go by incidental observations, and these suggest that by the age at which I begin to separate the infants from the mothers such an ability is already present. If, for example, the whole group is taken out of the cage and all returned but one the remaining animals get very upset.

AINSWORTH: It is extraordinarily difficult to demonstrate these things unequivocally with animals. I have a colleague, Silvia Bell, who is investigating object permanence with stumptail monkeys and she is having great diffiulty in applying the necessary techniques. If one separates mother and infant for the testing the infant is so upset that he cannot show interest in the proceedings, and if one allows the mother to remain she takes charge of the situation and herself removes the screens, covers, and so on.

BOWLBY: I am surprised that, in contrast to human infants, there is an immediate resumption of contact with the mother on reunion, even after many weeks of separation. Is this invariable?

ROSENBLUM: It is with these infants. Sometimes, however, it is delayed by the fact that the mother may want to resume her other social relationships first. We had two mothers who completely ignored their babies on first returning because they were so busy making contact with the other members of the group, and only when they had been fitted once more into the social hierarchy did they let the infant come back.

STEVENS: Did you collect any observations on the mothers' responses to separation?

ROSENBLUM: The mothers were put into a pen about 5 feet square and

7 feet high, and there we carried out some observations. The general finding was that both bonnets and pigtails did very little. They are agitated when the baby is first taken off them, and in the first hours of separation they vocalize a great deal, but after that they calm down very quickly and by the second day they behave as perfectly ordinary females. There is no postural change, no change in social or emotional patterns— absolutely nothing to differentiate them from other females. Eventually we stopped observing them.

STEVENS: What about the behaviour of the mothers when they were caged and put into the infants' pens? Did they signal in any way to the infants?

ROSENBLUM: That is hard to answer, for facial gestures directed to a clump of animals at a distance are difficut to determine, particularly gestures which have a certain ambiguity of meaning. The jaw thrust in the pigtail, for instance, is a gesture which appears as an attempt on the part of the mother to call the baby to her, but it is also found in a sexual context and in addition appears as a kind of submissive gesture. We recorded such gestures whenever we could be sure they were directed to the baby, and although they occurred with some frequency we found no clear-cut pattern. Several of the mothers were agitated, yet others showed no concern and appeared quite uninterested.

LAWICK-GOODALL: The literature on captive chimpanzee mothers also indicates that these animals show no seeking behaviour or distress when separated from their young. Yet in the wild, if a mother accidentally loses her infant, she shows much agitation, crying and looking for it for hours. It seems therefore that something happens to the mother in captivity which somehow reduces her distress and infant-seeking behaviour.

Fear of Strangers as a Function of Rearing Structure

LEWIS: The literature on human infants contains various discussions of the effects of fear of strangers when the child is reared in a polymatric as opposed to a monomatric setting. Can your data throw any light on this matter?

ROSENBLUM: Fear of strangers is very difficult to evaluate in these animals—for the same reason that object permanence is so difficult to test. One cannot tell the mother to keep quiet so that the baby's reactions may be observed, and consequently the latter's behaviour is inevitably confounded with what the mother does; and one cannot remove the mother without introducing the confounding influence of separation upset. If you are willing to accept an impressionistic conclusion, I believe that bonnets are much more accepting and affiliative with strangers than are pigtails. If bonnets are brought in from the wild and put together for the first time they begin to huddle very quickly and within 24 hours every animal will have huddled with every other animal. In pigtails, under the same circumstances, there is an enormous amount of fighting and hostility.

LEWIS: This seems to support the view that fear of strangers is a function of the family structure and the nature of the community. The phenomenon may not occur as readily or with as much intensity when the family structure includes a large number of relations. It would be interesting to examine, say, the Wolof of Senegal from this point of view.

Foss: The various investigators who have looked at this relationship in human infants have, on the whole, not found any evidence to support your statement.

LEWIS: I think it important to distinguish between recognition that a stranger has appeared and anxiety over the experience. We do know that anxiety as well as recognition occurs when a stranger moves towards the infant, so it is possible to make a distinction between these processes. Although awareness or recognition of a stranger occurs in all cultures, I am still not convinced that all family experiences produce anxiety in the infant when a stranger appears. Moreover, if it does not hold for humans but does hold for these primates, what possibility is there for ever making generalizations across species? And what accounts for the difference?

ROSENBLUM: I cannot answer those questions. At a descriptive level, however, I am sure that bonnet infants are much more likely than pigtail infants to establish a positive relationship with strangers. Sociologically, if not psychologically, the capacity to do that is more than just the opposite of fear of strangers.

Some Aspects of Mother–Infant Relationships in a Group of Wild Chimpanzees

JANE van LAWICK-GOODALL[1]

INTRODUCTION

In 1960 I initiated a long-term study of the behaviour of a small group of free-living chimpanzees, *Pan satyrus* (or *troglodytes*) *schweinfurthi*, in the Gombe Stream Reserve (now Gombe National Park) on the eastern shores of Lake Tanganyika. For the first $2\frac{1}{2}$ years I worked in the mountains, where it proved difficult to make consecutive observations on the same individuals as these apes are nomadic within a range of approximately 20 square miles and do not move about in a stable or semi-stable troop, but in small constantly changing temporary associations. Only a mother with her infant, and sometimes her young juvenile offspring, forms a stable unit over a number of years. Individuals forming these temporary associations, within a given area, recognize each other and may be said to form a main group or "community".

In 1963 a system of artificial feeding was introduced. After much trial and error we now feed bananas irregularly once every 2 to 3 weeks. This means that scattered individuals usually visit the observation area around the research camp when they are in the vicinity. Since 1964 observations on the behaviour of between 35 and 55 named individuals have been maintained regularly, either by myself or by assistants trained in my observation and recording techniques. In addition it has been possible to maintain fairly regular observations on the behaviour of

[1] This work was carried out in Tanzania and I am grateful to the Tanzania government, officials in Kigoma, and the Tanzania Game Department and National Parks for their co-operation. The work was financed initially by the Wilkie Foundation and subsequently by the National Geographic Society. Recently the Science Research Council has made a grant towards the research. I express my gratitude to all three organizations. I also wish to thank Dr. L. S. B. Leakey, who initiated the research, and my research assistants in the field.

11 different infants from birth onwards. Some of these infants are now in their sixth year of life (for further details see van Lawick-Goodall, 1968).

DEVELOPMENTAL COURSE OF THE MOTHER–OFFSPRING RELATIONSHIP

The female chimpanzee, in the wild, becomes sexually mature during her eighth or ninth year. After the start of the menstrual cycle there is a time lag of anything up to 2 years before conception occurs. In our group several young females have had one or two miscarriages before successful parturition.

I have defined the period of infancy as that time during which the youngster suckles, rides constantly or regularly on its mother's back, and shares her nest at night. For the first 4 to 6 months of life the infant normally remains in constant contact with its mother (unless it should happen to fall accidentally from her). During this period it is transported in the ventral position, clinging to the mother's belly. Some infants were supported by the mother (who used either one hand or walked with bent legs, thus supporting the infant with the thigh) for the first few days or even weeks of their lives; other infants seemed able to cling unaided soon after birth.

When the infant is 5 or 6 months old, mother–infant contact is usually broken, deliberately, for the first time. On those occasions when we have first observed this behaviour it has normally been the infant which initiated the break, letting go of the mother's hair as it sat or crawled beside her. Only once was it the mother who detached her infant's hand. It is at this stage in the infant's development that it takes its first unsteady quadrupedal steps, and makes its first attempts to climb thin branches or saplings.

Throughout the first 6 months the mothering techniques of different females showed considerable variation. Some mothers were very restrictive, pressing their infants firmly back into the ventral position when they tried to pull or push themselves from their mothers, whilst, at the other end of the scale, one mother was seldom seen to interfere with her infant's attempts at exploration and allowed it to creep through her groin and onto the ground behind her when only 9 weeks old. It cannot be too strongly emphasized, therefore, that an infant's independence and the development of its locomotor skills depend not only on its own physical development, but also on the behaviour of its mother. This may also be influenced by an elder sibling, as will be seen below.

Maternal behaviour differs also in the degree of solicitude and tolerance shown by individual mothers to their infants. Some mothers are quick to respond to the rooting behaviour of their young infants, cradling them in a position from which they can reach the breast; others fail to respond until the infant has given a soft whimper, with pouted lips, once or even several times. If an infant starts to slip when relaxing or sleeping on the mother's body, or loses its grip with a hand or a foot during locomotion, some mothers quickly push the child back into place but others fail to respond until the infant whimpers. And whereas some infants are permitted to pull themselves about all over their mothers' bodies, there are mothers who immediately detach their youngsters' hands when hair is pulled on their chins, inner arms, breasts, and so forth. Finally there is a marked difference in individual females as to the amount of playful behaviour directed towards their infants. Although the above data have not yet been systematically analysed for all mothers, a careful survey of the records suggests that the mothers who were the most restrictive in curtailing their infants' early movements were, at the same time, the most solicitous in other respects and, also, the most playful.

During the second half of the first year the infant's locomotor and manipulative skills develop rapidly, and by the time it is 1 year old it can walk and run reasonably steadily and climb slowly but efficiently through the smaller branches of trees. Throughout this period and, indeed, throughout infancy, similar differences in maternal behaviour can be observed in individual females. Our observations have not yet been continued over a long enough time period to say whether the characteristics of a given female's mothering behaviour remain constant towards successive offspring or whether they change as she gets older and more experienced.

Soon after mother–infant contact has been broken, mothers often walk a few feet from their infants and then wait for the latter to rejoin them. If the infant whimpers its mother usually hurries back to retrieve it. One very permissive mother, however, seldom returned to collect her child but continued for several yards followed by the crying infant until either she paused long enough for the infant to catch up or the infant managed to catch up and climb on by herself. Probably as a result, this child, for a period lasting over 2 months, seldom moved more than a few feet from her mother: during many play sessions at this time, when she was over 10 months old, she kept a tight hold on her mother's hair

FIG. 1. Old mother chimpanzee (Flo) plays with her 7-month-old infant (Flint). (Photograph Hugo van Lawick: copyright National Geographic Society.)

throughout. Even during the early part of her second year she normally started to whimper as soon as her mother got up to move off. Subsequently, however, her behaviour showed no obvious signs of insecurity though a thorough analysis of the existing data will be necessary before this statement can be substantiated.

A striking aspect of chimpanzee maternal behaviour, when compared with that of many other mammalian species, is the sparsity of pain-eliciting signals and the frequency of "pleasing" stimuli such as tickling and grooming. Physical punishment of the offspring is rare even when the latter becomes a partially independent juvenile. Most mothers frequently share food with their infants, and on many occasions will wait patiently for their children for up to 40 minutes after making a few unsuccessful attempts to remove them from a play session to travel to a new feeding area.

When infants or young juveniles persist in trying to attain a desired objective, such as a banana the mother is eating, mothers frequently react by tickling or grooming their child and thus distracting their attention from the desired food. This distraction behaviour is observed often during the period when young infants try to pull or push themselves from their mothers' bodies into the surrounding environment. Mothers were also observed to distract their infants when the latter tried to approach the nipple during weaning—a long-drawn-out process which may continue for over a year with the mother occasionally denying access to her breasts and occasionally permitting the youngster to nurse.

OBSERVATIONS OF FAMILY RELATIONSHIPS

As an illustration of chimpanzee social behaviour in general and the social development of infants in particular, a film, entitled "The Chimpanzees of the Gombe Stream Reserve", was shot between 1962 and 1966, by Hugo van Lawick.[2] Much of the film illustrated the relationship between the infant Flint and his 5-year-old sibling, Fifi. Observations began when the infant was 7 weeks old: Fifi, at first infrequently but gradually more and more often, approached Flo, the mother, in order to touch, play with, or groom Flint. If Fifi became rough Flo pushed her away, or distracted her temporarily by grooming or playing with her. When Flint was 13 weeks old Fifi began to try to pull him away from his mother: we first saw her succeed when Flint was 14 weeks old. Subsequently Fifi was permitted to take Flint more and more frequently, and

[2] This film was shown and discussed at the Study Group.

FIG. 2. Mother chimpanzee interferes when her 5-year-old daughter touches new sibling, moving her right foot and leg between the two offspring. Shortly after the picture was taken she moved her daughter's hand gently away. (Photograph Hugo van Lawick: copyright National Geographic Society.)

she often carried him for part of the way when the family was moving from place to place.

Flint took his first quadrupedal steps about a month earlier than all other infants studied to date, excepting his own sibling (born when he was 5 years old) who was, in her turn, pulled away from the mother both by Fifi and Flint himself. Both these infants, therefore, had the opportunitity and the motivation to move independently (as they crawled from sibling to mother) at an earlier age than other infants.

So far it has been possible to study only two other sibling pairs of comparable ages. In one such case the elder sibling was a male and was not seen pulling the infant away from the mother until she was over 6 months old. In the second instance the elder sister suffered from a "club foot" and seemed considerably upset by the new infant's birth. She was no longer permitted to ride on her mother, and had difficulty in keeping up when the family was on the move. She spent long periods of time, when the new infant was under 3 months, sitting close to and grooming the mother but paying little or no attention to her sibling.

On four occasions we have been able to observe the behaviour of infants whose mothers have died: in three of these instances the orphan was adopted by an elder sibling. One infant was only 14 months old at the time, and for the 2 weeks that she survived her mother she was constantly carried about by her 6-year-old brother. He also permitted her to share his food and his nest at night. At this age, however, maternal milk is the major source of food for the infant, and this one undoubtedly died of malnutrition.

The other two adopted orphans were between 3 and 4 years old. Both were adopted by elder sisters with whom they travelled and slept at night. One of them (Merlin) developed a number of stereotyped behaviours of the type usually associated with social deprivation in the laboratory chimpanzee, such as rocking, hair pulling, and hanging upside down from his feet for minutes on end. Also, soon after his mother's death, he began to show a decline in playful behaviour and an increase in grooming and submissive behaviour. Sometimes he was unusually aggressive for his age. About 18 months after his mother's death he died of a paralytic disease. The second infant (Beattle) also showed signs of lethargy and a low frequency of play behaviour, but otherwise her behaviour seemed normal; indeed, 1 year after her mother's death her play behaviour compared in frequency to that of any other normal 4-year old. The main difference in the social situation of these two youngsters lay in the fact that Merlin was only occasionally permitted (and only during the first month of his adoption) to ride on his 6-year-old juvenile sister's back, whilst Beattle, whose sister was an adolescent of about 8 years of age, constantly rode on her sibling. It is tempting to speculate that the added social security derived by Beattle from this constant physical contact helped to minimize the traumatic effect of her mother's death.

The fourth orphan, a 3-year-old female who had no siblings, also became lethargic and she, too, showed a low frequency of play behaviour very soon after her mother's death. She moved about either alone or with different groups of chimpanzees. She was observed regularly for about 2 months after her mother's death after which she was not seen and was finally presumed dead.

It seems possible, therefore, that the death of the mother, even during the fourth year of an infant's life, may cause profound psychological disturbance. Of course, we do not know whether the behaviour of these 3-year-old youngsters was influenced more by deprivation of

FIG. 3. Three-and-a-half-year-old chimpanzee infant, Merlin. This photograph was taken
about half a year after his mother died and shows one of his typical postures. He was
rocking slightly backwards and forwards at the time. The bare skin visible on the lower leg
shows where he has plucked out the hair. (Photograph E. Koning: copyright National
Geographic Society.)

maternal milk (none was weaned) or psychological disturbance following the mother's death. Two lines of evidence, however, suggest that nutritional dependence on milk was not, by itself, necessarily responsible for the changes in behaviour.

Firstly, Merlin, during a 4- or 5-month period before his death, and when he was extremely emaciated, showed an increase in play behaviour and his social interactions in other ways showed signs of becoming more normal. Secondly, and from a somewhat different viewpoint, we may consider the changes which occurred in the behaviour of the infant Flint after the birth of his younger sibling. Flint was weaned late—when he was 4½ years old and some 2 months prior to the new infant's birth. Until the time of her birth he had continued to ride on the mother, Flo, and share her nest at night. After the birth Flint continued to share Flo's nest, although she usually threatened him mildly when he made his first few attempts to join her each night. He then whimpered, more and more loudly, until she finally permitted him to creep in beside her and the infant. However, he only occasionally tried to ride on her back for the first few weeks of his sibling's life, and during this period there were no obvious changes in Flint's social interaction outside the family group.

When his sibling was about 2 months old, however, Flint began to show signs of listlessness and the frequency of his playful behaviour began to decrease (although not to the marked extent to which this occurred in the orphans). At the same time he tried to ride on his mother's back more and more frequently, and sometimes tried to take one of her nipples in his mouth. Each time Flo rejected him or refused to share food with him he whimpered loudly or threw "a temper tantrum", flinging himself onto the ground, rushing off waving his arms, and screaming. Flo and Flint were the only mother–offspring pair we have studied so far who have behaved with frequent aggression towards each other—when Flint hit and bit Flo in his tantrums she often seized hold of him and bit him in return.

These trends in Flint's behaviour persisted for the next few months, although he was almost always gentle with his sibling, and frequently carried her about and groomed her. When she was 6 months old she died and Flint's behaviour underwent a sudden change. He became once more full of life, his playful behaviour appeared to return to normal, and his mother once again permitted him to ride about on her back at will and, occasionally, to take a nipple into his mouth. (He was not observed to get any milk.) At the time of writing, Flint is 5 years 8 months of age, and still riding about on, and sleeping with, his mother.

Since it can reasonably be assumed that a $4\frac{1}{2}$year-old youngster is nutritionally completely independent of its mother, we may assume that it was Flo's rejection of Flint, following the birth of her new infant, which caused symptoms similar to those observed in infants who have lost their mothers. That, of course, suggests that the behavioural changes which occur in orphaned infants may be due, almost entirely, to psychological disturbance resulting from the death of the mother.

CONCLUSIONS

We plan to continue our study of these chimpanzees for at least another 20 years or so in order to cover the life spans of at least some of the individuals I knew as infants. Meanwhile data on infant development, particularly that concerning the mother–infant and sibling relationships, is being collected with increasingly refined techniques, so that reliable comparisons can be drawn in the future. Such a longitudinal study will help us, to some extent, to determine the effect of the personality of a mother on the subsequent social development of her offspring; we shall also investigate the effect of the social status of a mother, at the time when a given child is dependent upon her, on the child's ultimate social rank (and, as the status of a female may change with age, it should be possible to compare the different offspring of one mother in this way). I am hopeful, too, that we shall be able to correlate, to some extent, differences in females' maternal behaviour with differences in the way in which they themselves were mothered, and to find out whether older female siblings may be more efficient as mothers than the youngest female in a family who will have had less chance to "mother" infants before herself becoming a mother.

REFERENCES

van Lawick-Goodall, J. 1968. The behaviour of free-living chimpanzees in the Gombe Stream Reserve. *Anim. Beh. Monogr*, **1**, no. 3.

Discussion

Use and Development of Gestures

Stevens: When watching your film I was most impressed by the refined, almost civilized nature of the gestures which the chimps use towards one another. Have you worked out a vocabulary for such gestures, and have you formed some ideas as to the situations in which particular gestures seem to be appropriate?

LAWICK-GOODALL: Yes, chimpanzee gestures and postures—taken together with their calls—form a very clear-cut communication system. Gestures tend to occur in certain specific behavioural contexts: for instance, a submissive chimpanzee will crouch before a social superior, but a dominant individual will never crouch to an inferior. A subordinate may show submissive rump-presenting during a greeting; a dominant chimp will never present submissively to his inferior. When two particular "friends" greet each other after a separation they are most likely to embrace and kiss. And so on. There is, however, a good deal of individual variation in gestures: in a given context one chimpanzee may present, another may hold out its hand, and yet another is more likely to crouch and kiss.

FOSS: I believe there are local dialects in vocalization; do these occur in gestures too?

LAWICK-GOODALL: Yes. I saw some film material on chimpanzees in West Africa which convinced me of that. During a field experiment Dr. Kortland confronted a group of chimpanzees with a stuffed leopard which wagged its head. These animals showed the same self-reassuring contact behaviour as that which I have seen in our chimps in a similar context—embracing, kissing, holding hands, patting, and so on. In addition, however, one male stood, screaming loudly and with his hair on end—obviously frightened—and reached back with one hand towards another male standing behind him. In response this male mounted the gesturing chimp. This same gesture occurs in our chimpanzee society too, but in a very different context—for there it serves as a signal to an infant that a mother is about to move off. The infant responds by climbing onto the mother from the rear. There must surely be many other variations in gestures of this sort in different chimpanzee communities throughout the range of the species.

KAGAN: Aside from fear- or anger-provoking situations, do you find sex differences in the use of gestures? For example, in a situation when a male and a female greet each other, are both equally likely to vocalize?

LAWICK-GOODALL: There are no obvious sex differences in vocalization in this context—only rank differences. The greater the difference in the rank of two greeting individuals, the more likely it is that the subordinate will give submissive pant-grunt sounds. And again, there are individual differences: one of our females usually utters loud pant-*shrieking* sounds where others would merely pant-*grunt*. She is a particularly nervous chimp. If the animals are of equal dominance they may both emit pant-grunts. There is, however, considerable difference in the use of gestures from one sex to the other. Females typically present more frequently than males; males mount others (not in the sexual context) more frequently than do females; males turn their rumps to subordinates as a reassurance gesture more often than do females, and so on.

AMBROSE: At what age do greeting responses begin to appear and what form do they take?

LAWICK-GOODALL: Infants often respond to the approach of another chimpanzee with soft panting or hooting sounds from the third week. Usually they join in when their mothers make similar calls, but sometimes they call even when the mothers are silent. And when they are about 8 weeks old they usually start trying to reach out and touch other chimps. But really obvious greeting behaviour—when an infant arrives with its mother in a group, or when another individual arrives in the infant's group—does not usually occur until the youngster is about 6 months old. One 5-month-old infant was seen to kiss a newcomer in greeting; other infants first kissed about a month later. A 6- or 7-month-old infant may totter towards another in greeting and extend its hand. Sometimes the other individual then holds the infant's hand. Submissive presenting in greeting does not appear until the youngster is about a year old.

Chimpanzees' Responses to Separation

W. BRONSON: What happens when a youngster gets lost from its mother? LAWICK-GOODALL: The chimpanzee has a pretty effective communication system, but sometimes it does break down and this is one of those occasions. The child itself calls out, at first softly but, if it does not immediately see its mother, more and more loudly. If the mother hears the youngster she will return, but it may happen that, by the time she reaches the place from where the child was calling, it has moved away out of her earshot. If the mother had a loud call which the child could hear this would not occur. She may indeed call out when she first hears the offspring crying, but the sound is merely a soft "hoo" whimper—the sound which, in fact, serves to bring her infant into her arms when it is a few yards away. The sound is, however, totally non-adaptive to the needs of this situation. As a result a child may be lost for hours or days. One lost youngster (Fifi) moved around by herself for nearly 24 hours showing many signs of anxiety: she constantly erected her hair; she climbed many trees to stare around in different directions whilst crying loudly; and, as she hurried along, she often began to whimper quietly.

In the evening she came upon another mother whose child was a favoured playmate of hers; nevertheless, Fifi left them almost immediately and made a nest for herself. She whimpered and cried several times during the night. Fairly early the next morning Fifi joined a small group which contained her mature male brother. His presence seemed to calm her: she stopped raising her hair and whimpering and she ceased climbing trees to look around for her mother. Later in the day the group met up with Fifi's mother.

BOWLBY: After one of these long separations does the child cling to its mother more than normally?

LAWICK-GOODALL: The child certainly follows much more closely and appears very alert to the mother's movements, watching her all the time. When the mother gets up to move on the child usually abandons whatever it is doing to hurry after. I suspect, too, that there is an increase in social grooming (which does, of course, provide prolonged physical contact between mother and child), but we have not yet analysed our notes on this. I would point out that, for the most part, it is only when youngsters are over 5 years old, and only when their mothers have new infants, that they are liable to get lost. Before that the mother almost always waits until she is certain that her infant is following before she leaves a given feeding or resting place.

STEVENS: The hair erection that you observe when the infant is away from its mother seems an extremely useful overt sign of anxiety. It has been suggested that one of the forces that brings the child back to the mother each time after it has left her to explore is a slow build-up of anxiety—rather like an invisible string that periodically draws the child back, and that this is relieved when the child returns and reassures himself that the mother is still there. On the other hand, Harriet Rheingold has argued that the children she observed left the mother and explored the environment without any sign of fear or anxiety about being separated from her. Now, if we have an animal that erects its fur when anxious and does not erect it in other situations, we are provided with an excellent opportunity to make inferences about the role of anxiety during separation and exploration.

LAWICK-GOODALL: When a chimpanzee infant starts to explore the environment away from its mother's body it almost always erects its hair and, for the first few months anyway, it does appear anxious when out of contact with the mother. Certainly it turns and rushes back to her at the slightest unusual sound or movement. As the infant grows older it becomes increasingly less likely to erect its hair during exploration or other activities away from the mother; nevertheless, it still breaks off its activities from time to time in order to touch or sit close to her—almost as though constant renewal of contact with her is necessary to its wellbeing. The sudden deprivation of this source of security is undoubtedly one of the reasons underlying the psychological abnormality which may develop in a 3-year-old which loses its mother. Interestingly, this need for physical contact persists throughout life in the chimpanzee: adults, in moments of fear or anxiety, frequently reach out to touch another individual and this seems to reassure them in much the same way as an upset infant is calmed by contact with its mother.

Attachment and Affection in Chimpanzees

ROSENBLUM: Have you any ideas about which mothers are raising infants that are more or less attached, and, in general, what may account for differences in the intensity of attachments?

LAWICK-GOODALL: Only guesses at present. It appears that mothers who show the most affectionate behaviour towards their infants—fondling, playing, and grooming—produce offspring which remain more closely attached to the mother as they get older than the children of cold-natured and somewhat intolerant mothers. One mother (Flo) who is exceptionally playful and easy-going is very frequently accompanied not only by her infant and juvenile offspring but also by her adolescent and adult male offspring. And Flo is the only mother we know so far who shows a strong mutual bond of affection with her growing daughter. The sample, however, is far too small to permit definite conclusions. I should like to mention one other point: in general, chimpanzee mothers show a far greater range of affectionate behaviours towards their offspring, and far less physical punishment, than other primate mothers. I suspect that this may be a consequence of the specialized social structure of the chimpanzee. In chimpanzee society there is no stable group other than a mother and her younger offspring. Most young primates can leave their mothers for longer and longer at a time to join a play group; there are always several adults around them and, normally, several adult males close by. A young baboon, for instance, can safely play with his peers at any time and, for the most part, be assured of protection not only by his mother but also by adult males of the group. The chimpanzee infant, however, must remain with its mother if it is to receive adequate protection. Thus it is adaptive for the chimpanzee mother to be socially attractive to her growing child as this helps to ensure that it does not go wandering off with another youngster whose mother, in times of trouble, would ignore any child other than her own.

The Categorizing of Behaviour

GENERAL DISCUSSION

Problems in Response Interpretation

ROSENBLUM: The use of comparative material in a study group primarily devoted to human behaviour highlights the problem of how we decide that a particular pattern of behaviour should be put into one category rather than another. Take the box labelled "separation distress": we put into it not only such obvious phenomena as crying but also quite different forms of behaviour. What is more, we use the same label for responses in nonhuman species, which, phenomenologically, may bear little similarity to anything seen in babies. Distress vocalization may be fairly common in some animals, but heavily predated animals respond in quite different ways and do not vocalize when distressed. What justification have we for putting this diversity of responses into the same box? There are clearly dangers of adultomorphizing infant behaviour, but even greater dangers of anthropomorphizing animal behaviour.

FOSS: The usefulness of a category depends on what one wants to do with it. If it helps one's theorizing and research then it should be made available, and responses allocated to it accordingly.

KAGAN: We cannot, however, start off with specific responses and label them arbitrarily. We may use crying, because it is easy to convince our colleagues that it reflects distress, but there are other behaviours which also reflect the same state. It is the state that matters, not the response.

ROSENBLUM: But then we may get into an operational dilemma, for the same state may be indexed by diametrically opposed responses. The separated child may cry, but he may also lie passively without uttering a sound. Are we then to assume that a sign of distress is not crying but lying passively, so that by a kind of presumptive definition we decide that he is now in a state of distress? In clinical practice psychiatrists have to deal with the same dilemma: distress is indicated not only by general excitement but also by its opposite, flattened affect.

AMBROSE: In that case we ought to consider the use of physiological indices to define the underlying emotional state. Whatever the overt behaviour, these indices ought to differentiate at the very least between positive, stimulus approaching or maintaining tendencies and negative, stimulus avoiding or terminating tendencies.

SCHAFFER: We seem to be saying that it is the internal state that should provide us with our categories and that each unitary state is associated with a cluster of distinct physiological responses. I am not convinced that it is possible ever to locate such unitary states by physiological or any other means. It is sometimes suggested that by the use of physiological indices we can obtain access to the "real" internal events that define the states, implying that at the behavioural level we are dealing merely with somewhat unstable epiphenomena. In fact, if we did get down to a physiological level we would find ourselves in exactly the same quandary, picking up isolated measures that had to be interpreted and categorized by reference to concepts outside the measures themselves.

SCOTT: In dogs we have found that the precise relationship between physiological and behavioural indices depends very much on genetic constitution. We tested several different breeds under mildly frightening situations, measuring both their overt behaviour and physiological responses such as changes in heart rate. Cocker spaniels reacted with a great show of external emotional behaviour, crouching and vocalizing. Shetland sheep dogs tended to sit quietly, with little external display of emotion. Internally, however, the sheltie heart rate showed big changes but the hearts of the spaniels beat quite steadily. Thus external and internal emotional reactions do not necessarily show universally valid correlations.

Another experiment concerned distress vocalization as a result of separation. We isolated basenji and sheltie puppies overnight, keeping them away from their mother and litter-mates for 20 hours of the 24. Both breeds vocalized a great deal, the sheep dogs at a somewhat higher rate. When we placed them back with familiar animals the vocalizations ceased almost at once in both breeds. However, their subsequent behaviour was very different. The basenjis calmed down within a few minutes, and one could hardly tell that they had been away; but the sheltie puppies remained hyperactive for hours and even days. Thus one needs measures of both physiological and behavioural reactions, and one should expect wide variation among individuals in both the degree and significance of these reactions.

ROSENBLUM: I also feel that only limited understanding can be obtained from the use of physiological measures. If I see an animal stop playing and roll up in a ball I gain no further insight into what is going on by knowing that certain physiological measures have changed. To understand behaviour we must first determine the lawful relationships of various responses to one another and ascertain the psychological stimulus conditions related to these regularities. No amount of progress along the infinitely regressing path of "higher" (i.e. physiological) level of analysis can substitute for the establishment of these lawful relationships. If, for example, the same EEG pattern were found to accompany two quite disparate behaviours, such as movement to a returning mother and ingestion of a desired food object, should we therefore assume that these behaviours are equivalent and do we understand them or their ontogenesis any more fully? Similarly, will a distinction among physiological measures accompanying two apparently similar behaviour patterns lead us to allocate them to separate systems and inhibit further examination of their psychological communality? Until we establish the pattern of relationships at a behavioural level, psychophysiology in most instances is a powerful but rudderless ship sailing uncharted waters, whose captain can say no more than "We don't know where we are, but we are making excellent time."

Foss: Some physiological and anatomical work may add greatly to one's understanding. I am thinking particularly of von Holst's work with domestic hens, when by using electrical stimulation he was able to identify separate "centres" for different kinds of behaviour—for instance, for different kinds of fighting—and could on this basis show the behavioural effects of stimulating such centres strongly or weakly or of stimulating two at once. The degree of specificity of localization of function is not as great in mammals, but I cannot believe that parts of the brain are not closely associated with various distress symptoms; to know about their functioning and interrelations is bound to increase one's understanding.

Kagan: Let me put the problem in an experimental context. We have been observing the responses of 11-month-old infants to the mother making an exit through either a familiar or an unfamiliar door; although the babies cried more often when the mother left through the unfamiliar door, this was not the most dramatic difference—which was found rather in the length of time during which the infants stopped their play and studied the door. The issue is this: is there a continuum from a state during which the infant stares at the door, but not crying, to the state that accompanies crying? Do we not wish to call the former "distress"? If so, crying is clearly not the only index of the state. In any case, if the states are identical then "distress" may not be the best name.

Foss: Surely we ought to correlate all the supposed indices of this state. We might then find, for example, that some measures show a reciprocal relationship (when there is visual avoidance there is no crying and so on). We might thus conclude that some responses act as substitutes for others. Scott: I agree. The only way to discover which responses can usefully be put into the distress category is to test empirically whatever behaviour patterns are considered relevant, and thereby find out their inter-relationships and their functions. For instance, we have been studying the distress reactions of puppies to separation in order to determine which responses appear at particular ages and which particular aspects of the stimulus situation elicit them. We have found that from about 10 days of age the puppy starts to vocalize when it finds itself in an un-familiar nesting box, but the same reaction to the absence of familiar littermates does not appear till later. We suspect that this is because a puppy at this age, with its eyes still shut, cannot tell whether the other puppies are there or not; it is, therefore, the individual's developing sensory capacities which determine how he responds. In general, vocalizing is the most obvious reaction in puppies to stressful situations but not, of course, the only one—if the stress is much more severe, urination and defecation will also appear. I cannot see any problem here in making decisions about the nature of these behaviour patterns, provided one is prepared to test each one empirically.

Causal and Functional Levels of Analysis

Ambrose: When we use a term such as distress we ought to distinguish its use in a causal context from its use in a functional context. As far as the causal issue is concerned, we try to identify the stimuli that elicit the response—an internal pain, a loud noise, a strange object, and so on. In a functional analysis on the other hand, there is an implication that an organism is in distress, whatever the cause, that it needs help, and that such responses as crying serve the function of attracting the required help. But these are two separate issues and it is dangerous to confuse a causal analysis with a functional analysis.

W. Bronson: One can surely undertake causal analysis by examining what terminates the behaviour as well as what activates it. We may not know why a baby is crying, but if the mother comes and crying stops we can presume that the cause of the distress lay in her absence.

Kagan: The trouble is that if when a baby is crying (whatever the reason) he is given a novel toy, he may stop crying immediately. Yet he was not crying in order to be given a toy.

W. Bronson: In that case, and if boredom was not the causal factor, I assume that crying will resume and not finally terminate until the "right" stimulus is provided.

SCOTT: From a functional point of view, there is no reason why a given activity should not be allocated simultaneously to a number of categories at different levels of analysis. Vocalizing can be categorized as distress but also, at a more general level, as care-soliciting behaviour. Some time ago I developed a scheme of categories for classifying social behaviour in animals, and did this by surveying the behaviour of as many different species as possible (1956, *Ecology* **37,** 213). In one of the categories I placed a variety of behaviour patterns, all of which have the function of signalling for attention, and which I called etepimeletic behaviour. To get at the function of such responses one has to look at the consequences, because behaviour will stop only when adaptation has occurred; it is this which enables one to find some sort of communality among a great many quite diverse postural, gestural, and vocal response patterns.

Social Perspectives

Attachment Behaviour, Separation Anxiety, and Stranger Anxiety in Polymatrically Reared Infants

A. G. STEVENS

Horton Hospital, Epsom

INTRODUCTION

THE CONTROVERSY, HIGHLIGHTED by Bowlby in 1958, between learning theorists who believe that the development of social attachments depends on the satisfaction of primary visceral drives, and ethologically orientated theorists who consider attachment to be the expression of in-built, species-specific response patterns acting "monotropically", has in recent years lost much of its heat. In his reply to Lois Murphy's attack on his position in 1964 Bowlby argued that the controversy had become sterile through lack of data specifically collected to test the alternative hypotheses. "What is now needed," he wrote, "is much more systematic observation of attachment behaviour both in children brought up in ordinary homes and those brought up in atypical environments." The study on which the present paper is based was undertaken very largely in response to this suggestion.

MONOTROPIC RESPONSE PATTERNS IN A POLYMATRIC SETTING

The data which I want to present were collected at the Metera Babies Centre, Athens, between September 1966 and March 1967. The Metera is an intensive care institution for the protection and social rehabilitation of unwanted, mostly illegitimate, infants. It consists of eight attractive home-units, or pavilions, in each of which 12 infants are cared for by a large staff of qualified and student infant-nurses assisted by a small number of voluntary helpers.

In the course of the study, 24 children from three pavilions were observed both in their everyday environment and in an experimental situation. Their ages at the beginning of data collection ranged from 4 to 12 months (Table I); of the original sample of 24, 13 infants were still present at the end of the 6-month period, 11 having been removed earlier by adopting couples or by their natural mothers.

TABLE I. AGE DISTRIBUTION OF THE 24 CHILDREN IN THE SAMPLE AT THE BEGINNING OF DATA COLLECTION

Age in months	Number of children
4	4
5	4
6	5
7	6
8	1
9	1
10	0
11	2
12	1

Although the Metera children receive more intensive care than is possible in institutions with a lower nurse–infant ratio, each child is "mothered" by a far greater number of individual caretakers than is normal in family-reared infants. Over the whole 6-month period an average of 29 different mother-figures served in each pavilion and during each month of the study every child was fed by an average of 15 nurses, changed by 15, put to bed by 10, got up by 10, and bathed by seven different nurses. In broad agreement with these findings are those of a more recent study by Panayiotopoulou (personal communication) which indicate that every child in the Metera's care, irrespective of age or pavilion, receives mothering from approximately 13 different nurses per week and from approximately six different nurses per 24 hours. One must conclude, therefore, that the Metera infants are being reared in a polymatric situation.

The theoretical implications of the present attachment study are, I hope, not without interest. If the secondary drive theory of infant social attachment formation is correct then one might predict that infants reared in a polymatric setting such as obtains at the Metera, would develop multiple attachments, and the principle of monotropy would not hold. The Metera infants would not only fail to develop a strong, persisting bond with one preferred nurse but would fail to exhibit object-specific separation anxiety, and their wariness of strangers would be either mild or non-existent. Caldwell (1962) found children reared in much less widely polymatric environments than the Metera to be less affiliative and dependent and to display less affect in interaction with their mothers than infants from monomatric families, while Hunt (quoted by Schaffer, 1966) goes so far as to assert that "fear of strangers does not occur in children who have always been exposed to a large number of persons and that multiple mothering acts, therefore, as an inoculation against social shyness or fear." If, however, it is found that polymatrically reared infants do, nevertheless, develop strong specific attachments and exhibit marked separation and stranger anxiety, then it would suggest that ethologically orientated theory comes nearer than learning theory to explaining the observed facts.

That variations in upbringing are capable of influencing the timing, intensity, and appropriateness of social phenomena is, of course, not in question. Spitz (1950) drew attention to the failure of deprived infants to manifest fear of strangers, and Ambrose (1961) reported the absence of differential smiling in children similarly deprived. The Metera infants can certainly not be said to be suffering from maternal deprivation in the same sense as were the subjects of Spitz and Ambrose; indeed many of the ideals which the Metera seeks to embody in its intensive care programme grew out of careful study of Spitz's work. The focus of interest in the present attachment study is not how much mothering the Metera infants receive, but from how many mothers they receive it.

Should it be found that polymatrically reared infants fail to develop not only specific attachments but separation and stranger anxieties as well, then the consequences will be serious for Bowlby's theories and Metera children alike. "The complete absence of both anxieties," wrote Benjamin (1961), "would have highly pathological implications, representing a severe maturational deficit or the essential absence of a normal mother–child relationship in all its variations." Moreover, of the two children in the Tennes and Lampl (1964) study who showed minimal stranger and separation anxiety, one was found to be involved in a pathological relationship with its mother and the other "subsequently developed a rather severe convulsive disorder." Consequently if—as many workers suggest—attachment formation, separation anxiety, and stranger anxiety are normal, maturational milestones, then any social environment which precludes their development must be

A. G. STEVENS

regarded as bad; and, if the learning theorists are right, polymatrically organized institutions should either change their ways or close their doors.

PROCEDURE AND FINDINGS

Attachment formation was assessed according to the operational criteria developed by Ainsworth (1964) in her study of Ganda children and by Schaffer and Emerson (1964) in their Glasgow studies. Data on the pavilions were collected by a time-sampling method. A check list was used which embodied categories of attachment behaviour based on Ainsworth's differential criteria (e.g. differential smiling, differential vocalization, visual-motor orientation, following, lifting the arms in greeting, etc.). Nine 10-minute observations were obtained per month per child, giving a total of 540 minutes of observations on each child remaining at the Metera for the 6 months of the study. Each 10-minute observation period was divided up into 20 time intervals and, as a consequence, all categories were checked every 30 seconds. Care was taken always to record by a code letter the nurse to whom a response was directed.

Observations were made in the natural pavilion setting during the daily play period, 10 a.m. to 12 noon, when all nurses working on the morning shift were equally available to each child. Since nurses worked as many morning as afternoon shifts, the procedure of making morning observations only did not result in a weighting of attachment scores in favour of certain nurses at the expense of others.

In analysis of the pavilion data, a child was said to have demonstrated attachment to a given nurse if he had for 2 or more consecutive months directed a significantly greater number of attachment responses to that nurse than to any other nurse in the environment.

Schaffer's criteria of proximity seeking and separation protest were applied to data collected in the experimental setting where a child's responses were recorded through a one-way screen when he was left in a familiar room by different nurses from his pavilion. Strength of protest was scored and analysed in terms of:

(a) the child's age at the time of each experiment, and
(b) the identity of the nurse who brought him and left him alone in the experimental room.

On each occasion the child's responses to being approached, talked to, picked up, put down, and left by a stranger (a nurse from another pavilion) were also recorded.

TABLE II. NUMBER OF CHILDREN GROUPED BY AGE AT ONSET OF PERSISTING NURSE PREFERENCE BEHAVIOUR, SEPARATION PROTEST, AND STRANGER ANXIETY

Age in months	Persisting nurse preference	Persisting separation protest	Both preference and protest	Persisting stranger anxiety
4	1	1	—	—
5	4	2	—	—
6	3	—	1	—
7	3	4	3	2
8	2	6	4	5
9	1	1	—	3
10	1	—	1	—
11	1	1	1	2
12	1	3	1	1
13	—	—	—	—
14	—	—	—	—
15	1	—	1	—
Total number of children	18	18	12	13

Of the 24 children in the sample, 18 developed specific attachments on Ainsworth's criteria, and 18 on Schaffer's criteria, and 13 manifested stranger anxiety which persisted over 2 or more consecutive months. When Ainsworth's and Schaffer's criteria are combined, however, it is found that only 12 of the 24 children fall into both groups. For the purposes of data analysis, it is this group of 12 which is taken as showing unequivocal signs of having developed specific attachment (Table II).

In the case of two children, data for age of onset of specific attachment are unreliable because no data were available concerning attachments which may have been formed before the study began. When these two children are omitted the average age of onset of specific attachment

TABLE III. AVERAGE AGE OF ONSET OF PERSISTING NURSE PREFERENCE BEHAVIOUR, PERSISTING SEPARATION PROTEST, COMBINED PREFERENCE AND PROTEST, AND STRANGER ANXIETY

	Persisting nurse preference	Persisting separation protest	Both preference and protest	Persisting stranger anxiety
Average age (months)	6·8	7·7	7·5	8·4
Number of children	16	16	10	13

(judged by the combined criteria) is found to be 7·5 months and the age of onset of stranger anxiety is 8·4 months (Table III).

TABLE IV. AVERAGE SEPARATION PROTEST SCORES: COMPARISON OF ATTACHED AND UNATTACHED GROUPS

Age in months	Attached group		Unattached group		t values	p
	N	Mean score	N	Mean score		
4	0	—	4	0·8	—	—
5	0	—	8	1·0	—	—
6	1	2·3	12	1·0	—	—
7	5	3·1	15	0·2	5·94	<0·001
8	10	2·8	9	0·4	4·48	<0·001
9	10	4·1	7	1·8	2·04	<0·10
10	9	4·9	6	0·7	2·97	<0·02
11	5	3·6	6	1·2	1·32	<0·25
12	5	4·6	2	3·0	0·60	—

TABLE V. AVERAGE PROTEST SCORES ON APPROACH BY A STRANGER: COMPARISON OF ATTACHED AND UNATTACHED GROUPS

Age in months	Attached group		Unattached group		t values	p
	N	Mean score	N	Mean score		
4	0	—	4	0·5	—	—
5	0	—	8	1·4	—	—
6	1	4·0	12	1·0	—	—
7	5	5·6	15	0·9	5·15	<0·001
8	10	4·4	9	1·0	2·99	<0·01
9	10	6·3	7	3·5	2·02	<0·10
10	9	5·8	6	1·2	3·60	<0·01
11	5	5·4	6	3·9	0·79	—
12	5	5·6	2	4·5	0·28	—

When the sample is split in half, dividing it into attached and non-attached groups, it is seen that children in the attached group evince more intense separation protest and stranger anxiety than children in the non-attached group (Tables IV and V).

CONCLUSIONS

The average ages of onset of specific attachment and stranger anxiety in these polymatrically reared infants agrees closely with estimates made by other workers on children reared in predominantly mono-matric families (Freedman, 1961; Morgan and Ricciuti, 1969; Schaffer and Emerson, 1964; Schaffer, 1966; Spitz, 1950; Tennes and Lampl, 1964).

It must be admitted, however, that 12 members of the sample children developed only equivocal signs of attachment, and ten failed to show fear of strangers. However, such figures are misleading unless it is remembered that 11 of the children studied left the Metera before the 6-month period of data collection was over. Of these no less than eight belong to the non-attached group and it is possible that many of them left the institution before attaining the milestone of specific attachment. This argument is particularly credible in the case of the three unattached children who had left before reaching the age of 7·5 months (the average age of attachment onset in the attached group). Similarly, a large proportion of early leavers make up the group of children failing to develop fear of strangers (seven out of ten). It seems likely, therefore, that more members of the original sample would have demonstrated un-equivocal signs of attachment and of stranger anxiety had they remained in the institution for the whole 6 months of the study.

These findings are, I suggest, more in keeping with the theory that attachment behaviour is dependent upon the maturation of species-specific response patterns acting monotropically rather than upon the acquisition of instrumental responses reinforced by maternal gratifica-tion of primary visceral drives.

REFERENCES

AINSWORTH, M. D. 1964. Patterns of attachment behaviour shown by the infant in interaction with his mother. *Merrill-Palmer Q.* **10**, 51–58.

AMBROSE, J. A. 1961. The development of the smiling response in early infancy. In B. M. Foss (Ed.), *Determinants of infant behaviour.* Methuen, London.

BENJAMIN, J. D. 1961. Some developmental observations relating to the theory of anxiety. *J. Am. psychoanal. Ass.* **9**, 652–668.

BOWLBY, J. 1958. The nature of the child's tie to his mother. *Int. J. Psychoanal.* **39**, 350–373.

BOWLBY, J. 1964. Note on Dr. Lois Murphy's paper. *Int. J. Psychoanal.* **45**, 44–46.

CALDWELL, B. 1962. Mother–infant interaction in monomatric and polymatric families. *Am. J. Orthopsychiat.* **32**, 340–341.

FREEDMAN, D. G. 1961. The infant's fear of strangers and the flight response. *J. Child Psychol. Psychiat.* **2**, 242–248.

MORGAN, G. A. and RICCIUTI, H. N. 1969. Infants' responses to strangers during the first year. In B. M. Foss (Ed.), *Determinants of infant behaviour IV.* Methuen, London.

MURPHY, LOIS B. 1964. Some aspects of the first relationship. *Int. J. Psychoanal.* **45**, 31–41.

SCHAFFER, H. R. and EMERSON, P. E. 1964. The development of social attachments in infancy. *Monogr. Soc. Res. Child Dev.* **29**, no. 3, Serial No. 94.

SCHAFFER, H. R. 1966. The onset of fear of strangers and the incongruity hypothesis. *J. Child Psychol. Psychiat.* **7**, 95–106.

SPITZ, R. A. 1950. Anxiety in infancy: a study of its manifestations in the first year of life. *Int. J. Psychoanal.* **31**, 138–143.

STEVENS, A. G. 1968. "One of the greatest institooshuns": a description of the Metera Babies' Centre, Athens. *Clin. Pediat.* **12**, 8A–28A.

TENNES, K. H. and LAMPL, E. E. 1964. Stranger and separation anxiety. *J. nerv. ment. Dis.* **139**, 247–254.

Discussion

Maternal Stimulation in Polymatric Settings

ROSENBLUM: I wonder whether in this kind of polymatric situation the intensity of interaction might not be greater than in monomatric situations, so that, if one could in some crude way add up the total stimulation received by an infant, one might find that the infants you observed get a lot more stimulation per unit time than a single mother could ever provide.

KAGAN: The very high incidence of separation protest suggests this, for Stevens gets about 70 per cent, whereas in our studies at Harvard we never get more than 50 per cent in an experimental situation. Moreover, two students of mine carried out an investigation with infants in Guatemala, where the children are on their mother's backs and rarely parted from them. Here too the incidence of separation protest was approximately 50 per cent.

STEVENS: I have no measures of the total amount of stimulation received by each child, but my impression is that it would not approach that received by children from their own mothers.

AINSWORTH: These findings are easiest to interpret if we distinguish between an attachment relationship on the one hand and the attachment behaviours which mediate it on the other. The nature of the relationship may remain the same, yet its expression will be affected by a number of conditions like anxiety, separation, or illness, as a result of which a child may become more clinging and resist more the loss of the mother's proximity. Now there are some children who are chronically in this state, and I cannot help wondering if this does not apply to polymatrically reared infants. These children experience far more in the way of coming and going of people, so that sometimes the preferred figure is there and sometimes she is not, sometimes her place is taken by someone else, and also there is more distribution of the nurses' attention among a variety of children. As a result such a child may well be in a more chronic state of heightened attachment behaviour and more apt to protest at separations than a child who is at home with one mother, who has become used to her routine comings and goings, and feels confident either that he knows where to find her if he wants her or that he can expect her to return soon.

Individual Differences in Caretaking Activities

SCOTT: In one of our experiments on dogs we set out to measure genetic differences, so we ordered everyone who had anything to do with the dogs to treat them all alike and not to respond differentially. It meant that our people had to be essentially unresponsive to the dogs, and this was something that the girls in particular found extremely difficult. One result was that the kind of relationship which the puppies developed with their caretakers was very much shallower than the deep and complex attachment that a pet dog develops—they showed general excitement or pleasure with people, but not the close attention and variation in responsive behaviour that one sees in a house dog. Now I am wondering to what extent nurses in institutions, where they take care of other people's children, are able to interact differentially with these infants? Or do they, like the persons in our experiment, perform all caretaking activites very much in a routine way?

AINSWORTH: I would suspect that the main difference between poly-matric and monomatric rearing lies in the degree of sensitivity of the caretaker to the infant's signals and communications. David and Appell (in B. M. Foss (Ed.), *Determinants of Infant Behaviour*, 1961, Methuen, London) found that nurses in the polymatric situation of a baby home did not pick up the baby's signals as readily as did nurses in an experimental group who were giving infants individualized intensive care. It was therefore usually impossible for the polymatric nurses to make their responses contingent upon the baby's signals.

STEVENS: In any institution there is a danger that this may happen, and an institution can claim to be good only in so far as it seeks to prevent it At the Metera the nurses are encouraged to indulge in the little games which mothers and infants invent during changing, feeding and bathing. They try to make it as intimate a situation as possible and not just an automatic routine. But even so, Ainsworth's observations could well apply and, indeed, I think it is likely that the Metera nurses are not as sensitive to their infants' cues as are single mothers.

ROSENBLUM: What about punitiveness? May not the nurses be compensating too much in the direction of solicitude?

STEVENS: Yes, I would say that they do tend to inhibit their punitiveness. Certainly their standards of what is right behaviour for a Metera child seem to be very much more flexible and permissive than those I imagine they would adopt with their own children.

Determinants of Object Choice

BRONSON: Did you find that certain nurses tended to be selected as the infants' preferred person, and, if so, did they have any special characteristics?

STEVENS: I have only my own subjective impressions as to these characteristics, but I am sure that a nurse's relative popularity with the infants was very much determined by her sensitivity and responsiveness to their needs, especially their social needs. One factor I have looked into is the incidence of feeding by specific nurses. I have a record of every meal over a period of 6 months from which I can tell who fed whom. I have been trying to establish whether the nurse who is destined to become the infant's primary object of attachment gives more than her share of feeds in the preceding period, and it appears that this is not always the case. On the other hand, once the attachment bond is established, a nurse's feeding scores for 'her' baby go up dramatically. This happens, however, because it has become recognized by the other nurses that that baby belongs to that nurse and they will therefore leave him to her. The feeding association is thus a consequence of the attachment rather than its cause.

LAWICK-GOODALL: What about characteristics in children that determined their selection as attachment objects by the nurses? For instance, were infants in whom you did not detect any signs of attachment less attractive, either physically or psychologically?

STEVENS: Yes, you could say that there was a tendency in this direction, but the nurses' assessment of "attractiveness" sometimes struck observers as curiously eccentric. In my interviews with the nurses I tried to probe their feelings about various children, and from these it became clear that in each pavilion a very definite consensus existed concerning the desirable and undesirable characteristics of each child. These stereotypes naturally influenced the amount of attention paid to individual infants.

The Social Development of Two-year-old Children in Residential Nurseries[1]

JACK TIZARD AND BARBARA TIZARD

University of London

INTRODUCTION

THIS REPORT DESCRIBES one of a series of studies we are currently undertaking into the development of young children in different types of residential care. The overall purpose of the research is to explore relationships between (a) the organizational structure of different types of residential nursery, (b) the patterns of staff–child interaction found in establishments which are differently organized, and (c) the behaviour and development of children of different ages in different types of establishments.

The present study focuses upon some aspects of the social behaviour of 2-year-old children who are being reared in long-stay residential nurseries. They are compared with working-class 2-year-old children who are being brought up in their own homes by both parents in a relatively favourable environment, in which the mother is not working full time and in which there are no older sibs of pre-school age.

Concern in medical and psychological circles about the possible damage to the development of young children growing up in institutions has led in recent years to great changes in the organization of British residential nurseries. The most important of these changes have been the increasing emphasis placed on retaining links with the family and the attempts to approximate institutional care more closely to the family pattern. The typical British residential nursery today contains 15 to 25 children; it is organized into a baby unit and two or three "family

[1] Mrs. Anne Joseph acted as Assistant Research Officer in this project. The study was made possible by a grant from Dr. Barnardo's Society, and by the co-operation of the staff in nurseries under the auspices of Dr. Barnardo's Society, the Church of England Children's Society, and the National Children's Home.

groups" of six children. The "family groups" contain children of a mixed age range from about 12 months to the upper age limit of the nursery, which varies from $4\frac{1}{2}$ to 7 years. Each group has its own suite of bedroom, bathroom, and living room, with its own nurse, often called "the family mother", and assistant nurse. Two staff are on duty with the group each day. The living room is furnished more or less as it would be in a home, with adult rather than kindergarten furnishings, and is plentifully supplied with toys; outside is a large garden containing further play equipment. Staff on duty eat with the children, and the children have individual clothes and some toys of their own. Most nurseries are characterized not only by a high standard of physical care but also by a concern with the psychological well-being of the children.

Despite attempts to approximate to family life, the residential nursery differs in important respects from a real family environment. In the study reported below an attempt is made to assess the effects of the residential environment on the social development of 2-year-old children.

THE SAMPLES

Selection of the Nursery Group

The files of the three largest voluntary societies in England which provide residential care for deprived children were searched for children approaching the age of 2 years whose medical records showed that they had been healthy full-term babies, with no prenatal complications or difficulties during or after delivery, who had had no subsequent serious illness or hospitalization, and who had entered a residential nursery in good health before the age of 4 months and had not subsequently been moved. The experimental group was formed of the first 15 boys and 15 girls located who satisfied these criteria, provided that five of the boys and five of the girls were coloured. This proviso was made because large numbers of coloured children are taken into residential care and we wished to compare the intellectual development of the white and coloured children (Tizard and Joseph, in press).

All but one of the children were illegitimate. Half of them were visited by their mothers, who hoped to care for them later and did not wish them to be fostered meanwhile. The other half had been offered by their mothers for adoption, but this had not been considered feasible because of the child's colour, or because of some instance in the family history of epilepsy or mental illness. In only one case was this schizophrenia. It was hoped to foster these children eventually. No IQ data on the parents were available, and the occupation of a quarter of the fathers was unknown. One-third of the mothers were in skilled white-collar occupations, mostly as secretaries or bank clerks. All but one of the coloured children were of mixed race, with white mothers.

The Contrast Group

The files of the local health authorities in two London boroughs were searched for the names of 15 boys and 15 girls approaching the age of two who had been healthy full-term babies and had not subsequently been hospitalized. In order to ensure some homogeneity of culture only white English children were chosen and only those where the father was known to belong to the Registrar-General's social classes III to V, i.e. skilled, semi-skilled, and unskilled working classes. For practical purposes two further provisos were made: that the mother should not be working full-time, since our visits were made during the day, and there should be no older pre-school sibling (i.e. 3- to 4-year-olds) at home, since a pilot study had shown that reliable assessment was impossible if an older pre-school child was present. One-third of the group were in fact only children, eight had a younger sibling, and the rest had older siblings at school. Not all the families approached initially by post took part in the study. Attempts to call on those who did not answer our letter were unsuccessful, probably because the mother had gone to work or the family had moved. Three refusals were received. The group is thus in no sense a representative sample, but may be considered illustrative of children in small, well-functioning London working-class families. Two of the fathers were unemployed, and the housing was often poor by English standards—nearly half the families had no access to a bathroom; more than half had only one bedroom, so the children slept with the parents, and two families were living in condemned housing that was about to be demolished. Most of the families lived in two or three rooms in a house shared with one or two families; only 30 per cent lived in blocks of flats.

ASSESSMENT PROCEDURE

All children were seen within 2 weeks of their second birthday, an equal proportion of home and nursery children being seen in each of the 2 weeks preceding and following their birthday.

All the children were assessed in their own living room, with their mother or most familiar nurse present. Sixty per cent of both home and nursery children were visited by one experimenter, and 40 per cent by another. Both experimenters were women.

Response to Strangers

For the first 5 minutes of the interview the child sat on his mother's or nurse's lap, while she chatted to the experimenter. The experimenter then made a series of standardized overtures to the child and rated his responses. The assessment scale was adapted for use with 2-year-olds from one devised by Rheingold and Bayley (1959) for younger children. First the experimenter turned to the child, smiled, and said "hullo". Secondly, she opened a picture book and asked "Would you like to come and look at it?" Thirdly, she smiled at the child and asked "Would you like to come over here and sit on my lap and see?" At each of these three stages, and also at the end of the initial 5 minutes' chat, she rated the child's response to her on the following seven-point scale: (1) cries or runs away; (2) turns head away (definite avoidance) or clings to mother; (3) sobers, stares solemnly; (4) no response; (5) looks coy, or half smiles or comes reluctantly with urging; (6) definitely smiles or comes straight away without smiling; (7) smiles and vocalizes or approaches, smiling. Possible scores thus ranged from 4 to 28. At the end of the interview the final two stages of this test were repeated.

The rank order correlations between the scores of the two experimenters for each of the four stages, when interviewing a series of 20 children, ranged between $r = 0.92$ and $r = 0.96$, $p < 0.001$.

Response to Separation

After a few minutes' further conversation, the experimenter asked the mother or nurse to leave the room briefly, with the door ajar. The child's response to this separation was then rated on the following four-point scale: (1) child follows, looks miserable; (2) child follows, no emotion shown; (3) child stays, looks miserable; (4) child stays, no emotion shown. At the end of the interview the mother or nurse was again asked to leave the room, and the child's response was rated.

Attachments

These were assessed by the use of a scale adapted for older children from one devised by Schaffer and Emerson (1964) for infants. The mother or nurse was asked the following questions: 1. Is there anyone the child is particularly fond of? Whom else is he fond of? 2. Which people does he go up to of his own accord and climb onto their lap? 3. If h is sick or hurts himself, does he go to any particular person, or ask for any particular person? 4. Is there anyone he follows round the house, because he wants to be with that person? 5. Does he cry or protest if any particular person leaves the room? 6. Does he run to be picked up if anyone enters the room? 7. Does he cry or protest if any of these people leave the house? 8. If any of these people have been away for (a) the day, for (b) several days, is he clinging or difficult or hostile? The first question was treated as a lead-in, and not scored. That is, in order to be included in the list of preferred persons, the child must show one of the specified forms of attachment behaviour to substantiate the statement that he was "fond of him". Anyone mentioned in response to questions 2 and 3 was given a score of one. Each of the remaining questions was asked about all the people so far named, as well as about others, e.g. "Does he like to follow you around the house . . . and his father as well? . . . what about his grandmother? . . . would he follow his grandfather? . . . does he like to follow anyone else?" The answers for each person were rated on a four-point scale from 0 (never or hardly ever) to 3 (usually). A list of preferred persons was thus drawn up for each child, on the basis that he showed at least one of the specified forms of attachment behaviour in their presence. The preferred persons could receive scores ranging from 1 to 20, and the person with the top score was regarded as the child's favourite.

Number of Caretakers

Enquiries were made about the number of people who had looked after the child, i.e. given him general care including feeding, bathing and putting to bed (a) since the age of 4 months, (b) in the past 6 months. Only people who had cared for him for at least a week, or for at least 1 day a week for a period of months, were included.

Number of Adult Contacts

The mother or nurse was given a diary covering the next 7 days and asked to make a note of all adults with whom the child came into contact.

Number of Child Contacts

Enquiries were made about the number of children with whom the child had played in the past 2 weeks.

Incidence of Everyday Experience

The mother or nurse was asked about the frequency of certain experiences encountered by the child, her answers being rated on a

3- or a 5-point scale. The experiences which we covered fell into three categories: (1) play experiences, such as the frequency of walks or playing outdoors, watching TV, being read to and sung to, and using certain play materials such as large wheeled toys, pencils or crayons, water and sand; (2) social experiences, such as visiting other houses and having a meal with another family; (3) everyday aspects of the adult world, such as shopping, going in cars and buses, and visiting cafés.

Emotional Behaviour Patterns

The occurrence of emotional responses in certain key areas was investigated by asking the mother or nurse about the frequency of such habits as thumbsucking, nailbiting, headbanging, and rocking; how often the child had wet and soiled himself in the past 2 weeks; how often he had woken in the night in the past 2 weeks; whether he had food fads, messed about with his food, refused to try new food, or demanded to be spoonfed; whether he showed acute fear in any situation; how often he had temper tantrums and whether he was a problem because of destructiveness, jealousy, or attacks on other children.

Emotional Involvement of Mother or Nurse

An attempt was made to measure this by asking whether the child ever really upset them, and whether they ever felt really cross with him or worried about him.

RESULTS

Response to Strangers

The children living at home were significantly more friendly than the nursery children. After the experimenter had been in the room for 5 minutes 86·7 per cent of the home children approached her when invited, but only 50 per cent of the nursery children ($\chi^2 = 7\cdot7$, $p < 0\cdot01$). Of the home children 53·3 per cent then climbed on her lap but only 26·7 per cent of the nursery children ($\chi^2 = 4\cdot44$, $p < 0\cdot05$). The mean score of the home children on the whole scale was 19·17, S.D. 4·09, of the nursery children 15·63, S.D. 3·83 ($t = 3\cdot34$, $p < 0\cdot01$).

Although wary, none of the nursery children showed marked fear until they were invited to sit on the experimenter's lap, when 20 per cent of them cried and ran away. No home children did this. By the end of the session, when the invitation to approach the experimenter was repeated, the nursery children had become much bolder and 80 per cent were willing to do so. However, whilst 30 per cent of the home children approached eagerly on this occasion, none of the nursery children did so ($\chi^2 = 8.37$, $p < 0.01$). Similarly whilst 36.66 per cent of the home children smiled and chatted as they climbed on the experimenter's lap at the second invitation, no nursery child did this cheerfully ($\chi^2 = 27.80$, $p < 0.001$), and two ran away and cried.

Response to Separation

When left alone with the experimenter six nursery children ran out of the room on the first occasion, but no home children did this ($\chi^2 = 4.63$, $p < 0.05$). At the end of the session five nursery children were still unwilling to stay alone with the experimenter, but all the home children stayed cheerfully ($\chi^2 = 3.39$, N.S.).

Attachments of the Home Children

The mean number of persons towards whom the home children were said to show attachment behaviour was 4.13, S.D. 1.68. Parents and grandparents were mentioned most often. In 20 cases the top scorer was the mother, in another five cases both parents scored equally; in four cases (two boys and two girls) the father received the highest score, and in one case, where the father was away from home, the maternal uncle. The most frequently reported expression of attachment was following round the house; 66.7 per cent of the children were said to follow at least one of their favourite persons most of the day, and a further 20 per cent were reported to follow her several times a day.

Distress at brief separation from their mother, which is such a marked feature of young children, was already waning in these 2-year-olds. Fifty per cent of them were reported as usually crying if they saw her leave the house, and a further 10 per cent sometimes did so. However, only 6.7 per cent of the children usually cried if their mother left the room, although a further 36.7 per cent sometimes did so. Only 13.3 per cent of the group sometimes ran to be picked up if their mothers came into the room and none did so often. A third of the children were sometimes left for the day by their mothers with friends or relatives, but only one child was described as clinging or difficult on her return. None of the children had experienced longer separations within the past 2 months.

Attachments of the Nursery Children

A mean number of persons to whom the child showed attachment behaviour could not be calculated for the nursery children, since in every case the list of preferred persons included "anyone he knows well".

This was an ill-defined but numerically large category, comprising most of the nursery staff including cleaners and gardeners. The readiness with which a person was admitted to this category varied. Thus in some cases children were described as crying when "anyone who had spent a little while playing with them" left the room; but more often their attachments were confined to "anyone he knows well: but he won't go willingly to new staff for a week or so".

The number of persons the nursery children showed an attachment to was therefore large, but within this group all of them had preferences. The favourite person (i.e. the top scorer on the questionnaire) was usually someone whom the child saw somewhat infrequently. Thus if the child's natural mother visited at least once a week, she was always described as the preferred person; the child would be very excited to see her and distressed when she left. However, if her visits were less frequent the child would usually cry when she arrived and run away from her. In many of the nurseries a "special nurse" system operated. Each member of the staff had one or two children to whom she paid special attention by taking them out in her free time, buying them little presents, sometimes putting them to bed, or taking them to her home for a weekend. Since the staff member and child were rarely in the same group they would probably on most days spend only a few minutes together. The special nurse was invariably the child's preferred person, unless his mother visited frequently, but as described above the children also showed attachment behaviour to numbers of other staff.

The intensity of the attachment behaviour to both the preferred person and the rest of the staff was much greater than that shown by the home children. Thus, 33·3 per cent of the nursery children were said usually to cry when their favourite person left the room, and a further 46·7 per cent sometimes to do so; 30 per cent were said sometimes to cry when any staff working with them left the room. Sixty per cent of the nursery children were said usually to run to be picked up when their favourite person came into the room, and a further 33·3 per cent sometimes did so. Over half the children (55·3 per cent) were said sometimes to run to be picked up when the staff they knew well came into the room. On the other hand, according to the nurses, the children accepted that they go off duty, but 18 per cent of the children were said to cry if they saw their favourite nurse leaving the house. They were unlikely to know if she was out for the day, but 26·7 per cent were said to be clinging or to "playing-up" on her return after a few days' holiday. Following around the house, a characteristic form of behaviour in home-reared 2-year-olds, was not allowed in most nurseries.

Number of Caretakers

The mean number of persons who had looked after the nursery children for at least 1 week since the age of 4 months was 24·37, S.D. 5·52, and in the last 6 months 11·33, S.D. 3·55. The comparable figures for the home children were 2·23, S.D. 0·57, and 2·17, S.D. 0·70.

Number of Adult Contacts

Detailed records of the child's contacts with adults during the week following our visit were completed by 66·7 per cent of the mothers and 76·7 per cent of the nurses. The mean number of casual contacts (i.e. brief exchanges with strangers, e.g. in shops and buses) was 9·4, S.D. 7·7 for the home children, and 8·3, S.D. 6·9 for the nursery children. The range in both groups was from 2 to over 20, and it seems certain that these contacts were often under-reported. Apart from casual contact the nursery children came into contact with more adults than the home children. The mean number of other contacts, i.e. with familiar people, or longer contacts with strangers was 12·65, S.D. 5·96, for the home children, and 21·92, S.D. 7·02, for the nursery children ($t = 3·98$, $p < 0·001$). During the course of the week most nursery children would be spoken to by all the nursery staff, including cooks and cleaners, and by voluntary workers, and in some cases also by friends and relatives of other children and staff. The home children would typically see their grandparents, aunts and uncles, neighbours, and parents' friends.

Although the nursery children are in contact with more adults, their adult world is relatively undifferentiated in that the majority of people they know are uniformed or aproned females. Moreover the home children meet adults in a greater variety of situations. During the course of the week all the home children visited at least one other house with their mothers, and 60 per cent of them spent at least one period on their own with a relative or neighbour while their mother went shopping. No nursery child visited another house in the course of the week.

Number of Child Contacts

Of the nursery children 76·6 per cent had played with 11 or more children in the past 2 weeks. This was because all the children in the nursery usually played together in the garden, and because at certain times of the day two "family" groups might be pooled. Only 20 per cent of the home 2-year-olds had played with as many as 11 children ($\chi^2 = 22·85$, $p < 0·001$).

Incidence of Everyday Experiences

Confirmation of the more limited neighbourhood circle of the nursery child was obtained for the whole sample by questionnaire. Ninety per cent of the home children, but no nursery children, were said to visit another house at least once a week; 43·3 per cent of the nursery children had not, in fact, been in another house for at least 6 months. The nursery staff made determined efforts to widen the children's experiences in other directions, but the mean score of the home children for "experiences of the adult world" (frequency of visits to cafés, shops, rides in cars and buses) was significantly larger (12·9, S.D. 1·91, for the home children; for the nursery children 10·5, S.D. 1·8, $t = 4·89$, $p = <0·001$). On the other hand the mean score of the nursery children for play experiences was higher, although not significantly so, than that of the home children (38·3, S.D. 3·7; 36·7, S.D. 3·4; $t = 1·70$, N.S.). Nursery children were more often read to and sung to than the home children, and they more often played with sand, dough, paints, and wheeled toys.

Emotional Behaviour Patterns

No evidence of marked disturbance was seen in either group. Ninety per cent of the nursery children, but only 33·3 per cent of the home children, were said sometimes to suck their thumb or finger ($\chi^2 = 20·4$, $p < 0·001$). However, 46·7 per cent of the home children still had a bottle and 30 per cent a dummy, whilst no nursery child was offered these substitutes. There was no significant difference in the incidence of nailbiting, tics, nervous habits, head banging, or rocking reported by mothers and nurses, although playing with genitals was reported significantly more often by the mothers than by the nurses (73·3 per cent and 36·6 per cent respectively; $\chi^2 = 8·15$, $p < 0·001$). There was no significant difference in the incidence of mealtime problems—fads, refusal of new foods, demands to be spoon fed—which were infrequent in both groups. Sleep disturbances were much commoner amongst the home children: 36·7 per cent of the home children, but only 3·3 per cent of the nursery children had woken during the night at least 5 times a week in the previous 2 weeks. The incidence of temper tantrums was high in both groups, but did not differ significantly between them (at least one tantrum a day: home group 43·3 per cent; nursery group 53·3 per cent). Fewer nursery children were toilet trained: 93·3 per cent were still wet at least once a day, but only 60 per cent of home children ($\chi^2 = 9·32$, $p < 0·01$); 86·7 per cent of the nursery sample still soiled themselves at least once a week but only 56·7 per cent of home children ($\chi^2 = 6·65$,

$p < 0.01$). Destructiveness (tearing up books, scribbling on walls, etc.), jealousy, and fearfulness (panic in certain situations, e.g. when meeting dogs) were reported with equal frequency in both groups.

Emotional Involvement of Mothers and Nurses

Not unexpectedly, significantly more mothers than nurses said that they often felt really cross with the child (66·7 per cent and 26·7 per cent respectively, $\chi^2 = 9.64$, $p < 0.01$), that he often really upset them (36·7 per cent and 13·3 per cent; $\chi^2 = 4.36$, $p < 0.05$), and that they did not always feel happy about the way they had handled him (56·7 per cent and 23·3 per cent; $\chi^2 = 6.94$, $p < 0.01$). More mothers than nurses smacked the child at least once a day (56·7 per cent and 26·7 per cent; $\chi^2 = 5.55$, $p < 0.02$) and told the child they would not love him if he was naughty (23·3 per cent and 3·3 per cent; $\chi^2 = 5.19$, $p < 0.02$).

CONCLUSIONS

The gross emotional disturbance which has been described in children reared in large groups in inadequately staffed institutions (e.g. Flint, 1967) was not found in these 2-year-old children. To be more precise, disturbance was not reported by their nurses, but in subsequent observational studies in 13 residential nursery groups (Tizard, Joseph, Cooperman and Tizard, in preparation) nothing was seen to contradict this finding. Gross disturbance amongst young nursery children, in the authors' experience, is not seen in children who in early infancy enter residential care of the type described. In certain respects, however, the development of the nursery children differed from that of home-reared London working-class children. Fewer 2-year-olds had achieved control of their bowels and bladders, despite systematic attempts at training, usually begun at the age of 9–12 months. Language retardation was present but was not in most cases severe (Tizard and Joseph, in press). Thumb and finger sucking were much more common in the nursery, but many home children still had a feeding bottle or dummy. Sleep disturbances were rare amongst nursery children. The major area of difference between the two groups lay in their relationships with their caretakers and with strangers. Nursery 2-year-olds were less willing to approach or to stay alone with strangers than were home-reared children, and with familiar adults they were in certain situations more clinging. Their social behaviour might thus be considered in some respects immature, except that, unlike a home-reared 18-months-old child, they tended to show attachment to a wide range of adults.

However, their attachments, although somewhat diffuse, were not indiscriminate: each child had a hierarchy of preferences, as did the home-reared children.

Despite attempts by the nurseries to approximate to family life, differences between them and real families are so numerous that a variety of possible explanations for the atypical behaviour of nursery children can be advanced. Among the differences measured in this study were the lack of neighbourhood experiences of nursery children, the multiplicity of their caretakers and peer contacts, and the more limited emotional involvement of caretakers. The shyness of the nursery children is most readily accounted for in terms of the narrower range of their social experiences. Although they have contact with larger numbers of both adults and children than do home children, these occur mainly within the physical setting of the nursery, with the child in his familiar peer group. Our experimental social situation, in which the child was alone with two adults, one of whom was a stranger, is one which is much less familiar to the nursery child than to the home child. The home-reared 2-year-old comes into contact with fewer people, but he is used to meeting them in a wider variety of settings, and even to staying alone in other peoples' houses. Some support for this argument comes from the significant correlation found within the nursery group between experiences of the outside world (visiting, going to shops, etc.) and willingness to approach a stranger ($r = +0.427$, $p < 0.02$).

The diffuseness of the nursery children's attachments is not un-expected in view of their multiplicity of caretakers. In all the nurseries which we visited large numbers of staff care for the children; on an average, 24 nurses had looked after each of our 2-year-olds. During a 5-day observation period we found that an average of 6·3 nurses (range 4–11) had worked on each group. This figure excludes night staff (unless it was their responsibility to dress the children) and nursery school staff. The large numbers stem in part from the practice of partially staffing the nurseries with students who work only 3 days a week and who move from group to group. However, apart from this, an ever decreasing working week, lengthening staff holidays, and the needs of staff to move because of marriage, promotion, or a variety of personal reasons, mean that multiple caretaking is an inescapable aspect of residential care.

No attempt was made in any of the nurseries we visited to reduce the number of adults handling each child by assigning the care of particular children within the group to particular members of staff. Thus a child might be dressed by a different nurse each day, and if four nurses worked on one group during the day a child might be dressed by one, toileted by a second, taken for a walk by a third, and put to bed by a fourth. It was not uncommon for child-care tasks to be allocated by seniority—e.g. the most junior nurse on duty would be assigned the task of dressing any child who had wet his bed, or changing children who were subsequently wet or soiled. It is therefore not surprising to find that the nursery children's attachments were more diffuse than those of home-reared children. The 2-year-old nursery child cannot predict who will look after him each day, and indeed any one of the nursery staff may at times care for him.

The caretaking in the nurseries we visited tended to be not only multiple but detached. That is, the staff tend to avoid prolonged verbal or physical one-to-one interactions with the children, and to discourage, usually by distraction, any attempt by a child to engineer such an interaction. In a subsequent 5-day observational study in 13 nursery groups, staff talk to the children was found to express pleasure or affection only 2 per cent of the time, and displeasure or anger only 3 per cent of the time. Affectionate physical contact was seen only 1·3 per cent of the time. In reply to questioning, few nurses admitted to experiencing the frequent feelings of anxiety and hostility towards their charges which many mothers described. During intelligence testing we frequently had to ask mothers not to prompt, assist, or berate their children, but this was never necessary with the nurses.

There would appear to be no inevitable reason why multiple care-taking should be impersonal, but we found the social climate of the nurseries implacably opposed to the development of one-to-one relationships, outside the "special nurse" system. The problem of what kind of relationship should exist between children and the staff caring for them was discussed with the matron in charge of each nursery visited. Almost all of them believed that close relationships should not be allowed to develop, because these were potentially damaging to the children and created difficulties for the staff. It was argued that if a child became closely attached to the nurse who gave him day-to-day care he would suffer a great deal when she left or went off duty, and he would find it difficult to relate to his mother or foster mother if he left the nursery. From the point of view of the staff, since they work for a limited number of hours each week, and in addition since most nurseries are training centres, numbers of different people must handle the children and their work is made very difficult if the child cries for one particular nurse. Moreover, if the staff working with the children are encouraged to become "involved" with them, acute rivalry problems develop within the group and the children become difficult to manage. The "good" nursery child is therefore one who makes few demands on the staff, but responds to all; the "difficult" child who makes demands of a particular nurse is considered spoilt, and both nurse and child are unpopular.

In this situation one would expect the children's attachment behaviour to be not only diffusely directed but very weak, if not indeed extinguished from lack of reinforcement. In some nurseries, in fact, 2-year-olds appear to be uninterested in adults; they spend the day playing in a self-contained and usually contented manner with toys. However, our study showed that the attachment behaviour of the majority of the nursery children was more intense than that of the home children; unlike the home-reared 2-year-olds they often ran to be picked up when staff entered the room, and cried when they left. To account for this finding one must suppose that some intermittent reinforcement of attachment behaviour occurs. It is especially likely to occur in those nurseries with a "special" nurse system. This system represents an interesting attempt to compensate for impersonal group care by giving each child a nurse who is responsive to his demands *outside* the group situation. If the group nurse is like the *metapalet* in a *kibbutz* nursery, who gives impartial but impersonal care, the "special" nurse corresponds to the *kibbutz* mother. She does not work on his group, takes no responsibility for his daily life, but only "sees him to spoil him" as one puts it. The depth of the relationship is very varied. Unlike the *kibbutz* mother, however, the "special" nurse spends minutes rather than hours each day with "her" child, appears at irregular intervals, disappears for days or weeks when off duty, and leaves the district when her training is complete.

Assuming that the child's attachment behaviour is intermittently reinforced, it seems likely that it is tied to the immature form of demanding attention when the adult enters and leaves the room by the lack of autonomy of the nursery child. In the private family the 2-year-old has typically long ago abandoned crying when his mother leaves the room; instead he follows her around the house. In almost all nurseries the 2-year-old is not allowed to follow staff, but may leave the room only *en bloc* with his group for a particular purpose. The home-reared 2-year-old can confidently predict the return of his mother, should she leave the house without him. In the nursery the staff come and go at irregular and unpredictable intervals, often disappearing for days or weeks or indeed for ever. In these circumstances the 2-year-old has as little control over the source of his social satisfactions as a non-mobile infant, and it is not surprising to find that his attachment behaviour assumes an immature form.

These observations relate only to children of 24 months in a particular social organization. We have reason to believe that the children's relationships with one another, and with adults, change as they get older, and that the nature of their social relationships depends on the specific manner in which residential care is organized rather than on "institutional" care as such. In subsequent work we have therefore attempted to compare the behaviour of children who are being cared for in nurseries which have differing social structures.

REFERENCES

FLINT, B. M. 1967. *The child and the institution.* University of London Press.
RHEINGOLD, H. L. and BAYLEY, N. 1959. The later effects of an experimental modification of mothering. *Child Dev.* **30,** 363–372.
SCHAFFER, H. R. and EMERSON, P. E. 1964. The development of social attachments in infancy. *Monogr. Soc. Res. Child Dev.* **29,** no. 3, Serial No. 94.
TIZARD, B. and JOSEPH, A. In press. Language development of young children in residential care. I. A study of children of twenty-four months.
TIZARD, B., JOSEPH, A., COOPERMAN, O. and TIZARD, J. In preparation. Factors affecting the language development of children in residential nurseries: an observational study.

Discussion

Substitute Attachments

FOSS: Children can get attached to things as well as to people—things like dolls and ornaments and pets. I was wondering if there is any relationship, either of a direct or of an inverse kind, between attachments to property and attachment to a person.

TIZARD: That I cannot say, but the nurseries we investigated certainly did their best to supply children with their own toys and clothes and possessions. All the children had one or two soft toys of their own, but only about 20 per cent of them insisted on taking them to bed, and it was rare to see soft toys being carried around.

STEVENS: There can be cultural differences in this respect, for in the Greek setting in which I studied institutionalized infants there was far less emphasis on private property and far more on sharing. The Greek people in general are tremendously community oriented: there is a kind of natural communism abroad, and as a result you have the idea, for instance, that the baby should be shared with the group and that all objects are group-owned. Greek nurses, one finds, tend to sit in a circle, with each child facing the group and his back to the nurse, instead, of, as here, facing her or at least sitting sideways on. In consequence toys and other possessions are also regarded as belonging to the group and not to any particular individual.

SCOTT: Has anyone studied the attachments formed between children raised in an institution? This is really an ideal setting to observe whether they can obtain such satisfactions from each other when these may not be available from adults.

STEVENS: Older children may do so, but in the course of my investigation I was much impressed by how few signals were directed by the infants to other children. I had expected far more, particularly among un-attached children, but instead, when no nurse was available they tended to occupy themselves manipulating toys and exploring the physical environment rather than interacting socially with each other.

TIZARD: I can confirm this. At 24 months other children were seen as rivals or ignored. In our observational study we found that 2-year-old nursery children, although always surrounded by other children, spoke to them only 3·6 per cent of the time. There was no evidence that they attempted to form attachments to anyone other than adults.

SCHAFFER: This would argue against those theories which suggest that an animal or child will form an attachment to whatever object it happens to associate with frequently, and particularly so if the object is a highly salient one. Other children tend to be perceptually very salient creatures, but the crucial difference between them and an adult is that it is far more difficult for an infant to build up reciprocal relationship with another child. When an infant signals by, say, smiling or crying, another child is unlikely to respond like an adult. A young child especially will probably take no notice, and so the relationship will lack the reciprocity which is the hallmark of an attachment.

ROSENBLUM: What about self-directed attachments? I have particularly noted the degree to which various forms of self-directed behaviour occur in my animals when they are separated from their mothers, and I am wondering whether such behaviour can at least in part have certain things in common with the kinds of attachment behaviours that are outwardly directed.

TIZARD: There is certainly no necessary relationship between the two, in the sense that you must get self-directed behaviour in deprived children. On the contrary, we were impressed by the lack of autoerotic activities of all kinds among long-stay children.

Behavioural State in Deprived Children

AMBROSE: Did you find any overall difference in behavioural state between your two groups? Institutionalized children have often been described as either more apathetic or more hyperactive than home-reared children.

TIZARD: We found that the nursery children were on the whole more apathetic. This was, however, very much related to the amount of freedom allowed by nurseries to the children. One was far more likely to find it in the nurseries that operated a block treatment system, where everyone went to the toilet together or went out for walks together.

RICHARDS: We must be careful in interpreting such differences in state. Institutionalized children come from populations that are much more prone to perinatal complications, and one would therefore expect to find a much higher percentage of babies who are apathetic or hyperactive. Illegitimate children in particular are known to be a high risk group when compared with other children of the same social class.

KAGAN: On the other hand, Papousek has told me informally that among children in Prague nurseries, with mothers who have had good antenatal care but have to work, apathy is a prominent characteristic.

TIZARD: In any case, we did our best to eliminate those children from our sample for whom there were any medical data to suggest prenatal or perinatal complications.

Social Class Differences in Child Rearing during the First Year[1]

JEROME KAGAN AND STEVEN R. TULKIN[2]

Harvard University

INTRODUCTION

THE CHANGES THAT have occurred over recent years in our view of the parent–child interaction is one instance of two more general ideas that have altered our attitudes towards a wide variety of behavioural phenomena. We acknowledge, first, the intimate interaction between organisms in a common setting and no longer regard the mother–child dyad as a game of unidirectional billiards in which the mother acts on the child who, in turn, acts on a younger sibling who, in turn, acts on a rattle. The ethological research on imprinting has supported this view, for the mother goose does not tempt her newborn to follow her. The infant walks after her and in that act contributes to a dynamic relationship between the two.

A new respect for the determining influence of social structure and physical setting also pervades theorizing about the family. Each member of the family lives in a specific ecology that controls the behaviour of all participants. The mother in a ten-room house is less likely to hear her infant cry than a parent in a two-room apartment. Hence, the former is less likely to habituate to the cry than the latter. Similarly, the infant in a family with three older sisters, in contrast to a first-born, will be nurtured less often by the mother, merely because a 10-year-old sister is available for help. Since the lower class child's differential pattern of treatment results as much from the structure and setting in which he lives as it does from the specific rewards and punishments parents

[1] This work was supported by research grant HD4299 from NICHD, U.S. Public Health Service, and a grant from the Carnegie Corporation of New York.
[2] Now at the State University of New York, Buffalo, New York.

administer, social class has become an increasingly popular variable in developmental psychology.

This paper summarizes some recent research on the relation between social class and the caretaking practices of the mother towards her infant. Since we do not view social class as an independent variable in the traditional sense, it is helpful to indicate why it was chosen at all. The developmental psychologist is interested in the covariation between the practices and attitudes of the caretaker, on the one hand, and the psychological development of the child, on the other. This general concern blankets two specific questions: (1) the relation between the caretaker's attitudes and her actual practices, especially the interaction among her ego ideal for the child, her expectancy of attaining that ideal, and her behaviour towards the child; and (2) the relation between her caretaking practices and specific outcomes in the child.

In order to obtain some initial clues as to the form of these relations it is helpful to study caretakers who are at the extremes of the variables regarded as significant. We might note, incidentally, that much of the ambiguity in research generalizations on parent–child relationships may be due to the selection of samples that occupy a restricted range on the critical independent variables. The content of the ego ideal the mother sets for her child, her expectancy of attaining it, and the likelihood that she will attempt to sculpt the child in accord with this ideal are important influences on the child's growth in all social settings. It is believed, further, that mothers of different classes in the United States show dramatic variation on these three dimensions. We study mothers of different social classes not because class *qua* class is a causative agent, but because we believe there are clusters of attitudes, expectancies, and practices that are correlated with class membership. This strategy is an economical first step in attacking major problems. This empirical procedure is often used by comparative and physiological psychologists. Harlow and Harlow (1966), for example, compared the effects of isolation versus no isolation on the psychological development of monkeys. By initially looking at the extremes of a particular dimension, they obtained an approximation of the topography of the effect. After a hypothetical mechanism is inferred, more detailed study of the dynamic variables can be initiated as a next step. Membership in a social class represents a continuing mosaic of experience, and it is not obvious which sets of conditions are most influential for the psychological development of the child. Social class is not an explanatory construct. But the parent's sense of effectiveness in being able to control the environment and to mould the young child's interest and talents, which covaries with class membership, is a potentially powerful influence on the child's behavioural and cognitive profile. The strategy of examining differences in caretaking practices and behavioural profile for children from varied classes is, therefore, potentially valuable.

CROSS-SECTIONAL STUDY OF 10-MONTH-OLD INFANTS

The data to be reported come from a recent cross-sectional study conducted by Steven Tulkin, supplemented by information gathered on a longitudinal sample that has been followed for several years. Some of the data from the second study were reported at the first in the series of these study groups (Kagan, 1969a). The earlier longitudinal data persuaded us that cross-sectional studies were necessary.

Subjects

The sample consists of 60 ten-month-old, first-born, white girls living in the Boston–Cambridge area. We chose to study girls in this first investigation because social class generally covaries in a more lawful manner with the developmental profile of girls than boys. We shall consider this interesting issue later. Thirty of the children were middle class; 30, lower class. Criteria for the definition of middle-class status were that either one or both parents had graduated from college and that the father was in a professional job; for lower class, that either one or both parents had dropped out of high school and neither had attended college, or that the father was working at a semi-skilled or unskilled job. Only four of the 30 parents had finished high school and five of the fathers and one of the mothers had not even attended high school. Among the middle-class families, by contrast, both parents in 22 of the 30 pairs of parents were college graduates. The occupations of the lower-class families included truck driver, labourer, parking lot attendant, clerk; the occupations of the middle-class group included engineers, college faculty members, teachers, businessmen, computer specialists, and lawyers. About one-third of the sample were Catholic and two-thirds Protestant. The names of all subjects were obtained from local hospitals' birth records, paediatricians, and Well Baby Clinics. The families were told about the study either on the telephone or by letter. Although the actual co-operation rate was similar for the two classes, there were many more families who were not reachable in the lower-class group; typically these were from the lowest part of the social class scale. About 30 per cent of those who were approached from each class group declined to co-operate.

Procedure

The observer made two separate visits to the home, each lasting about 2 hours, during which he took 10-minute breaks after every 20-minute observational epoch. For every 5-second period (signalled by means of an inconspicuous battery-powered device) the observer noted, on a pad marked off in blocks, the events that corresponded to an *a priori* code designating categories of mother and child behaviours. Thus, if the mother bent down and picked up the child, the observer would note the code for "mother picks up child" followed, perhaps, by the code for "baby smiles". When these data were analysed the investigator knew that these two events had occurred within a 5-second period in that particular temporal sequence.

A. Variables Coded in the Home

The primary variables coded are defined briefly below.

Maternal Behaviour

1. Kiss. Mother kissed child.
2. Initiate physical contact. Mother patted child on head, picked child up, took child's hand, etc.
3. Passive holding. Mother carried child; child sat on mother's lap.
4. Tickling and bouncing. Mother tickled child or threw child in the air in playful manner.
5. Vocalization. Mother spoke to child (categorized by the location variable, see point 15 below).
6. Reward. A special subcategory of vocalization used to indicate high affect or praise in response to an achievement behaviour (e.g. "What a good girl!").
7. Instruct. Mother issued a command in a directing tone (e.g. "Come here!").
8. Encourage. Mother's order was more suggestive than in point 7 above, and usually involved an act that had already begun (e.g. "That's right. Come on. Give it to Mommy.").
9. Prohibit. Mother interfered with or stopped an act that had already begun (e.g. "Stop that, don't go near that!"). Categorized as prohibitions which were verbal only, physical only, or both verbal and physical.
10. Punish. Mother physically punished child, usually by slapping her hand.
11. Give food. Mother gave food to infant.

12. Entertain. Mother held attention of child by either non-verbal sounds, body movements such as peek-a-boo, or holding the attention of the child through a toy—such as shaking a rattle. If words were used in conjunction with an entertainment behaviour, both codes were recorded.

13. Give object. Mother gave child an object and made no effort to hold child's attention.

14. Imitation. Mother copied exactly a behaviour of the child (categorized as verbal imitations or physical imitations).

15. Location. Distance of mother from infant, coded each time it changed: (a) face to face, eye to eye; (b) within 2 feet; (c) more than 2 feet away.

Infant Variables

1. Play. Child picked up or moved object with her hands. Object had to be moved; passive holding was excluded, as was a non-moving object in the mouth.

2. Inspect. Child stared at or examined inanimate object, studying details; could be environmental object such as furniture, rug, or toy.

3. Positive vocalization; categorized according to whether the child was playing, moving, or doing neither.

4. Negative vocalizations. Fretting, fussing, whining.

5. Cry.

6. Touch mother. Infant touched mother.

7. Offer object to mother. Infant unambiguously attempts to hand an object to mother.

The primary observer taught the coding system to another male and then both visited the homes of ten infants. Each of the ten homes in the reliability sample was observed for 2 hours and percentages of agreement were computed on each variable. Percentages were based on tallies from each page of the coding booklet (representing $2\frac{1}{2}$-minute epochs). The formula was the ratio of agreements per $2\frac{1}{2}$ minutes to total number of agreements and disagreements. A percentage was computed for each infant. The range was 70 to 100 per cent, and all median percentages were above 80 per cent.

Pearson product-moment correlations were also computed between the coding of the two observers. Within-subject correlations were computed for six child behaviours only, because frequencies for other variables were too low. Between-subject correlations, based on the total number of tallies for each subject over the 2-hour period, were computed for all variables. Between-subject correlations and medians for within-subject correlations were all 0·90 or higher.

B. Laboratory Assessment

Within a few days of the home observation the child and mother came to the laboratory. The staff who assessed the child had no knowledge of her behaviour in the home and were not told about the social class of the family. In only a few cases could the staff tell with certainty the social class of the family from either the dress or deportment of the mother. The child was placed in a high chair behind an enclosure with the mother sitting to the right and behind the child and the following episodes were administered:

Episode 1. Meaningful speech. During the first episode a tape recording of meaningful and non-meaningful speech was played to the child. There were four stimuli in this episode: high meaning sentences read with high or low inflection and nonsense words read with high or low inflection. These sentences were read by two different female voices with foreign accents (one Chinese and one Spanish). Half the subjects heard one voice, and half the other voice. The choice of foreign voices was based on the assumption that these two accents would be equally strange to all subjects. Each stimulus was presented twice, and all subjects heard the sentences in the same order. The variables recorded included vocalization, fretting, orientation towards the speaker baffle, orientation towards the mother, orientation towards a stranger who was seated to the left of the child, heart-rate deceleration, and general activity.

Episode 2. Mother's voice. The second episode included tape recordings of the voice of the subject's mother and the voice of another subject's mother (hereafter called the stranger) reading a fairy-tale. Each subject heard the voice of a different stranger from her own group, either middle class or lower class. As in the first set of auditory stimuli, the passages were 20 seconds long and separated by a 10-second interstimulus interval. All the children heard the passages in the same order and the variables recorded were the same as those described above.

Play behaviour. Following two other episodes, not described here, mother and infant were taken to another part of the building to a carpeted room $9\frac{1}{2} \times 11\frac{1}{2}$ feet square. Initially the child was given a 2-minute adaptation period designed to accustom her to the room. Three single toys were presented in succession, each one for 4 minutes. The toys were: a small piece of smooth wood; an attractively coloured bug; and a chime ball. After the child had played with each toy for

4 minutes, two conflict trials were presented. Each conflict trial lasted 4 minutes and consisted of presenting one of the single toys simultaneously with a toy the child had not seen previously. The two toys were presented at equal distances from the child and about 2 feet apart. The bug was presented with a steamship, and the chime ball was presented with a hanging xylophone. Each was presented for 4 minutes. Prior investigations of the preferences for all toys were obtained on an independent sample. These data indicated equal attractiveness for each member of the pair presented to the infant. Therefore the choice of the novel toy cannot be attributed to any intrinsic attractiveness.

RESULTS

A. Differences in Maternal Behaviour in the Home

The major differences between the lower- and middle-class mothers involved vocalization and duration of interactive episodes. The middle-class mother spent more time in a face-to-face posture with the infant, more time talking to her infant, usually within 2 feet of the infant's face, and she issued more distinctive vocalization to the infant (see Figs. 1, 2, and 3). A distinctive vocalization was coded when the mother was

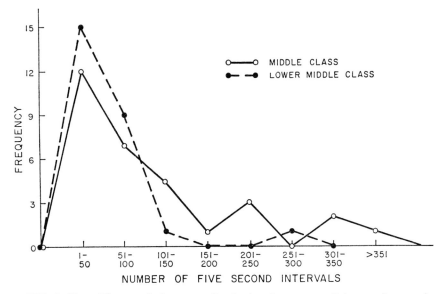

FIG. 1. Class differences in frequency distribution for amount of time mother was in face-to-face orientation with infant.

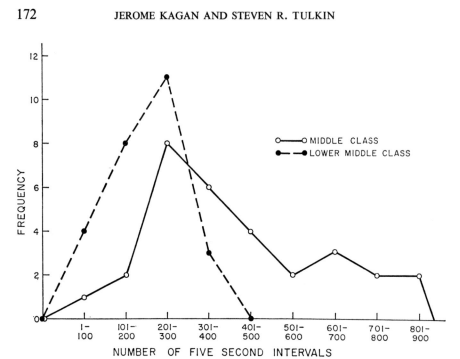

FIG. 2. Class differences in frequency distribution for amount of maternal vocalization to infant.

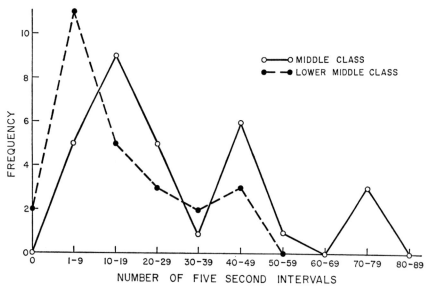

FIG. 3. Class differences in frequency distribution for amount of distinctive maternal vocalization to infant.

talking to her infant in a face-to-face position but was not providing any other sensory input, either visual or tactile. This last result replicates a similar class difference observed in mothers of 4-month-old infants.

Mean scores (number of 5-second units) for the two groups of mothers appear in Table I.

TABLE I. CLASS DIFFERENCES IN MATERNAL BEHAVIOUR[1]

	Lower middle class	Middle class	p
Location of mother			
Within 2 feet of child	1,424	1,525	N.S.
Face to face	53	111	<0·05
Maternal verbalization			
Within 2 feet of child	149	329	<0·001
Percentage reciprocal vocalization	19	38	<0·05
Imitation	4	12	<0·001
Encourage walking	10	26	<0·05
Verbal reward	0·9	6	<0·01
Amuse the child			
Entertainment	56	99	<0·01
Physical contact			
Kiss	4	5	N.S.
Hold	210	265	N.S.
Tickle, bounce	21	31	N.S.
Duration of interaction			
Q_3 for positive interaction	3·9	4·6	<0·001
Mean of the 3 longest interactions	8·9	11·4	<0·05

[1] Scores refer to mean number of 5-second units.

The middle-class mothers were more likely to entertain their children with objects, to encourage walking, and to reward them for mastery. However, there were no class differences for kissing, total holding of the infant, tickling and bouncing of the infant, non-verbal interaction, or verbal prohibitions. The higher rate of vocalization among middle-class mothers held not only for vocalizations that were reactions to the infant's babbling, but also for spontaneously initiated verbalizations towards the infant.

There were also class differences in the mother's response to irritability in the infant. Middle-class mothers were more apt to respond to fretting or crying, and with shorter response latencies. Further, the strategy chosen to placate the infant was class related. Middle-class mothers responded verbally, while working-class mothers were likely to offer the child a bottle or a cracker. Less than one-third of the middle-class mothers offered the irritable infant food, in contrast to two-thirds of the lower-class mothers who responded in this manner on one occasion or more.

B. Infant Behaviour in the Laboratory

Episode 1. Meaningful versus non-meaningful speech. There were no class differences in absolute reactivity to each of the stimuli. However, when one compared the reaction to the most meaningful stimulus (high meaning–high inflection) with reactivity to the preceding stimulus (low meaning–high inflection) class differences emerged. Middle class,

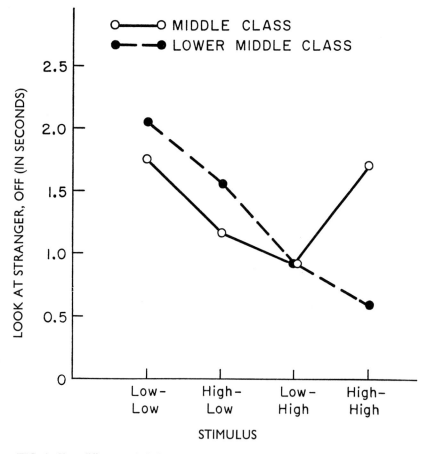

FIG. 4. Class differences in infants' orientation to the stranger following termination of meaningful and non-meaningful speech.

in contrast to lower-class, infants quieted more dramatically to high meaning-high inflection than to the preceding stimulus ($p < 0.05$), and were more likely to look at the stranger following termination of high meaning–high inflection ($p < 0.10$). Most infants looked at the stranger following termination of the first stimulus, but this interest gradually waned. When high meaning–high inflection occurred on the fourth trial the middle-class infants increased their orientation to the stranger, but lower-class subjects did not (Fig. 4), which suggests either that the middle-class infant was better able to differentiate meaningful from non-meaningful speech, or was more likely to inquire about the source of the meaningful speech. We shall return to this possibility later.

Mother's voice versus stranger's voice. There were no significant class differences in the mean scores for each of the variables considered separately, but the second-order differences differentiated the classes. Middle-class infants quietened more to the mother's voice than to the stranger's voice, and, upon termination of the voice, vocalized more following the mother than the stranger. Comparisons between the classes were both significant ($p < 0.05$ for quieting and $p < 0.10$ for vocalizing following the passages). Further, middle-class infants looked at the mother following termination of her voice and looked at the stranger following termination of the stranger's voice. That is, the middle-class infant showed more appropriate orientation following the termination of each voice than did the lower-class infants (see Figs. 5 and 6). Lower-class children gradually habituated orientation to the mother over the first four stimuli, but showed increased looking at the stranger. However, the "looking" was not related to the voice they had just heard. Moreover, the tendency to quiet during the stimulus and to orient towards the correct person following termination were positively correlated for middle-class, but not for lower-class subjects. That is, the middle-class infants who looked more at their mother following the termination of the mother's voice had quietened more while listening to the mother's voice ($r = 0.32$, $p < 0.10$). This class difference may mean either that the lower-class girls did not recognize the difference between the two voices or that they did not care to inquire about the source of the voices.

Our preferred interpretation is that all the infants were alerted by the obvious acoustic differences between the two voices. The middle-class infant wanted to resolve the discrepancy and to determine, if possible, the source of the voices. The lower-class children did not have this mental set.

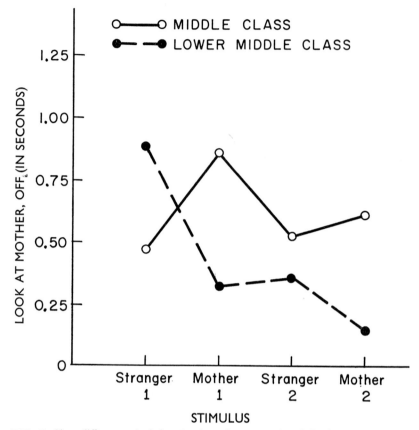

FIG. 5. Class differences in infants' orientation to mother following termination of mother's or stranger's voice. (Numerals on the abscissa refer to the first and second presentation of the voice.)

Play behaviour. The play session revealed no class differences for mobility, proximity to the mother, or duration of play with the toys. There was, however, a difference on the conflict trials. Middle-class subjects showed more vacillation before they made their final choice of toy. The middle-class subjects shifted their gaze about 2·2 times, in contrast to 1·4 for the lower-class subjects. We interpret this difference to reflect two processes—a tendency to retrieve past experience in the service of resolving discrepancy, and inhibition in a new situation. An unusual event tends to provoke an infant to attempt assimilation in order to reach cognitive equilibrium. The pairing of a novel and familiar toy is an "odd event", but children differ in their need to assimilate this discrepancy and, therefore, in the disposition to retrieve the relevant cognitive structures that might aid assimilation. This interpretation resembles the one used to explain the differences between middle- and

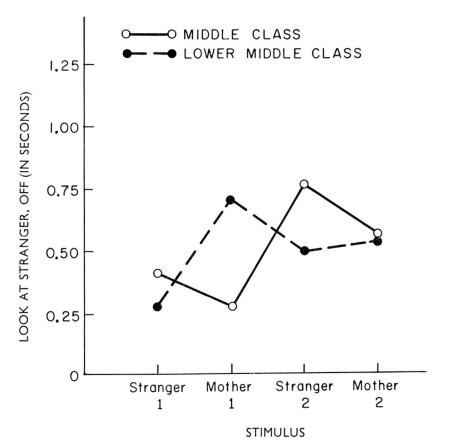

FIG. 6. Class differences in infants' orientation to stranger following termination of mother's or stranger's voice. (Numerals on the abscissa refer to the first and second presentation of voice.)

lower-class infants on the two auditory episodes. We recognize the conjectural nature of this interpretation, but note the provocative implication that a primary difference between middle- and lower-class children may rest in their desire to understand discrepant experience.

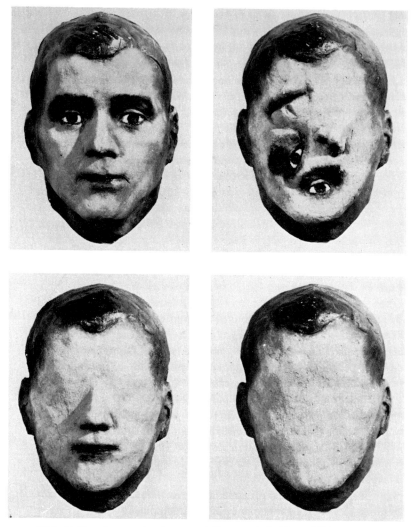

FIG. 7. Clay face masks shown to infants at 4, 8, 13, and 27 months.

LONGITUDINAL STUDY

Data from a longitudinal study initiated in 1964 corroborate these conclusions. Subjects were 150 first-born white boys and girls living in the Boston area. The families ranged from lower middle- to upper middle-class, but the lower middle-class group was higher in education and vocational role than the cross-sectional sample reported on above.

A. Fear to Faces

In one of the episodes the subject saw a set of clay faces as illustrated in Fig. 7, at 4, 8, 13, and 27 months. At 8 months of age significantly more upper middle- than lower middle-class infants showed fearful crying to the unrealistic masks. We interpret this finding to mean that the upper middle-class infants had a stronger need to assimilate the discrepant mask. They noted the disarranged face and tried to assimilate it to their schema for a human face. Those infants who could not accomplish this assimilation became anxious. Anxiety occurs when the child is alerted by a discrepant event, attempts to assimilate it, but is unable to do so. The lower middle-class child, it is suggested, noted the discrepancy but was less likely to attempt the assimilation. Thus the tension born of the initial alerting dissipated, and anxiety did not occur. The upper middle-class child tried, but was unable, to assimilate the scrambled face and, as a result, became anxious and cried. When the child's cognitive structures are mature enough to permit interpretation of discrepant events, fear does not appear. It is to be noted that no child cried when these same faces were shown to them at 27 months of age.

B. Fixation Time

We have suggested in an earlier publication (Kagan, 1969b) that after 11 to 12 months of age duration of fixation time to discrepant events is controlled primarily by the richness of hypotheses activated in the service of assimilation. Long fixations reflect persistent activation of a rich nest of hypotheses. For girls there was a positive correlation between social class and fixation time to the faces at 27 months ($r = 0.33$, $p < 0.01$), but not at 4 or 8 months. When the stimuli were transformations of human forms (rather than faces) the significant correlation between class and duration of attention emerged at 1 year ($r = 0.36$, $p < 0.01$ for girls; $r = 0.21$ for boys). Moreover vocabulary score at 27 months was positively correlated with duration of fixation at 27 months.

C. Changes in Vocalization

Non-morphemic vocalization during the first year of life reflects, among other things, the excitement generated by an interesting event. Excitement often accompanies or follows a successful assimilation of discrepant experience and may index the degrees to which the infant is involved in the dynamic process of understanding his experience. Analysis of vocalization patterns to the faces and forms presented to the longitudinal sample revealed a larger increase in vocalization across the period 8 to 13 months for upper middle-, than for lower middle-class girls. Lower middle-class girls showed no change in vocalization across this 5-month period; upper middle-class girls displayed a 50 per cent increase ($p < 0.01$ for class differential).

CONCLUSIONS

The data from both studies are concordant in suggesting that a Caucasian child born to a mother with less than a high school education behaves differently from a middle-class child, even before the first birthday. We have interpreted these differences in terms of a set to explain discrepancy and richness of cognitive structures. It is assumed that differences in parental treatment are partially responsible for the children's profiles. The middle-class mother unconsciously plays theme and variations with her infant. She repeatedly tickles him on the tummy until his excitement wanes and then she shifts the locus of stimulation to the face, or changes modality entirely. She is continually transforming her voice, her position and her presentation of toys in the service of keeping her infant happily surprised. This play keeps both partners happy. It also may be teaching the infant to be alert for surprise; to expect a transformation on a standard; to maintain a state of alerted attentiveness towards the outside world.

The middle-class mother also engages in longer episodes of verbal interaction which should facilitate the articulation of schemata for human speech and strengthen the tendency to emit vocalizations in states of attentional excitement. Although the argument linking the class differences in the mother's actions with observed differences among the infants lacks the logical rigour of a commanding explanation, these propositions are, at least, intuitively reasonable.

The closer covariation between class and cognitive development for girls than for boys is puzzling. Duration of attention during the second year of life increases in vocalization, and quality of vocabulary are all more closely yoked to social class for girls than for boys. Other investigators have also reported closer covariation in girls between social class and indices of cognitive development. Hess and his colleagues (1969) have reported significant partial correlations between maternal verbal IQ and the 4-year-old black girl's IQ score, with maternal social class controlled ($r = 0.39$, $p < 0.01$ for girls, but only 0.15 for boys). The same pattern emerged when this analysis was restricted to black working-class families. In a longitudinal study on Hawaii, 231 boys and 254 girls from the island of Kauai were given the Cattell Development Scale at

20 months of age and the Primary Mental Abilities at $10\frac{1}{2}$ years of age. Both parental IQ and education were more highly correlated with the girls' Cattell scores than with those of the boys (0·3 for girls, 0·1 for boys). Although this sex difference had diminished by age 10, the index of social class was still more strongly correlated with the Primary Mental Abilities scale for girls than for boys ($r = 0·34$ versus 0·24) (Werner, 1969). Finally, in a recent study, 34 boys and 33 girls of pre-school age were observed in six different pre-school programmes, including a Headstart setting, a day care centre, an experimental school, and a typical suburban nursery. Each child was observed three times for 20 minutes over a 3-month period. The behavioural variables included dependency, attention-seeking, dominance, affection, and hostility towards children or adults, as well as pride in mastery and role playing. None of the variables reliably differentiated lower- from middle-class boys, while four approached significance for the girls. The middle-class girls sought adult attention more often, but were less likely to direct peers or to test adults. The middle-class girls seemed to have a more positive relationship with adults than the lower-class girls (Ogilvie, 1969).

The typical interpretation of the sex by social class interaction in older children usually invokes an assumption about the girls' stronger identification with the goals of the family. But this dynamic is not operative at 1 year of age. Hence we must seek other explanations.

It is possible that there is greater variability across social class levels in maternal reactions towards daughters than towards sons. Most mothers in this culture, whether they be high school drop-outs or college graduates, believe and hope that their sons will develop independence, responsibility, and a reliable vocational skill. Lower-class mothers of daughters project their sense of impotence on to their daughters and are less likely to stimulate, encourage, or reward the daughter's simple accomplishments. Observations of lower middle-class mothers when their infants were 4, 10, and 27 months affirm this suggestion. As noted in the above cross sectional study, middle-class mothers spend more time engaging in distinctive face-to-face vocalization and entertainment with their daughters than do lower-class mothers. But this class difference may not hold for sons. Additional support for this idea comes from home observations on our longitudinal sample made when the children were 27 months old. A female observer visited the home on two occasions for a total of 7 hours, and recorded units of interaction that focused on the child's violation of maternal standards for appropriate behaviour and the mother's reaction to those violations. The data were in the form of descriptive statements of the interaction. These descriptions were typed and coded by two independent observers who had no knowledge of the social class of the mother and had never visited the home. The intercoder agreement was generally high. Most of the variables did not reveal dramatic sex or class differences or sex by class interactions. However, the few class differences that emerged occurred for daughters, not sons. Well educated mothers of girls, for example, were most likely to criticize incompetent behaviour. If one computes only those incidents which provoked the mother to criticize or punish the child, less than 1 per cent involved incompetent behaviour among lower middle-class boys, upper middle-class boys or lower middle-class girls. However, 2·4 per cent of all punishments were for incompetence among middle- and upper middle-class mothers of girls. Well educated mothers of daughters were three times more likely than poorly educated ones to chide the child for not performing to the standard held by the mother. No comparable class difference occurred for sons. This difference was specific for task competence, for the well educated mothers were generally more tolerant of other kinds of violation by their daughters. These empirical findings suggest that mothers of daughters are more divergent in their acceleration of intellectual skills than mothers of sons. As a result, there should be greater covariation between maternal education and level of cognitive development in daughters than in sons.

A second interpretive stance posits less variability in temperamental disposition among girls than boys. Let us assume that there are more boys than girls who are extremely irritable, alert, active or lethargic. Infants at the extreme of a psychological dimension should be less influenced by specific caretaking experiences than those who are more typical. It is more difficult to engage in long periods of reciprocal vocalization with a highly mobile, highly apathetic, or highly irritable baby. The mother who initiates such action will influence the child less than one who initiates the same sequence with a less extreme child.

The best support for the notion that experience affects girls' cognitive development in a more lawful fashion comes from a study in which amount of face-to-face contact with mother and infant was correlated with attention to faces. Observations of mothers of 3-month-old infants were made in the home and the amount of face-to-face contact quantified. Soon after the home observation the infants were brought to the laboratory and shown achromatic representations of faces and geometric stimuli. There was no relation between face-to-face contact in the home and fixation time to the geometric forms for either sex. However, the relation between face-to-face contact and fixation time to the faces was 0·61 for girls but −0·10 for boys (Moss and Robson,

1968). Perhaps the greater variability in temperament or maturational development of boys is responsible for this difference. At the moment it is not possible to decide whether the cause of this sex by class inter- action is greater variability among the boys, or greater class differences in maternal treatments towards girls than boys. The data favour the latter interpretation.

It should be noted that social class covaried with vocabulary, atten- tion, and vacillation in a conflict situation but was not related to spontaneous talking, excitability, or smiling. Class was related more clearly to cognitive than to affective dimensions, and it is not claimed that there is a higher correlation between social class and all aspects of development for girls.

The infant is being influenced continually by parental practices which are monitored by attitudes towards the child and expectancy of attaining the parents' ego ideal for the child. During the first half year of life the visible effect of these maternal differences is subtle, but by 2 years of age verbal competence, sustained attention, and inhibition—the hall- mark of white middle-class values—appear to be more salient for the middle- than for the lower-class child.

REFERENCES

HARLOW, H. F. and HARLOW, M. K. 1966. Learning to love. *Am. Scient.* **54**, No. 3, 244–272.

HESS, R. D., SHIPMAN, V. C., BROPHY, J. E. and BEAR, R. M. 1969. *The cognitive environments of urban preschool children.* Graduate School of Education, University of Chicago, Chicago, Ill.

KAGAN, J. 1969a. Some response measures that show relations between social class and the course of cognitive development in infancy. In A. Ambrose (Ed.), *Stimulation in early infancy.* Academic Press, London and New York.

KAGAN, J. 1969b. Continuity in cognitive development during the first year. *Merrill-Palmer Q.* **15**, 101–120.

MOSS, H. A. and ROBSON, K. 1968. Maternal influences in early social visual behavior. *Child Dev.* **39**, 401–408.

OGILVIE, D. M. 1969. A conceptual framework for the evaluation of social behaviors of preschool children. Unpublished manuscript. Graduate School of Education, Harvard University, Cambridge, Mass.

WERNER, E. E. 1969. Sex differences and correlations between children's IQs and measures of parental ability and environment ratings. *Devl Psychol.* **1**, 280–285.

Discussion

Sex Differences in Developmental Variability

LEWIS: We have already discussed the possibility that sex differences may affect early behaviour, either through the mother's differential treatment or through basic genetic differences in the infants themselves, or both. Therefore let me just emphasize that your findings for girls need not necessarily also hold for boys. There are indeed some definite indications that the same kinds of relationships do not apply to boys. We have just finished a study looking at variables similar to yours, centred on a play situation and employing both male and female subjects from middle and lower classes. One of the things we found is that there are no class differences except for the number of times these 1-year-old infants turned and vocalized to the mother: this was about four times less frequent among the lower class than among the middle-class subjects. A most interesting finding, however, is that there appears to be a sex variable by class difference interaction. While girls of both classes show more attachment behaviour than boys, the sex-linked difference in middle-class infants is greater than it is in lower-class infants. This suggests the possibility that lower-class parents differentiate less between their male and female children than do middle-class parents.

KAGAN: That is not, however, inconsistent with our findings; it is an additional finding, and is another indication that there is a sex difference in variability. Several investigators have established that a better relationship between parental practices and the child's cognitive behaviour exists for girls than for boys, and there is little doubt now that girls generally display a more lawful developmental sequence. Let us just consider two (not mutually exclusive) explanations. One is cultural, and states that in Western society there is a greater differentiation between lower- and middle-class mothers in their practices towards daughters than towards sons, because mothers are more likely to project their personality on to a girl than on to a boy. A lower-class mother without a high school education will assume that her daughter will end up like her and will, therefore, not attempt to accelerate, mould, reward, and instruct as much as the middle-class mother. With a boy, on the other hand, the lower-class mother maintains a hope that he might make it in society and she behaves with him in a way more similar to the middle-class mother. A second possible explanation is biological and is based on the suggestion that girls are less variable than boys on constitutional dimensions. This is true for anthropometric variables and it seems also to be true for psychological variables. Most of the measures in our longitudinal study (visual fixation times, vocalizing, etc.) showed greater stability for girls than for boys. Consider a trait like irritability-apathy. At the extremes we should have more boys than girls, and it seems to me that the effect of environmental experience on these boys will therefore be distorted. If there are more boys with extreme temperamental traits, the theoretically expected co-variation between experience and outcome which you find in girls will be attenuated. The female is a more stable organism and reflects with greater fidelity the mosaic of experiences that occur to her.

BOWLBY: It is true, is it not, that the male phenotype is more varied? HIRSCH: There are data to this effect. But on the whole I would be reluctant to make the generalization that males are more variable. There are sex differences in variation, but their nature depends on the particular function: in the case of some traits it might be the male that is more variable, but in others the female might show the greater variability.

Class Differences in Maternal Expectations

BRODY: How did you obtain your data on maternal expectations? KAGAN: We conducted an informal interview, in which we asked questions like "When your child is 10 years old, what are the three or four things you would really like him to be?" If, for example, the mother said that she hoped the child would be good in school, we tried to find out how confident she felt that this would come about. All interviews were recorded and subsequently rated. The data are crude, however, and we do not intend to give them salience in the final analysis. BRODY: They may be crude and yet meaningful. We have also been trying to get data about maternal expectations, both with regard to immediate things like weaning and toilet training and with regard to their aspirations for the future. As far as immediate things are concerned, lower-class mothers were just as hopeful as middle-class mothers, but this did not hold for the more distant future. The middle-class mothers mostly expected their children to go to college and do well, whereas the more usual hopes that a lower-class mother had even for a highly intelligent child was that he should, for example, become a good carpenter. And the further we went on in reference to the child's age the less optimistic the lower-class mother was and the lower her aspirations. I thought that was very meaningful material. KAGAN: Our lower-class mothers were also pessimistic about the possibility of their children attaining the ideals they had for them. Yet the ideals themselves were close to those of the middle-class mothers.

The Usefulness of the Social Class Variable

SCOTT: I would like to question the usefulness of examining data in terms of social class differences. I fear that sorting people into two or three classes is really a very artificial procedure and that the end result is actually to obscure differences of a more meaningful nature. What impressed me about your data was not that you got differences but that you did not get very big differences in many cases. Probably the most significant variable here is something we might refer to as the "culture" of the parents, or, in other words, the store of information to which they have access. Now this might be the result of all sorts of factors, such as the level of education attained, the family's geographical location, personality characteristics, and so on. As a result, class assumes a different meaning in the Southern States of the U.S., where the main division is between Negroes and whites, than, say, in New York or Boston.

SCHAFFER: Kagan never pretended that class is a causal factor or anything but a starting-off point for further analysis. Of course it is a global concept; on the other hand it has been shown that it can usefully highlight differences which one can then further explore and trace back to their associated antecedent conditions. In some of our work on attachment formation, for instance, we found class differences, but after looking at these more closely we decided that they were mostly explicable in terms of the physical living conditions in which infants of different classes were reared. If the child lives in one room with the rest of the family and is never separated from the mother by more than a few feet he is likely to develop a rather different set of expectations from the child whose cognitive world includes several different rooms and who quickly learns to expect mother's frequent disappearances from his immediate visual field. The advantage of the class concept is that it helps to direct one's attention to variables such as this.

KAGAN: At the moment class is one of the most sensitive indices we have of the mother's sense of her own effectiveness in society. I know of no better index—if I did I would use it. Moreover, it is this variable which highlights some of the crucial differences in cognitive performance. A 6-year-old middle-class child shows greater language proficiency, reflection, and vacillation than a lower-class child of the same age. These are the hallmarks of the middle-class ideal, and it would appear that one can already isolate these differences in the first year of life.

A Comment on the Social Context of Mother–Infant Interaction

M. P. M. RICHARDS[1]

University of Cambridge

INTRODUCTION

UNTIL VERY RECENTLY studies of mother–infant interaction have been rather narrowly focused on the mother (or her absence) and her infant, and we have paid little attention to other members of the social group or to cultural factors that may influence the interaction. Without this narrow focus, it is hard to see how progress would have been as rapid as it has been (c.f. Bowlby, 1969). Lately, however, the direction of research has been greatly modified and there is much discussion of the social and cultural climate in which a child grows up. To a large extent this has not been an internal development of the subject, but has been brought about by outside social and political pressures, particularly through Project Headstart. Though we may feel that it is appropriate to respond to such pressures and change the direction of our research, to do so may give rise to some rather special problems as we may not have the necessary conceptual framework to tackle the new area. When psychologists were asked to work on "cultural deprivation" and the "disadvantaged" and so broaden their view of mother–child relations to include the whole social context, they were faced with quite a new range of problems for which their methodology seems to have been inadequate or inappropriate.

The discussion which follows has grown out of our work on mother–infant interaction and its social context (Richards and Bernal, 1971). Many of the problems we have had to face are common to American research on cultural deprivation and I shall illustrate my argument with

[1] The author expresses his gratitude to Judith Bernal, Kenneth Kaye, and Joanna Ryan for many helpful comments on this material.

examples from the latter. First I shall try to isolate some of the conceptual problems in the investigation of the social context of mother–infant interaction and child development, and then, tentatively, to put forward some ideas about how we may approach them.

There is fairly general agreement that the roots of cultural deprivation are to be found very early in childhood—at least this seems to be taken as a working hypothesis for most studies. Thus in a report of one of the earlier intervention programmes, Klaus and Gray (1968) state that "the home conditions of a child [is] the situation which created the original deficit", and so part of their programme attempted to "bring the mother up to providing a home situation analogous to that of a more favoured middle-class child, the one who makes the so-called normal progress on attitude and achievement tests."

THE PROBLEM

Lacking a more suitable paradigm, most investigators have approached the problem of deprivation as if it were a laboratory experiment. An experimental ("deprived", "disadvantaged", "lower-class") and a control ("middle-class", "advantaged") group are selected and then contrasted on one or more items of the children's behaviour. Any differences that are found are related either to some environmental measure that was taken (e.g. an aspect of mother–child interaction) or to some supposedly established characteristics of one of the groups, to provide an "explanation" for the children's behaviour. There are some studies which are genuine experiments: for instance, those which set out to assess intervention programmes by giving different treatments to subgroups of homogeneous populations. I am not referring to studies of this kind but to those which have the more general aim of isolating the conditions that lead to cultural deprivation. This pseudo-experimental paradigm carries with it a number of unfortunate assumptions:

1. The paradigm is prejudicial and contains an inherent value judgment. The control (middle-class) children are treated as normal while the others are assumed to lack something (that is they are deprived) which causes them to behave in another way. This assumption is clearly present in the passage from Klaus and Gray (1968) quoted above and similar sentiments may be found in almost any writing on the subject.

2. It is implicitly assumed that the children in the two groups are inherently similar before the experiment starts; that is to say, all the differences between them are created by environmental influences. Such an assumption was not too surprising in the environmentalist

climate of the early sixties (for example, Hunt, 1961) but there is overwhelming evidence against it. The distribution of a wide range of pre- and perinatal factors that have been shown to influence child behaviour and mother–infant interaction is highly related to social status. Though it may be a sensible educational strategy to concentrate on the purely environmental factors it cannot be an adequate basis for research. Kagan (1969) states that "The lower-class mothers spend less time in face-to-face mutual vocalization and smiling with their infants; they do not reward the child's maturational progress, and they do not enter into long periods of play with the child. Our theory of mental development suggests that specific absence of these experiences will retard mental growth and will lead to lower intelligence test scores." These are "theories" of development that must be questioned as they are clearly incomplete.

3. A typology is employed which is assumed to be universal or nearly so. Studies of deprivation have been carried out in widely separated geographical localities with very varied samples. Data from these studies are used to describe *the middle-class* and *the lower-class* child without regard for the cultural and geographical differences within each group. An extreme example of this fallacy is the use of Bernstein's (1961, 1967) distinction between the elaborated linguistic code of middle-class children and the restricted code of working-class children in England to "explain" social status differences in the United States (e.g. Cazden, 1968). To anyone familiar with accounts of working-class life in England (e.g. Hoggart, 1957) and the States (e.g. Clark, 1965), the similarities will seem few indeed. More direct evidence of the problem comes from the study by Lesser and associates (1965) of cognitive abilities in middle- and lower-class children from four sub-cultures in the United States. In each subculture the various abilities followed similar patterns in the two socio-economic groups but showed no similarities across the subcultures or within the class samples.

The typology of social class follows in part from the assumption that the varied criteria used to select the two groups will give comparable and repeatable samples across space and time. These criteria include place of residence, income, type of school attended, race, enrolment in an intervention programme, or one of the synthetic social class scales. When interstudy comparisons are made it is implied that these criteria will have the same significance whenever and wherever the study is conducted. No evidence is produced to justify this assumption and there is much to challenge it.

TOWARDS AN ANSWER

Let me try to restate the problem. Children from varying social backgrounds differ in their school performance and characterization on a wide range of psychological tests. We wish to relate these differences between the children to some aspect or aspects of their backgrounds. The interaction of child and social context is a two-way process. The child is not simply a passive being, he actively goes out into his environment and selects from it, and in turn may modify it. Thus any studies of the social context of the developing child must consider both the child and his social context. Children are born with varying behavioural characteristics and these are not randomly distributed among children of different subcultures. This point has been persuasively argued by Birch (1968) who has indicated that many factors such as prematurity, obstetric complications, and malnutrition, which are known to influence a child's behaviour, are highly correlated with criteria of social position. For example, the percentage of non-white premature births in the United States is about twice that of whites (Baumgartner, 1962). English data (Butler and Bonham, 1963; Butler and Alberman, 1969) show that geographical variation is superimposed on the social class differences. This variation among children at birth must be taken into account in comparisons of children from different subcultures as well as the observed differences in the environment. In part, this is merely an acknowledgment that the environment not only operates directly on the child after birth but also through effects on the mother's reproductive capacity. We have indications that these congenital factors interact with environmental factors. Ucko (1965) found that children who suffered perinatal anoxia were more upset by changes in their family situation than children who had less traumatic births.

These considerations lead to the conclusion that longitudinal studies are required in which individual differences between children are assessed as soon as possible after birth, before the extra-uterine environment–child interaction has confused the picture. Some enormous practical difficulties exist here, though the development of neurological examinations for newborns (Prechtl and Beintema, 1964; Thomas et al., 1960) provides one hopeful method.

A recurrent problem in cultural deprivation studies is the wide disparity in the two groups that are compared. Such disparity means that there are innumerable differences in the backgrounds of the children, any or all of which may be significant in their development. Perhaps we could select our sample in a much more efficient way.

Instead of taking widely differing social groups, we could look at differences within one relatively homogeneous population. This would be analogous to a comparative psychologist moving from the comparison of species to a consideration of variation within one species. We might profitably move from comparisons of the ghetto with the campus to an examination of the variation within one or other of the groups. In this way many of the environmental and congenital differences between the children are eliminated and we may more easily find those that really matter for development. At the same time we should lose the dangerous simplicity of the typology of the middle-class and lower-class child and its superficial suggestion of wide generality. One objection to the suggested approach is that widely differing groups are required to produce significant differences in measures of behaviour. If that is the case, and I have no reason to believe it, the problem lies in the crudity of our methods. It is surely more sensible to try to improve our methods than to remain content with inadequate ones which require us to use highly inefficient and misleading strategies of research.

Even if we work within a very circumscribed subculture, there is still the problem of deciding which environmental factors to investigate. In the absence of a general theory that links environmental factors and the child's development, there is always the danger that correlations we find between the child's behaviour and his environment are coincidental and are unrelated to differences between the children. As it is clearly impossible to measure every aspect of the children's background, we need some way of choosing those factors that are likely to be important. This seems to be an insoluble problem but it may be ameliorated by examining as many likely factors as is feasible and by working simultaneously at several levels of analysis. Since we are dealing with the social context we have to consider social facts. However, we do not suppose that a man's income level can *cause* his child to develop in a particular way. But among a restricted group of people living in a limited geographical area, different income levels may be associated with certain attitudes towards child rearing, and these attitudes in turn may be related to particular behaviour patterns directed towards the child and characteristic responses to the child's behaviour. The building of chains of this kind seems to provide a possible way of ordering the many features of the environment that could be investigated. It provides a multilevel analysis without being reductionist.

At the outset I suggested that some of the difficulties of the cultural deprivation work were caused by our departure from the developing path of our subject under social and political pressures. This is certainly not the whole story and it may imply a rather over-optimistic view of the state of psychology. Some problems appear to be the direct consequence of trying to build a science of psychology which closely resembles the physical sciences. In the study of chemical reactions it is not necessary to consider the individual identity of the atoms: any hydrogen atom may substitute for any other hydrogen atom. In such situations the comparison of groups rather than individuals provides very powerful experimental procedures. But mother–child diads and child–environment diads are each unique and we are very far from being able to account for a significant proportion of the variance between them. This imposes severe limitations on strategies of research based on group rather than on individual comparisons. Summarizing the behaviour of a group of people in terms of some central tendency may leave us with only rather trivial statements and will not lead to an understanding of individual differences. I am not trying to argue that the methods of validation in psychology are necessarily different from those in the physical sciences but there is little doubt that the means of discovery and the methodology required for psychological problems are not those that have proved so useful in classical physics and chemistry.

REFERENCES

BAUMGARTNER, L. 1962. The public health significance of low birth weight in the U.S.A., with special reference to varying practices in providing special care to infants of low birth weights. *Bull. Wld Hlth Org.* **26,** 175.

BERNSTEIN, B. 1961. Social class and linguistic development: a theory of social learning. In A. H. Halsey, J. Floud and C. A. Anderson (Eds.), *Education, economy and society.* Free Press of Glencoe, New York.

BERNSTEIN, B. 1967. The role of speech in the development and transmission of culture. In G. J. Klopf and W. A. Hohman (Eds.), *Perspectives on learning.* Mental Health Materials Center, New York.

BIRCH, H. G. 1968. Health and education of socially disadvantaged children. *Devl Med. Child Neurol.* **10,** 58–599.

BOWLBY, J. 1969. *Attachment and loss. Vol. 1: Attachment.* Hogarth Press, London.

BUTLER, N. R. and BONHAM, D. G. 1963. *Perinatal mortality.* Livingstone, London.

BUTLER, N. R. and ALBERMAN, E. D. (Eds.). 1969. *Perinatal problems.* Livingstone, London.

CAZDEN, C. B. 1968. Three socio-linguistic views of the language and speech of lower-class children—with special attention to the work of Basil Bernstein. *Devl Med. Child Neurol.* **10,** 600–612.

CLARK, K. B. 1965. *Dark ghetto, dilemmas of social power.* Gollancz, London.

HOGGART, R. 1957. *The uses of literacy: aspects of working-class life with special reference to publications and entertainment.* Chatto & Windus, London.

HUNT, J. McV. 1961. *Intelligence and experience.* Ronald Press, New York.

KAGAN, S. J. 1969. Inadequate evidence and illogical conclusions. *Harvard educ. Rev.* **39**, 274–277.

KLAUS, R. A. and GRAY, S. W. 1968. The early training project for disadvantaged children: a report after five years. *Monogr. Soc. Res. Child Dev.* **33**, No. 4, Serial no. 120.

LESSER, G. S., FIFER, G., and CLARK, D. H. 1965. Mental abilities of children from different social class and cultural groups. *Monogr. Soc. Res. Child Dev.* **30**, No. 4, Serial no. 102.

PRECHTL, H. F. R. and BEINTEMA, D. 1964. *The neurological examination of the full-term newborn infant.* Clinics in Developmental Medicine No. 12. Spastics Society/Heinemann Medical Books, London.

RICHARDS, M. P. M. and BERNAL, J. F. 1971. An observational study of mother–infant interaction. In N. Blurton Jones (Ed.), *Ethological studies of human behaviour.* Cambridge University Press.

THOMAS, A., CHESNI, Y. and SAINT-ANNE DARGASSIES, S. 1960. *The neurological examination of the infant.* Clinics in Developmental Medicine No. 1. Spastics Society/Heinemann Medical Books, London.

UCKO, L. E. 1965. A comparative study of asphyxiated and non-asphyxiated boys from birth to five years. *Devl Med. Child Neurol.* **7**, 643–657.

Maternal Stimulation and Social Responsiveness of Infants

SYLVIA BRODY AND SIDNEY AXELRAD

The City University of New York

IMPRINTING AS A FORM OF HUMAN LEARNING

SEVERAL EXPERIMENTS IN imprinting during the last decade touch upon specific connections between sensory and emotional arousal and adaptive behaviour in animal infancy (Green and Gordon, 1964; Lemmon and Patterson, 1964). We expect the same condition to hold for an imprinting process that takes place in human infants.

Imprinting is of obvious survival value for the species as well as for the individual. It makes mothering possible in species where the infant organism must take an active role in being mothered. It also sets one of the conditions for the choice of a sexual partner. The fact that extra-species objects can be imprinted does not speak against the survival value of imprinting. The fact that imprinting is a special form of learning does not speak against its biological function, for statistically, during the critical period and in a state of nature, the imprinting object will belong to the animal's own species. And as various observers have noted, there is no reason to believe that the human species should be exempt from this kind of process (Ambrose, 1963; Benjamin, 1961; Gray, 1958; Hess, 1959; Scott, 1963).

If, as seems likely, an imprinting-like phenomenon exists among human infants, the infant's smile appears to us to be too mature a response to be regarded as an example of that phenomenon. Our contention is rather that there are two major critical periods of socialization among human infants: the first, in which there is imprinting to the human species in general, may be signified by the ability to fixate, visually or auditorily, as observed by sharp increases or decreases of body movement (limbs, head, facial features) or of activity level, and by visual pursuit of the human object. In this first period the ability to fixate is prerequisite to the ability to smile. The second critical period, in which there is imprinting to the mother or her surrogate, may be signified by the ability to discriminate the mother or her surrogate from other human objects. It would be shown by the immediacy of the smiling response to her above others.

The appearance of the smile may be a result of a kind of practice, or work, i.e. an expenditure of effort for an end other than the activity itself. If so, it is experienced by the infant as a relief of tension. The relief would lie in the achievement of familiarity of a percept: it occurs when no further effort is necessary to attain the percept. It effects a habituation of the hitherto unfamiliar. It is as if the organization of the hitherto amorphous world into patterns and Gestalten permits an easy and pleasurable discharge of tension. Smiling proceeds from perception of a mechanically patterned object to a discriminatory response to more and more specific stimuli: i.e. from the most general configuration of the human facial features to the face of the specific mother (Gough, 1962).

Referring back to the phenomenon of imprinting, we propose that in its initial phase imprinting for the human species in general is likely to be as swift and irreversible as Scott (1963) reports it to be for birds. We suggest that visual fixation upon the human face presented at very close range and especially when reinforced by the human voice, plus visual pursuit movements, may be the human equivalent of following among animals. Human infants can locomote, as it were, only with their eyes in the first weeks of life. Among older infants the second phase of imprinting—marked by recognition of, and smiling approach towards, the mother—may indicate a process far more complex and reversible. A 6-week to 6-month period of primary socialization as suggested by Scott (1963) seems too gross. It is in accordance with our observations rather to divide the primary socialization period into at least the two major phases we have alluded to, the first beginning with fixation and pursuit movement, the second beginning with discrimination of the mother *qua* object. Many mothers have reported the latter to occur in the fourth month.

It follows from these considerations that imprinting, or its counterpart in the human species, is a special form of learning, and may involve a hypercathexis of primary percepts: that is, it may involve a perception of objects as not yet apart from the self, and a perception which succumbs to a truer object cathexis at a later point of maturation, when objects come to be recognized as separate from the self and as "interfering" with the object–self unity. Imprinting in the human would thus be seen as a form of object cathexis, perhaps the simplest kind of affective bond, first to the species and then to the mother, subsequently to other parental objects. The "interference" of percepts of external objects, the rise of secondary narcissism, might be viewed in relation to the onset of anxiety arousal and early conflict—a process in some ways analogous to the onset of fear and the ending of imprinting in lower species.

We propose that two kinds of sensory arousals, one dominant in each of the two phases of socialization, may occur. The first arousal is automatic, is close to an unconditioned reflex, and touches off an innate releasing mechanism. It promotes the onset of the critical period for the first phase of socialization during the first 6 weeks of life and strengthens the imprinting response to the species; it ends some time in the fourth month. The second arousal occurs when there is a perception of inner tension, and a perception of motor capacity to discharge tension or to summon relief from tension. This second kind of arousal promotes the onset of the critical period for the second phase of socialization, and so for the perceptual consciousness of the mother—which, we propose, is normally completed in the seventh month.[1]

MATERNAL INFLUENCE UPON INFANT SOCIALIZATION

We wish to suggest that data obtained by us on infants during the first 6 months indicate that those infants whose perceptual consciousness of the mother has been highly reinforced show high social responsiveness to people in general, and that the converse is true for infants whose perceptual consciousness of the mother has been poorly reinforced. It follows that high stimulation at the proper critical period advances high perceptual consciousness.

Subjects

The data are drawn from interviews and observations of 122 infants studied in the Infant Development Research Project.

All pregnant women, white, native born, in good health, married and living with the fathers of their prospective infants, and expecting to deliver the infants in the hospital where the research was conducted, were identified with the help of the Prenatal Clinic nurses and the obstetrical records, and were invited by the social worker of the project to participate in a study of normal infant development. They were told

[1] A fuller discussion appears in Brody and Axelrad (1970).

that the aim of the project was to learn about the effects of environment upon early development; that their participation would require bringing the baby to the Project offices in the hospital three times during the baby's first year, allowing us to take films of his feeding, and to test him; we should also wish to ask the mother many questions about his development. Approximately 70 per cent of the mothers accepted the invitation. The population of mothers in the final sample $(n = 122)$ consists of a self-selected group of primiparae and multiparae, from all socioeconomic classes, and of infants born to them at a large metropolitan hospital in New York City between the end of 1963 and the beginning of 1966. Distribution of the cases by social class, using the Hollingshead two-factor index of social position (Hollingshead and Redlich, 1958) was approximately normal.

To be included in the sample the neonates had to be of normal, fullterm, spontaneous birth, with normal Apgar ratings. The Apgar scores were made routinely by the attending obstetrician and recorded by him or by the obstetrical nurse, along with the complete medical record of labour and delivery. It would have been desirable to have a member of the Project staff present during the delivery of each prospective subject, and trained to make the Apgar ratings. Practical difficulties of staff availability, and of hospital regulations made it necessary, however, to rely upon the medical staff for a judgment of the infant's normality. As a result, scores were not recorded in some cases, but in each of these cases the infant's perinatal and postnatal condition were found to be normal by both the obstetrician and the paediatrician (the latter required by the hospital), and the infant was retained in the sample.

We wished our sample to be composed of infants assumed by usual clinical evaluations to be normal. Since we had no opportunity to estimate the presence or the significance of soft neurological signs of impairment in the neonate we preferred to make use of a common run of mothers and infants, excluding those who showed any detectable biological or psychological abnormality.

Only those cases have been used in which the mother's report was adequate for rating and appeared to be reliable, contained no contradictions, and could be supported by our own observations. Cases in which the maternal stimulation was deemed moderate were also excluded, as the effects of moderate stimulation were most likely to be influenced in either direction by paternal or sibling stimulation— phenomena that were difficult to assess even during several home visits. This left a sample of 77.

The Physical Setting

The observation room was 18 by 16 feet, air-conditioned, and sound-proofed. False windows were covered with venetian blinds and brightly coloured curtains. The floor was of cork tile for extra sound-proofing. The ceiling was equipped with fluorescent lights to provide maximum light and minimum heat, and arranged to maintain an overall light of 160-foot candles. A one-way mirror, 2 by 3 feet, was set into the front wall, approximately 4 feet from the floor. Behind the mirror, in the camera room, two Auricon Cine Voice II Sound-on film cameras (16 mm) were set on a table and on heads which allowed for a complete horizontal and vertical sweep of the room in a 180° arc. The cameras were automatically timed so that both reels of film could be run without interruption for a total of 100 minutes, and were adapted to run at 16 frames per second. The cameras were set in operation by a remote control switch placed inconspicuously at the side of the interviewer's desk in the observation room; a switch in the camera room allowed for operating the cameras from there as well. Another remote control panel was placed in the secretarial office, to inform camera personnel when the camera was turned on (to check on focusing, reloading, lighting, and camera operation).

Most of the furniture in the room was easily movable and could be arranged in any way the mother chose when she fed her baby. She was free to sit in any one of a number of chairs; and either to hold the baby on her lap or to place him in an infant seat, or in a crib, a baby-tenda, or a high-chair.

Procedure

The mother and infant were observed in the above settings at 6 weeks, 6 months, and 1 year. Filmed observations were obtained of their behaviour in a number of situations, particularly during a feeding session.

An observer greeted the mother and baby on their arrival at the observation room and tried to help them to feel at home. The mother was asked to make herself comfortable, to do what she liked with the baby. Having tried to put her at ease, we observed her for a little while. She was then asked when she would like to feed the baby, since she had been expressly invited to do so, and to have the feeding of the baby filmed. We wanted her to feel free to feed when it was most convenient for her, so the decision was left to her. Filmed observations were then begun.

From the observations thus obtained we derived a number of indices, including Maternal Stimulation and Infant Responsiveness. The following categories were used for these variables.

Maternal Stimulation

High: Mother reports generally high attentiveness during day, with frequent vocal, tactile, and kinesthetic stimulation; and a great deal of play, rough or gentle, occurring independently of routine care.

Low: Mother reports attentiveness mainly for routine care; few or no attempts to play with or communicate with infant; infant left alone while awake for long periods, rarely held or only in limited situations, e.g. while mother watches television.

Infant Responsiveness

High: Infant initiates smiling or smiles easily and often, and shows visual and vocal interest in both mother and observer.

Moderate: No initiation or ease of smiling; mild or sporadic vocal communication, but both can be elicited by mother or observer.

Low: No initiation or ease of smiling, and little or no reciprocal smiling at, or vocalization to, mother or observer.

Results

The association between maternal stimulation and the infants' social responsiveness at 6 months is given in Table I. Because of the low frequency in several cells the data of Table I had to be grouped in order

TABLE I. MATERNAL STIMULATION AND SOCIAL
RESPONSIVENESS AT SIX MONTHS

| Maternal stimulation | Infant responsiveness | | | Total |
	High	Moderate	Low	
High	31	2	2	35
Low	4	6	32	42
Total	35	8	34	77

to calculate statistical significance. When high and moderate infant responsiveness were combined, a chi-square of 38·8 (d.f. = 1, $p < 0.001$) was obtained; when moderate and low responsiveness were combined, a chi-square of 48·1 (d.f. = 1, $p < 0.001$) was found.

Of 35 infants who at 6 months were indicated to have had abundant stimulation by their mothers, 31 reacted in the observational setting with high degrees of responsiveness. Two, whose responsiveness was moderate, had mothers who were overactive and dominating in their stimulation; and two whose responsiveness was low, both had mothers who overwhelmed the infants with continuous childish physical play. Of the 42 infants who were stimulated little or not at all by their mothers, 32 showed little or no social responsiveness. Four infants in this group of 42 were highly responsive: all four received high stimulation from the father, siblings, or other adults. Of the remaining six, whose responsiveness was moderate, five received considerable attention from siblings or adults.

It is clear that there is a significant relationship between degree of social stimulation by the mother and social responsiveness of the infant at 6 months.

These findings are only suggestive as to the complexity of perceptual development in early infancy. Nevertheless it is reasonable to apply them to our propositions regarding the significance of visual perception for the socialization process. Thus we might say that under 2 months, and approximately before the social smile appears regularly, the infant may fixate upon the human face and also upon other familiar inanimate stimuli; and that at about 2 months the facial movements that compose the smile present a novel aspect to the infant's perceptions and may facilitate an imprinting response to the species: for in the ensuing 3 or 4 months the smile configuration that was first responded to in the mother or her surrogate grows more and more familiar, and the smile of non-mothers comes to be imbued with the attractive aspect of novelty. So human faces are responded to during the 3- to 6-month period liberally, generally, and without differentiation. All friendly overtures are welcomed by the infant, and he may work hard to elicit attention from persons who are slow to pay him court. The capacity for such reciprocal responsiveness might be said to consolidate the first phase of the socialization process, as we have outlined it.

At about 6 months the infant discriminates the mother from other persons. If now he prefers her and grows more wary of others, it might be because now a new variety of maternal attributes or features, those that are visually more complex are better perceived and attended to. The 6- to 9-month period, approximately, is that in which the infant is quick to grab at the mother's hair, to poke his fingers into her mouth, to slap at her face. He is excited, we might say, by those aspects of her figure that heretofore he has seemingly neglected. And this vivid response to the mother as an individual, to the mother as a specific imprinting object, would consolidate the second phase of the socialization process. One is tempted to imagine a continuous, spiralling process of socialization and learning, according to levels of curiosity, activity, and gratification achieved in the course of infancy.

INFANT SOCIALIZATION AND STRANGER ANXIETY

Except in a few recent studies, stranger anxiety has been treated as a normative event unrelated to the stimulation history of the infant. The hypothesis we wish to examine is that stranger anxiety is a function of the relationship between mother and infant, and that stranger anxiety itself is not a unitary phenomenon but one which has many gradations.

Subjects

The relevant data were obtained from the Infancy Development Research Project referred to above. All 122 subjects were observed for evidence of stranger anxiety at 6 months and at 1 year.

Procedure

In the observational setting previously described, the stranger, who was the observer, sat at a desk about 10 to 12 feet from the mother. She made no particular overtures to the baby, other than maintaining a friendly facial expression, or offering a pleasant, quiet "hallo" as was socially appropriate. There was initially little physical proximity, but we did not remain at a remote silent distance. We just tried to be naturally tactful and polite and behaved in a manner that appeared to make mother and baby comfortable.

Observations were obtained for a period of not less than $2\frac{1}{2}$ hours, often closer to 4 hours. Behaviour during feeding and during the administration of an infant development test was not taken into consideration for the purpose of testing for stranger anxiety, but responses to the stranger at all other times, whether the infant was resting or playing, were considered.

Results

Logically and actually, there are three possible main responses to strangers: to be positively outgoing, either spontaneously or reactively; to respond negatively, either spontaneously or reactively; or to show no visible response. These coarse groupings did not contain all of the observations of behaviour shown by the infants to strangers. The infants showed eight kinds of responses, within two main general categories of *Positive Responsiveness* and *Apprehensiveness*. The former category includes all infants who were *Spontaneously* or *Reactively Outgoing*, as shown by smiling and/or vocalizing (reactions 1 and 2 below). Infants in the latter category were those who were not Spontaneously or Reactively Outgoing. All infants (in both categories) could in addition have shown certain specific response patterns, namely *Customs Inspection, Unchanging Soberness, Mild General Anxiety* and *Strong General Anxiety*, as defined below (reactions 3, 4, 5, and 6). Infants who showed no differentiation in behaviour at sight of the stranger were classified in the Apprehensive group. Tables II to VI deal only with reactions that could be contradicted in the research setting. Tables VII and VIII deal with the category of *Specific Avoidance*, which could not be checked in the research setting, and is treated separately.

To repeat: the primary classification of infants was either Positively Responsive or Apprehensive. All the infants could in addition show certain specific reaction patterns, such as Soberness and Mild General Anxiety. When this occurred, the infant was classified according to the most fearful of his reactions, and his other reactions were eliminated from immediate consideration. Thus there is no overlap in the categories cited in the following tables.

The eight specific reaction patterns are defined as follows.

1. Spontaneous outgoingness. The infant initiates social overtures, often coyly or flirtatiously at first, and later with ease.

2. Responsive smiling or vocalizing. The infant does not initiate social communication but responds to overtures by the stranger. This includes mechanical smiling, observed in nine infants at 6 months and in five at 12 months. Probably the latter behaviour is equivalent to the "propitiating smile" described by Benjamin (1961).

3. Customs inspection. The infant quietly and steadily regards the stranger, "sizes him up", with no loss of composure but with temporarily reduced activity; he may then smile, or return to a previous activity, or continue to watch the stranger, yet with no sign of uneasiness.

4. Unchanging soberness. The infant maintains an apprehensive watch on the stranger, and his facial expression is uneasy. His activity is sharply reduced, and there is no return to good humour or to other objects as long as the stranger is present.

5. Mild general anxiety. The infant reacts with mild but pervasive distress in the form of whimpering, turning away, or restlessness; and the distress is rekindled by eye contact, by physical proximity to the

stranger, or by touch. Cautiousness is maintained and activity is minimal as long as the stranger is present.

6. Strong personal anxiety. The infant reacts with acute and prolonged distress in the form of fearful clinging, crying, or panic, and avoids looking at the stranger. He can hardly be comforted as long as the stranger remains present.

7. Specific avoidance. The infant freezes or withdraws physically at the sight of specific persons (the doctor, an elderly neighbour), or of familiar persons with unusual appearance (grandmother when she puts on her glasses), or when suddenly approached by, say, a visiting relative. This behaviour was only reported, not observed.

8. No differentiation. The stranger (staff observer) seems to go unnoticed or is responded to as if perceived to be no different from the mother.

Table II shows that at age 6 months 95 infants were either Spontaneously Outgoing and/or Responsive to the stranger (Positively Responsive), and 27 were neither. At 12 months, 90 were Outgoing and/or Responsive (Positively Responsive), and 32 were neither. The number of infants who were Positively Responsive Only (no other reaction observed) falls from 51 at 6 months to 31 at 12 months, and the number showing Customs Inspection rises at 12 months correspondingly. It appears that at 12 months fewer infants were indiscriminately social, and more showed capacity for calm visual appraisal of the stranger. The greater frequency of Soberness at 6 months may reflect a wariness that in succeeding months matures to Customs Inspection.

TABLE II. POSITIVE RESPONSIVENESS AND APPREHENSION AT
6 MONTHS AND 1 YEAR

Primary classification	Specific reaction patterns			
	Six months		One year	
	Positively responsive	Apprehensive	Positively responsive	Apprehensive
Positively responsive (no other reaction)	51	0	31	0
Apprehensive (no other reaction)	0	4	0	3
Customs Inspection	25	6	47	7
Soberness	12	9	3	7
Mild anxiety	6	5	7	11
Strong anxiety	1	3	2	4

Chi-square for 6 months = 43·30 (d.f. = 5, $p < 0.001$).
Chi-square for 1 year = 50·65 (d.f = 5, $p < 0.001$).

Of the 27 infants observed to be Apprehensive at 6 months, 11 were reported by their mothers normally to be Positively Responsive, but in four of the latter cases neither the mother nor we observed any additional degree of awareness of the stranger as such. Of the 32 infants observed to be Apprehensive at 12 months, six were reported normally to be Positively Responsive; but all six were also reported, and four were observed, to show some additional degree of awareness of the stranger. The maternal reports about Apprehensive infants were thus less broadly positive at 1 year than at 6 months.

Although Positive Responsiveness may be construed as showing positive capacity to accept the stranger, Apprehensiveness need not in itself be construed as absence of the capacity, or as evidence of anxiety. Depending upon the context in which the infant is neither Spontaneously Outgoing nor Responsive, his behaviour may signify a capacity for cautiousness, or a temporary indisposition. Customs Inspection, however, does appear to us to signify that an effort is being made to work through a normally anxious reaction to the stranger. It indicates that the infant recognizes the stranger as different and is working visually towards a judgment of the stranger's acceptability. Since this act of judgment is a resultant of major infantile advances in ego development, we feel it would be confusing to describe it solely as a reaction of anxiety *unless one explicitly means signal anxiety.* We therefore prefer to retain the name *stranger anxiety* only for those instances where the infant reacts with overt fear visible in prolonged stillness or soberness, or prolonged restlessness, or turning away or clinging; or audible in whimpering, crying, or screaming.

Of the 35 infants who showed high social responsiveness to maternal stimulation at 6 months (Table I), all 35 were in the group of 95 infants who were Positively Responsive to strangers at 6 months. Only one of the 35 was in the group of 19 who showed overt anxiety.

Of the 34 infants who showed low social responsiveness to maternal stimulation at 6 months (Table I), 19 fell into the group of 95 who were Positively Responsive to strangers at 6 months, and 15 fell into the group of 27 who were Apprehensive of strangers. However, of the 19 in the Positively Responsive group, only two were Spontaneously Outgoing to strangers at 6 months; the other 17 showed variable degrees of positive responsiveness, ranging from reactive to rote responsiveness, and only eight showed Customs Inspection as well as responsiveness.

High stimulation by the mother appears to lead to high social responsiveness, at least at 6 months. The two together seem to make for an absence of stranger anxiety at 6 months.

Low stimulation by the mother appears to lead to low social responsiveness at 6 months, and in turn to a more cautious response to the stranger, either in the form of overt anxiety or of a passive approach.

These findings suggest that stranger anxiety at 6 months is not a normative event, but is a phenomenon related to the stimulation history of the infant, and one which may have pathogenic significance.

Accordingly, we regard Positive Responsiveness and Customs Inspection as normative and benign reactions to strangers; nondifferentiation as an absence of positive reaction but of equivocal import without knowledge of its context; and Soberness, Mild Anxiety, and Strong Anxiety as indicative of stranger anxiety. Statements about stranger anxiety following here refer only to the latter three reactions, unless otherwise noted.

Thus, Table III shows that in the Positively Responsive group of 95 infants, at 6 months, 76 reacted to the stranger with equanimity and 19 with anxiety.

TABLE III. REACTIONS TO STRANGERS: POSITIVE RESPONSIVENESS VERSUS OVERT ANXIETY AT 6 MONTHS

| Primary classification | Specific reaction patterns | | |
	Positive responsiveness and Customs Inspection	*Overt anxiety*	*Total*
Positively responsive	76	19	95
Apprehensive	6	17	23[a]
Total	82	36	118

Chi-square $= 25\cdot505$ (d.f. $= 1$; $p < 0\cdot001$).
[a] Four of the 27 infants in the Apprehensive group showed no differentiated reactions.

In contrast, in the Apprehensive group of 27 infants, only six reacted with equanimity (Customs Inspection) and 17 with anxiety. Four did not differentiate the stranger in any way. The same relationship obtains at age 12 months (Table IV): of 90 infants in the Positively Responsive group, 78 reacted to the stranger with equanimity, and 12 with anxiety. In contrast, in the Apprehensive group of 32 infants, only seven reacted with equanimity (Customs Inspection) and 22 with anxiety. Three did not differentiate the stranger in any way.

At both 6 months and 12 months, stranger anxiety was significantly more frequent among infants who were neither Positively Responsive nor showed Customs Inspection.

TABLE IV. REACTIONS TO STRANGERS: POSITIVE RESPONSIVENESS AND CUSTOMS INSPECTION VERSUS OVERT ANXIETY AT 1 YEAR

Primary classification	Specific reaction patterns		Total
	Positive responsiveness and Customs Inspection	Overt anxiety	
Positively responsive	78	12	90
Apprehensive	7	22	29[a]
Total	85	34	119

Chi-square $= 44 \cdot 43$ (d.f. $= 1$; $p < 0 \cdot 001$).

[a] Three of the 32 infants in the Apprehensive group showed no differentiated reactions.

Of 66 infants who reacted with Customs Inspection and no stranger anxiety at both 6 months and 1 year, 60 were in the Positively Responsive group and six in the Apprehensive group, a significantly smaller proportion (Table V).

Of 14 infants who showed stranger anxiety at both 6 months and 1 year, eight were in the Positively Responsive group and six in the Apprehensive group, a significantly higher proportion (Table VI). This reaffirms the greater susceptibility of Apprehensive infants to show stranger anxiety over a prolonged period of time and to fail to experience, through Customs Inspection, signal anxiety in an adequate degree.

At 6 months, 28 infants were reported to show fear of specific persons. Of these, 23 were in the Positively Responsive group and five in the Apprehensive group (Table VII). As seen above (Table III), in the Positively Responsive group as a whole at age 6 months 19 infants

TABLE V. CUSTOMS INSPECTION AND NO STRANGER ANXIETY IN POSITIVELY RESPONSIVE AND APPREHENSIVE GROUPS AT 6 MONTHS AND 1 YEAR

Primary classification	Specific reaction patterns		Total
	Customs Inspection and no stranger anxiety	Stranger anxiety	
Positively responsive	60	35	95
Apprehensive	6	21	27
Total	66	56	122

Chi-square $= 14 \cdot 3$ (d.f. $= 1$; $p < 0 \cdot 001$).

TABLE VI. STRANGER ANXIETY ONLY IN POSITIVELY RESPONSIVE
AND APPREHENSIVE GROUPS AT 6 MONTHS AND 1 YEAR

| Primary classification | Specific reaction patterns | | |
	Stranger anxiety only	Other	Total
Positively responsive	8	87	95
Apprehensive	6	21	27
Total	14	108	122

Chi-square $= 3 \cdot 84$ (d.f. $= 1$; $p < 0 \cdot 05$).

showed stranger anxiety and in the Apprehensive group as a whole
17 did so. Thus of 6-month-olds reported or observed to show fear of
strangers of any kind of degree (Table VII), a significantly higher
proportion of the Positively Responsive group showed Specific Avoidance than showed stranger anxiety. That is, of 42 infants in the Positively
Responsive group, in whom fear of strangers was evident at 6 months,
in 23 the fear was limited to specific persons. In contrast, of 22 infants
in the Apprehensive group in whom fear of the stranger at that age was
evident, in only five was the fear limited to specific persons.

TABLE VII. SPECIFIC AVOIDANCE AND STRANGER ANXIETY IN
POSITIVELY RESPONSIVE AND APPREHENSIVE GROUPS AT 6 MONTHS

| Primary classification | Specific reaction patterns | | |
	Specific avoidance	Stranger anxiety	Total
Positively responsive	23	19	42
Apprehensive	5	17	22
Total	28	36	64

Chi-square $= 7 \cdot 01$ (d.f. $= 1$; $p < 0 \cdot 01$).

At 1 year, 53 infants were reported to show Specific Avoidance. Of
these, 44 were in the Positively Responsive group and nine in the
Apprehensive group (Table VIII). As seen above (Table IV) 11 infants
in the Positively Responsive group showed overt stranger anxiety at
1 year, and in the Apprehensive group 22 did so. Thus, among 1-year-
olds reported or observed to show stranger anxiety of any kind or
degree, again in the Positively Responsive group a significantly higher
proportion of infants showed Specific Avoidance. That is, of 55 infants
in the Positively Responsive group in whom fear of the stranger was
evident, 44 showed Specific Avoidance. In contrast, of 31 infants in the

Apprehensive group in whom fear of the stranger was evident, nine were reported to show Specific Avoidance.

TABLE VIII. SPECIFIC AVOIDANCE AND STRANGER ANXIETY IN POSITIVELY RESPONSIVE AND APPREHENSIVE GROUPS AT 1 YEAR

| Primary classification | Specific reaction patterns | | Total |
	Specific avoidance	Stranger anxiety	
Positively responsive	44	11	55
Apprehensive	9	22	31
Total	53	33	86

Chi-square $= 21.7$ (d.f. $= 1$; $p < 0.001$).

To the extent that the maternal reports are accepted as reliable, the indications are that infants who are spontaneously or reactively outgoing show fear of discrete aspects of strangers more than apprehensive infants do so. This may imply that positively responsive infants perceive Gestalten earlier or better, or achieve a higher degree of visual discrimination, than do infants who are negatively responsive. For the latter, stranger anxiety may take a more general or more inchoate form.

STRANGER ANXIETY AS A DEVELOPMENTAL INDEX

Since our data regarding infants' reactions to strangers include observations made and reports cited only at age 6 months and 1 year, and refer only to current or to recently observed behaviour, no inferences can be made about the normative peaks of Customs Inspection or of Stranger Anxiety. It is noteworthy, however, that if we differentiate the benign inspecting behaviour from patently fearful behaviour, we see that at 6 months 82 infants (Table III) and at 1 year 85 infants (Table IV) showed no stranger anxiety. The distinction between the two kinds of reaction is important because Customs Inspection implies early ego functioning of a more mature nature and the emergence of a preparedness for signal anxiety.

It appears that at any period of infancy understanding of stranger anxiety requires consideration of a large number of variables in addition to infant-age, namely such complex factors as drive endowment, maternal behaviour, and maternal attitudes. To the latter material, information about a variety of data must be added: the infant's state when the stranger is sighted; whether in the presence of the mother or of another familiar person, or when alone; where the stranger is seen; the manner of the stranger's approach; the frequency with which the infant has been in the presence of strangers; the behaviour of the mother in the stranger's presence; the quality and quantity of external stimulations usually available to the infant; the length of time necessary for the infant to recover a positive mood if he has been disconcerted by the stranger; and the stability of his recovery.

REFERENCES

AMBROSE, J. A. 1963. The concept of a critical period for the development of social responsiveness in early human infancy. In B. M. Foss (Ed.), *Determinants of infant behaviour II*. Methuen, London; Wiley, New York.

BENJAMIN, J. D. 1961. Some developmental observations relating to the theory of anxiety. *J. Am. psychoanal. Ass.* **9**, 652–669.

BRODY, S. and AXELRAD, S. 1970. *Anxiety and ego formation in infancy*. International Universities Press, New York.

GOUGH, D. 1962. The visual behaviour of infants in the first few weeks of life. *Proc. R. Soc. Med.* **55**, 308–310.

GRAY, P. H. 1958. Theory and evidence in imprinting in human infants. *J. Psychol.* **46**, 155–161.

GREEN, P. C. and GORDON, M. 1964. Maternal deprivation: its influence on visual exploration in infant monkeys. *Science, N.Y.* **145**, 292–294.

HESS, E. H. 1959. Imprinting. *Science, N.Y.* **130**, 133–141.

HOLLINGSHEAD, A. B. and REDLICH, F. C. 1958. Social class and mental illness. Wiley, New York.

LEMMON, W. B. and PATTERSON, G. H. 1964. Depth perception in sheep: effect of interrupting the mother–neonate bond. *Science* **145**, 835–836.

SCOTT, J. P. 1963. The process of primary socialization in canine and human infants. *Monogr. Soc. Res. Child Dev.* **28**, No. 1, Serial no. 85.

Discussion

The Nature of Maternal Stimulation

RICHARDS: I would like to bring in a note of caution about the use of what I regard as very loaded labels of behaviour. Take the word "stimulation", which has so many connotations derived, for instance, from the work on early stimulation of animals and from studies of so-called deprived children who are said to "lack stimulation". I would like to ask what this alleged entity is, because it is our experience that if one watches mothers with their babies and measures the sort of obvious things which people seem to regard as stimulation, like talking, smiling, touching, and so on, one is lumping things together under one global heading that do not necessarily belong together. A mother may show a lot of talking but little touching, and vice versa. Rather than prejudging the various component parts one should try and find out what the function of each is and not settle the question before we begin. A point that brings this up is your distinction, Dr. Brody, between adequate and inadequate mothers. On the basis of about 6 hours of observations obtained during the first 10 days we tried to rate mothers on the scale that you published some time ago (S. Brody. 1956. *Patterns of Mothering*. International Universities Press, New York), but found ourselves unable to do so, because in some respects a mother's behaviour might fit into one category while in other respects it would fit into another category.

BRODY: The scale you refer to I should now regard as unsatisfactory, but it was set up so that one could get different measures for speech, touch, and so forth. These would not be lumped together.

RICHARDS: Nevertheless, you do use phrases like "smoothly adapting to minimal cues". Now we have mothers who during feeding might well be described like that but who, in other situations, are utterly different. When putting the baby to sleep, for instance, they do not seem to respond to what we would perhaps regard as cues of the baby wishing to be left alone and instead start playing with him. So you cannot have general scales referring to such dimensions as responsiveness or adequacy.

AXELRAD: Ainsworth, I believe, has found that the behaviour of the mother in the feeding situation is prototypical.

AINSWORTH: That was certainly our impression for the first 3 months of life. We undertook a classification of mother–infant interaction in the feeding situation, based on a cluster analysis of a multiplicity of features (M. D. S. Ainsworth and S. M. Bell. 1969. In A. Ambrose (Ed.), *Stimulation in Early Infancy*. Academic Press, London). By this means we were able to identify nine patterns which could be ordered roughly in terms of the extent to which the baby was permitted to be an active partner or the mother was the dominant one in their feeding transactions. We also rated the mother in terms of 22 maternal care variables including, for instance, her perception of the baby, the appropriateness of her social interaction with him, the amount of physical contact, and the effectiveness of her response to his crying. We found close correspondence between these ratings and the patterns of interaction in feeding. For example, the mothers who permitted their babies to be active in determining timing, pacing, and termination of feeding were the same as those who gave much physical contact and who were effective in terminating crying. In addition, there were substantial positive correlations among the maternal-care variables themselves. Thus, on the assumption that mothers might well differ in their modes of interaction, we rated separately the amounts of physical, visual, and auditory-vocal contact, but found these ratings to be very highly intercorrelated. This congruence of measures holds not only for the first quarter-year of life but for the whole of the first year. It appears that configurations of mother–infant interaction that become established early in the first year have a pervasive influence which continues to colour many facets of interaction. Therefore, although I agree with Richards about the value of detailed behavioural studies, I am not disturbed as he is about the lack of specificity of the measures used by Brody and Axelrad.

G. BRONSON: There seem to be two sorts of difficulties about the word 'stimulation'. One is that it refers to a multidimensional concept, in that one must take into account not only a total quantity of excitatory input but also such features as the timing, pattern, and quality of stimulation. And the second difficulty is that in the past studies of early stimulation have been based on the assumption of the infant as a *tabula rasa*, and have therefore viewed the mother–infant relationship as a unidirectional process. This we can no longer do: it might very well be, for example, that certain babies produce inadequate mothers for themselves.

AXELRAD: We chose quite deliberately to study what the mother brought to the situation, for I don't think we know yet how to isolate and measure what the baby brings with him. The behavioural measures which we obtained at age 3 or 4 days, derived from the neonatal scales of Graham *et al.* (1956. *Psychol. Monogr.*, **70** (22), No. 428), just did not differentiate among infants at the age of 1 year, whereas the mothering variables did.

SCOTT: It is possible that a genetic hypothesis might account for this. In other words, one would expect that there would be genetic differences in your behavioural phenomena and that they might well be correlated between mother and offspring.

AXELRAD: The interesting thing is that at 6 weeks of age we have few significant correlations, whereas at 6 months and at 1 year we have many. The simplest hypothesis to account for this is to relate it to the growing influence of the mother; otherwise you have to have a rather complicated series of hypotheses about genetic factors which fail to show up at 6 weeks but do show up from 6 months on.

SCOTT: In our work with breed differences in dogs we found many cases where genetic influences appeared only after a considerable period.

For example, clear-cut breed differences in reaction to inhibitory training appeared only after several weeks. Again, in humans the parent–offspring correlations in IQ become progressively greater as the child grows older. The point is that a genetic hypothesis as well as the maternal influence hypothesis can account for such data.

Application of the Imprinting Model to Human Behaviour

ROSENBLUM: If, in our ignorance, we regard it as useful to think of the first phase of the infant's relationship with the mother as representing something which parallels what has been described as imprinting in lower animals, I am surprised that so little attention has been paid to what the mother actually does at that phase. If you are to imply that visual fixation plays a crucial part in the formation of the relationship, then one ought to have a lot of critical empirical data on such specific aspects of the mother's behaviour as where her face is when she approaches the infant, the rapidity of these approaches, and so on. There is reason to believe that the same visual stimulus which would elicit positive orientation and interest and thereby perhaps facilitate an imprinting effect during a gradual approach might produce disturbance or actual avoidance in response to more rapid approaches. Similarly, the distance and angle at which the mother's face is held during contacts with respect to the infant's most effective focusing distance need to be taken into account as possible influences on any imprinting-like process.

RICHARDS: I doubt whether the concept of imprinting is at all helpful in attempts to understand human social development. Imprinting was originally defined by Lorenz as a type of learning quite different from other kinds of learning, yet one by one his criteria have now been disposed of and imprinting has been shown not to be in any sense unique. It is special only because it is the first learning, not because the process itself is different in any way from other learning: indeed it is now regarded as a type of perceptual learning. Now if we simply mean that the first perceptual learning is different from later perceptual learning, then the notion of imprinting may well be applicable to human infants. At the same time, if that is all we mean, the word should be dropped, because to many people it has other connotations which cannot be carried across species. Moreover, imprinting is nowadays often defined in operational terms—that is, one puts a bird in a certain situation and then certain things happen. That definition cannot be used for human infants because operationally we use quite different situations and quite different things happen. In terms of perceptual and motor characteristics babies are not like chicks, and to regard visual following in the one as equivalent to locomotor following in the other is quite unjustified. So it would really be rather surprising to find similarities between the two species except at a very general level of perceptual learning.

Foss: I wonder if you are right in saying that there is nothing special about imprinting. For instance, massed practice is better than spaced practice for strengthening imprinting, which is rather unusual; also, the reinforcement in imprinting is pretty difficult to spot. But the most important thing is that this concept has drawn attention to a class of phenomena and to various analogies which one would otherwise have overlooked.

Scott: It is the fact that the reinforcement in imprinting is internal while in other forms of learning it is external that made this phenomenon so puzzling at first. If a young animal is separated from familiar individuals and places it becomes emotionally distressed, as indicated by vocalization, and this is relieved when the young animal returns or is returned to the familiar individuals and places. In terms of reinforcement, he is punished for separation and rewarded for reunion. There are no external rewards or punishments. The animal must, of course, be able to distinguish unfamiliar objects and individuals in order that the emotional reinforcing mechanisms may come into play. The results seem to be different from ordinary conditioning because environmental factors do not appear to have any effect on the organism. If the young animal is able to move towards or away from familiar things, the result is a particular kind of operant conditioning. Apart from the special nature of the reinforcing mechanism, associative learning processes should operate in the same way in this case as in any other.

Richards: I will not deny that the work on human development has benefited from the work on imprinting. But let us look at it in a biological context: when the chick hatches it must be able to follow the mother immediately, otherwise it will not survive. So there is very strong selection pressure to produce some mechanism which will lead the chick to form a bond with the mother. With human infants there is no such immediate urgency, so the mechanisms that are built-in and functioning from the beginning will be subject to very different selection pressures and are therefore unlikely to resemble those in a chick.

Scott: Even when we can demonstrate the existence of early built-in mechanisms we have to ask whether they are relevant to later development. One of the obvious features of an animal like a dog is that its behaviour in the neonatal period is adaptive to neonatal life alone. Its sucking and distress vocalization are useful only in the presence of a nursing mother. Then in the transition period the puppy undergoes a metamorphosis towards adult behaviour, at the conclusion of which it has developed behaviour adapted to adult social life. Natural selection processes must therefore operate in two directions, one adapting the animal for very early life, the other for adult life. One of the consequences of this is that the behaviour found in the early stages will not necessarily lead into the behaviour of the latter part of life, but may be purely transitory and bear no relationship to future response patterns.

BOWLBY: It seems to me that the value of Lorenz's work is that he has drawn attention to a particular kind of development in a rather impressive and dramatic manner and given us a useful shorthand label to refer to it. Once you start examining imprinting you find that most of the characteristics listed by Lorenz are untrue or only partially true, but even so we are still left with a "syndrome" of several important features none of which is unique on its own but which together form a rather unusual pattern that merits a special name. As long as we understand that imprinting refers to a "syndrome" of developmental processes rather than to a single process, the label seems to me to serve a useful purpose.

The Nature and Development of Fear

GENERAL DISCUSSION

Problems in Defining Fear

BOWLBY: We have already discussed fear on a number of occasions, and indeed it is one of the most frequently investigated aspects of early social behaviour. I am interested in how to define fear and how to distinguish it from such related concepts as anxiety or distress. In common usage the word fear generally implies some movement away from the object, but that does not hold for anxiety or distress. For fear, in other words, the basic criterion tends to be avoidance or escape, and we classify all those actions as fearful that are highly correlated with avoidance behaviour.

AMBROSE: There is a lot to be said for confining the meaning of fear operationally in this way. The only difficulty arises when we look at it from a functional point of view, in that the behaviour is supposed to have the function of changing the relationship between the subject and the feared object by withdrawal. There are so-called fear responses that do not involve withdrawal, such as appeasement postures which are designed to change the behaviour of the object. Again, what about approach behaviour such as that found in Hinde's (1954. *Proc. R. Soc.* **B.142,** 306) description of the mobbing response of the chaffinch to the owl? We find here a very close link between fear and attack which needs to be taken into account.

SCHAFFER: From a functional point of view the aim common to such activities is stimulus termination. When one approaches it in this way, one can bring together withdrawal and attack under the same heading as well as, for that matter, such other activities as freezing.

LAWICK-GOODALL: In non-human species fear may sometimes take a form that, on its own, cannot easily be interpreted without ambiguity. Hugging in chimpanzees is an example: it may be referred to as a fear response, but only because it occurs in a fearful context and because it is associated with subsequent running away. Yet the same response also occurs when these animals come across a large pile of food; then we would interpret it quite differently. Similarly what is referred to as a fear face is indistinguishable from a copulation grin. The response on its own, therefore, does not necessarily enable one to distinguish fear from other emotional states such as general excitement.

RHEINGOLD: This example shows rather nicely that we cannot define fear merely by reference to moving away or looking away or freezing. We must know more about the total situation. An organism may move away for reasons other than fear alone—it may be satiated after prolonged exposure to the situation and be motivated by boredom. Terms like avoidance and escape, however, indicate that we are reading something into the act of moving away, and this we cannot do on the basis of the behaviour pattern alone. We are forced to take into account the context in which it occurs, that is, the total interaction between the organism and the stimulus field. This makes our task much more complex but it saves us from arbitrarily interpreting a response in terms of what we think the organism must be experiencing.

AINSWORTH: One example of this difficulty takes us back to the strange situation, where moving away from the mother may have a quite different connotation from moving away from a stranger.

RHEINGOLD: I see the value of using moving away as a response index, for it can be seen, measured, and recorded. But to regard it as an example of avoidance or fear introduces a quite different set of complications.

BOWLBY: This is borne out by a study in which Hamburg's group (D. Hamburg et al., 1958. Archs Neurol. Psychiat. 79, 415) investigated the reliability of observations on the emotions of patients during sessions lasting 3 hours on four successive days. The point Hamburg emphasizes is the need for observers to be able to see, first, the context and, secondly, the sequence in which any particular behaviour and emotional expression occur. With that knowledge, reliability of observation is high. Without it, observers tend to misinterpret what is going on and so to disagree.

LEWIS: I suggest that, apart from looking at context and sequence, our research strategy should also examine multiple responses at any given time. Observation of clusters of responses may increase the probability of identifying internal states with similar behavioural patterns. I have data, for example, which indicate that two kinds of female infants tend to touch their mothers a great deal, namely girls who themselves are touched a lot by their mothers and rejected girls. The internal state motivating the infants' behaviour may be quite different: in one case the pleasure of contact, in the other the fear of the mother leaving. Observations of single behaviour patterns—facial expression, for example, or the touching response itself—cannot identify which underlying state is affecting the behavioural sequence. On the other hand, multiple responses might well do so.

SCOTT: Yes, it is artificial to use a single index as the behavioural criterion of the internal state. One ought to think in terms of patterns of behaviour; that is, the total attempt of the organism at adaptation.

LEWIS: A further difficulty needs to be taken into account, namely that presented by the problem of individual differences. If a distinction is made between the internal state and the overt response, then one must allow for the fact that children develop idiosyncratic ways of reacting to one and the same state. Two infants may both be feeling equally fearful, but one reacts more vigorously than the other and therefore runs away more quickly. This is because one is a basically vigorous infant while the other is more placid. This difference in a dimension not directly related to the fear experience can produce quite different overt behaviour. Unfortunately inferences have to be made about the internal state on the basis of the overt behaviour, so that idiosyncratic responses must also be explored and taken into account.

KAGAN: One way round this is to test each child before the experiment on a known set of events that everyone agrees will elicit fear and obtain each individual's standard motor responses. Then it is possible to allow for individual differences in the experiment.

RICHARDS: We seem to be assuming that there *is* something called fear and that all we need do is to search for a suitable definition. I think that is the wrong way round, that one has to begin with a description of behaviour in its social context. This descriptive phase of the work need not, and probably should not, depend on common language categories of behaviour. Description requires a theoretical framework. For some situations the concept of fear may form a useful part of our descriptive and theoretical scheme, but then the concept will exist only within this framework. Only when it is anchored in this way can we begin to make decisions about such details as how to determine whether an organism is fearful or not.

Levels of Emotional Responsiveness

G. BRONSON: From an evolutionary point of view it is obviously important that every organism should be equipped with means for avoiding hazard. In very simple organisms it may be merely a reflexive pulling back, or brief immobility. For survival in diversified environments, however, we must postulate a prolonged state, rather than a stimulus-bound response, to facilitate complex behaviour sequences; at this point one can introduce the concept of fear. To survive in a still more complex environment it would be useful to be able to anticipate impending hazard; such foresight we call worry or, if the feeling is rather more vague, anxiety. All of these techniques for avoiding hazard presumably emerged at different points in the evolutionary scale, but all are still operative in the human being. Sometimes we respond at a very primitive level, sometimes at a more sophisticated level, and often, I suggest, one finds a mixture of techniques of different degrees of sophistication in a single situation.

This perspective may give us a way of distinguishing between the terms 'distress', 'fear' and 'anxiety'. Distress would be the most primitive emotional state in that it can be elicited without previous learning by unpatterned stimuli such as pain or loud noise. Fear represents the next level in that it requires previous experience and involves the processing of complex patterns; and finally anxiety, which is the most complex and most characteristically human, implies a sense of foreboding and is not limited to a concern with the immediate perceptual environment. The three states may well tie in with different levels of the nervous system and emerge at different ages in the course of development.

KAGAN: Our task is then to fill in the following matrix:

	Event	State	Behaviour
Distress			
Fear			
Anxiety			

In other words, each of the three levels of emotion must be specified in terms of antecedent events, the nature of the emotional state, and the resulting behaviours.

W. BRONSON: One further term ought to be added to this matrix, namely the "field" in which the action is taking place. If the context of the event allows for alternative ways of coping with it, both the affect and the behaviour that are evoked will surely be modified, even under conditions of identical state and event.

BOWLBY: We are short of words to describe all the states we want to describe. The usage proposed by Gordon Bronson is good but it cuts across another usage. For example, fear can be used to refer to not liking, wanting to get *away* from something that you do not like the look of; and anxiety can be used to refer to wanting to get *to* something and being unable to do so, as in the case of separation anxiety. It was in this latter sense that Freud used the term anxiety, though he built a very complex theory to account for it because he could not believe that difficulty in getting to something could possibly produce anxiety.

ROSENBLUM: As empiricists we have to start with some kind of classification that lends itself to investigation, and I suggest for this purpose an arbitrary two-way classification involving, on the one hand, stimuli that induce either approach or avoidance and, on the other hand, availability or non-availability of stimuli. We can then set out to measure the responses to each set of circumstances and choose our labels accordingly. Thus, for example, crying and rapid movement after the removal of a stimulus would be classified differently from the same behaviours observed in conjunction with the presentation of a stimulus. The former might be considered anxiety; the latter, fear. Similarly, cessation of crying and more casual movement following removal of a stimulus would be interpreted and labelled differently from the same set of behaviours when observed after the appearance of a stimulus. This sort of scheme might enable us to categorize and label sets of behaviour more operationally in terms of antecedent and current conditions and thereby reduce the ambiguity of our terms.

Conditions Evocative of Fear

KAGAN: I suggest that fear results from a sequence in which an individual encounters an event which alerts him and which he cannot avoid, and for which he has no response. Alerting is a special state which is neither fear nor distress, but it can lead into fear if the individual has no coping response available. If he can make such a response, fear will not be experienced.

RHEINGOLD: But if he cries, is that not a response?

KAGAN: I regard crying as a reaction to the fear-state. It is in this light. moreover, that we can view the relation between discrepancy and fear, If an individual has previous experience of an event he can make an appropriate response and will not experience fear. If, however, he has no relevant schemata, the discrepancy between input and past experience can result in fear.

FOSS: How does one differentiate between an event that is discrepant and one that is completely novel?

KAGAN: It is a Gestalt problem for which at the moment we have no metric. In general terms, if there is some relation between the event and a relevant cognitive representation we regard it as discrepant; if there is no such relation, it is a novel event.

FOSS: Can there ever be a novel event? Cannot everything be categorized?

KAGAN: As we mature the number of novel events decreases, but for the very young many events are novel.

RHEINGOLD: Would you be willing to make a quantitative statement about the relationship between the degree of discrepancy and the strength or latency or frequency of the organism's response?

KAGAN: The relation is curvilinear: up to a point, the greater the discrepancy the greater the response; beyond that point the response decreases again. I would predict, for instance, that a stranger who looks like the mother will be approached; that a stranger of different colour, dress, and appearance would elicit maximum fear; but that an object that is not human at all would elicit only minimal fear.

AINSWORTH: The crucial difference is probably not so much in terms of appearance as in behaviour. In home visits, for instance, if you act as a spectator rather than a participant observer, you are behaving abnormally from the infant's point of view, and so you do not become "part of the furniture" and are much more likely to get a fear response. If, on the other hand, you occasionally respond to the infant he can go ahead and ignore you after a while.

RHEINGOLD: Some of our findings may be relevant here. We have data on a situation in which the mother and infant are in a room, the infant showing no fear. The door is then opened to another room, and in it is either a toy or a person who has already spent some time with the child, playing with him and administering a developmental test. If the room contains only a toy, all infants go immediately into the room and promptly make contact with the toy. If the room contains the person, however, the majority will not enter it and none will make contact with her. The infant may have looked at her when he was still with his mother, smiled, and even played peek-a-boo, but as he comes to the doorway he looks down and may turn around and retreat, or if he does enter the new room will do so with his head down. Now, explain that to me in terms of discrepancy. One can talk about ambivalence, or separation anxiety, or fear of strangers, but I consider none of these as offering a satisfactory explanation and find the whole phenomenon perplexing.

ROSENBLUM: What is the person doing?

RHEINGOLD: She is smiling, but is otherwise not responsive. There are, of course, other variables to manipulate, and we intend, for example, to investigate what happens when the person is responsive on his own schedule, cajoling and calling, or when he is responsive only to the child's own behaviour.

KAGAN: I agree that it is perplexing. One might suggest that it is discrepant for a child to enter a strange room and see a person who is unresponsive, who does not talk but merely sits looking at him. In the film with which Mary Ainsworth illustrated her investigation we saw how wary the children were of the stranger as long as she remained unresponsive. But as soon as she began to talk to the mother, the children relaxed.

SCHAFFER: I doubt if unresponsiveness as such is necessarily the source of the fear. In our investigation of fear of strangers we used a procedure in which the adult made contact with the infant in a series of steps extending from simply appearing in front of the child through smiling, talking, and touching to picking the child up. To the adult mind it might appear that the first of these steps, involving an unresponsive, unsmiling adult staring at the child, would be the most fear-provoking; yet we found that it rarely gave rise to any avoidance responses and that it was generally one of the subsequent steps, especially one that involved physical contact, which elicited fear. In other words, if one is to explain this in terms of discrepancy or incongruity, the basis of the discrepancy lies not so much in any static attributes of the stranger but in the fact that certain forms of stimulation that are generally offered by the mother now emanate from an unfamiliar person. It is the stranger's behaviour, not the lack of it, that gives rise to fear.

RHEINGOLD: Moreover, the toy in our experiment was not responsive either, yet all infants made contact with it.

ROSENBLUM: That would give you another interesting variable to investigate, namely to have the person face the other way.

RHEINGOLD: We plan to do that too.

FOSS: The notion of discrepancy underlying fear comes from Hebb's observations of chimpanzees' responses to such objects as another animal's head without body or an anaesthetized chimp. I wonder if Jane Lawick-Goodall has made any such observations of chimps in the wild?

LAWICK-GOODALL: During a polio epidemic we had a crippled chimp, with no use in either leg, that was attacked several times very vigorously by the other mature males. On that occasion it was not too clear that the attacks were prompted by fear. On another occasion an adolescent male came back who had lost the use of one arm and was therefore unable to walk quadripedally. As his legs were not strong enough for bipedal walking he went along in a shuffling movement, and as he came up the path for the first time a group of six chimps caught sight of him and immediately ran to each other and put their arms round each other with big fear faces. The chimp did not realize they were scared of him, looked behind him, also made a fear face, and tried to join the others for physical contact, whereupon they all ran away.

Foss: Is it true that a lot of animals actually kill abnormal members of their own species?

Lawick-Goodall: Yes, I believe they do.

Foss: Then what makes you say it is fear?

Lawick-Goodall: In this group fear was shown by the whole sequence of behaviour of the animals rushing towards each other, embracing with a fear face, and then running away.

Basic Processes

Attachment and Separation in Dog and Man: Theoretical Propositions[1]

J. P. SCOTT

Bowling Green University

IN THIS PAPER I shall try to develop a theoretical explanation for the formation of primary social relationships and social attachments. For brevity's sake I shall not attempt an extensive review of the literature, but simply state that the basis for this theory is the evidence derived from a large number of experiments and observations demonstrating the development of social emotions which appear very early in both the dog and in human beings. Other developmental mechanisms and processes also enter into the process of attachment, but these two emotions—distress at the absence of the familiar and fear of the strange —are the most important.

EMOTIONAL DEVELOPMENT IN THE DOG

Major periods of development. The early behavioural development of the dog can be described in terms of three periods, each based on a major developmental process. The *neonatal period*, beginning at birth and extending through the first 2 weeks of life, is marked by the establishment of the process of neonatal nutrition, or nursing. All behaviour in this period is adapted to the conditions of early infancy, when survival depends upon almost complete maternal care. At approximately 2 weeks there begins a second major process, that of transition to behaviour adapted for the more independent conditions of adult social life. The resulting *transition period* principally includes changeovers to the adult forms of nutrition and locomotion, but also involves the development of the capacities for the next major process, that of forming

[1] Research reported in this paper was in part supported by Grant HD-3778 from the National Institute of Child Health and Human Development.

emotional attachments both to places and to social objects. This process goes on most rapidly between approximately 3 and 12 weeks of age, with a peak between 6 and 8 weeks. The period corresponding to this process may therefore be called the period of *primary socialization.*

Emotional reactions at birth. During the neonatal period the puppy reacts with distress vocalization to any form of physical discomfort, particularly hunger, pain, and cold. There is no external evidence of pleasurable emotions, although the act of nursing is obviously a rewarding one. Nor is there any indication of fear.

Development of distress vocalization in reaction to the absence of the familiar. During the transition period the puppy begins to show distress vocalization to a new stimulus, the absence of the familiar. The vocalization rates of a puppy placed in a strange room by itself are three or four times as great as the rate when the puppy is left alone in a familiar room (Scott and Bronson, 1964). There is at first no evidence of fear of strange objects or individuals introduced into a familiar place.

The reaction to the absence of the familiar is fully developed by 3 weeks of age, when average vocalization rates of 140 per minute are recorded. The response continues on this high level up to 8 weeks of age and then gradually declines. Older puppies and even adult dogs still show distress after separation from the familiar, but in other forms in addition to vocalization.

Positive approaches to strangers. Also in the transition period, tail wagging appears, accompanied by approach and investigation of any potentially social object (Scott and Fuller, 1965). Any new inanimate object is also approached and investigated, but ordinarily tail wagging does not take place. Tail wagging, of the rapid horizontal sort, has the function of signalling a friendly and non-aggressive approach and persists throughout the lifetime of the dog. In the early socialization period it has the function, along with approach and investigation, of making contact with other individuals and stimulating interaction with them, thus making possible the establishment of social relations.

Fear of the strange. At approximately 7 weeks there begins the development of a strong and persistent fear reaction to strange individuals introduced into a familiar environment. Up to this time the puppy will give a momentary fear or startle reaction to loud sounds or sudden movements, but such reactions tend to die out quickly and habituate readily, being followed by a positive approach. After 7 weeks, fear reactions to strangers last for longer periods and have the effect of preventing the puppy from forming an attachment to individuals with whom there is only casual contact. The development of this reaction is most clearly illustrated in puppies which have been reared in large areas apart from human beings (Freedman *et al.*, 1961).

Genetic variation. All these emotional reactions show variation between breeds and between individuals within breeds (Scott and Fuller, 1965). Nevertheless, a similar emotional development takes place in all puppies.

EMOTIONAL DEVELOPMENT IN HUMAN INFANTS

Periods and processes in human development. Human newborns are somewhat better developed sensorily and somewhat less advanced in motor capacities than puppies, but both are born in a very immature state in which a high degree of maternal care is necessary for survival, and the same basic general development processes take place in both. The human neonatal period, during which neonatal nutrition is established, lasts until approximately 6 weeks. Beginning at this point developmental processes occur in a different order from that in the dog, since the process of primary socialization, or emotional attachment, takes place before the transition in the methods of nutrition and locomotion. The beginning of the period of socialization is marked by the appearance of the social smile, and the period ends at approximately 8 months with the appearance of a fear reaction to strangers which coincides approximately with the first changes in locomotor ability (Scott, 1963). A marked change in reactions to separation occurs at about the same age (Schaffer, 1958).

Emotional development. The appearance of crying in reaction to a strange place occurs at approximately 2 months, according to the original work of Bayley (1932). During the period of socialization, contact with other individuals is established through vision and social smiling. A considerable change in the amount of time spent on visual fixation occurs at about 2 months, coinciding with an increase in smiling to the human face. As Ambrose (1960) has shown, the amount of smiling is somewhat greater to a familiar face, such as that of the mother, than to a stranger. Finally, the development of the fear reaction to strangers has been well authenticated by various writers (e.g. Schaffer, 1966; Bronson, 1968; Morgan and Ricciuti, 1969).

In general, emotional development in the dog and human being are similar, the chief difference being that the signal for positive contact appears in the face in human infants and at the opposite end in canine infants. The appearance of distress vocalization in response to the absence of the familiar, and the fear reaction to the strange, follow a similar order in canine and human infants, and serve to delimit the period during which primary social attachments are most readily formed. A similar emotional development is seen over a much shorter period in chickens and ducklings, which show distress vocalization and later fear reactions during the time of formation of the first social attachment. The process of social attachment in birds is usually called imprinting. Since these various social species are widely different in origin, one can conclude that among vertebrates there are only a few basic emotional reactions, and that their functions tend to evolve in similar ways. Rather than create new reactions in each species, evolution has made economic use of a relatively few basic capacities found generally in the nervous systems of vertebrates.

A THEORY OF EMOTIONAL ATTACHMENTS

On the basis of the above evidence we can develop a theory concerning the mechanism by which social attachments are produced in infant human beings. Although the theory was first suggested by an examination of canine development (Scott, 1967), it is based on phenomena which also occur in human development and hence is independent of the evidence derived from other organisms.

Basic mechanism. The basic mechanism is emotional distress stimulated by the absence of the familiar. This is an almost reflex reaction which appears as soon as the infant is able to discriminate between the familiar and the unfamiliar, and is manifested in the human infant by crying. Distress is relieved by the reappearance of familiar objects or individuals. Thus this relatively simple emotional reaction acts as an internal reinforcing agent, punishing the infant when familiar individuals are absent and rewarding him by its disappearance as contact is re-established. Ordinarily such separations occur only for short periods during early development, with the result that reinforcement occurs over and over again. This mechanism in itself is sufficient to account for the facts of emotional attachment.

Following the principles of learning, motivation for attachment should be strengthened by repeated reinforcement produced by prolonged contact and many short separations. There may in addition be a positive emotional reaction of pleasure resulting from social contact, but this has not been established as yet. Reinforcements of the external sort, such as food, warmth, contact, etc., modify behaviour and emotional reactions within the social relationship once it is established, but ordinarily they do not serve to produce the constant contact which first establishes the relationship. Furthermore, food has been shown to be unnecessary for attachment to take place, in such widely different nonhuman animals as chickens (Hess, 1959), dogs (Brodbeck, 1954), and monkeys (Harlow, 1958). The object needs only to be present and noticed for attachment to take place.

Other mechanisms that are involved in the formation of emotional attachments function as follows. The smiling response, combined with visual investigation, is the mechanism by which social contact is initiated. The response of fear of strangers delays or even prevents social contacts, with the result that at a later age an infant does not readily form attachments to strangers, i.e. individuals other than those to whom attachments have already been formed. All three emotional responses—distress vocalization at the absence of the familiar, differential rates of smiling, and presence or absence of fear responses—can be used as indicators of the presence and degree of emotional attachment to particular individuals. Furthermore, it can be predicted from our knowledge of widespread genetic variation in human populations that there will be marked individual variation in the amount of emotional responses in any standard situation. We should also expect the expression of these emotional responses to be modified by previous experience.

INTERACTION OF PROCESSES

A distinction may be made between processes and mechanisms, the latter including more or less fixed behavioural and emotional reactions. Apart from the process of attachment itself, the principal processes which affect it are those of familiarization and habituation.

The process of familiarization. The emotional reaction of separation depends upon familiarization and the ability of the infant to discriminate between familiar and unfamiliar objects. Familiarization in turn depends upon the behavioural reaction (or mechanism) of investigatory behaviour stimulated by novelty. Investigatory behaviour is a preferable term to exploratory behaviour, since the latter implies gross bodily movement, whereas in the human infant investigation may be largely confined to eye movements and reception of auditory stimuli. Familiarization results from the repetition of stimuli and their subsequent recognition, and to this extent is a perceptual process. At the present time we do not know the number of repetitions required to produce familiarization in infant animals, but we have some evidence concerning the time that is required. Cairns and Werboff (1967) found that young puppies began to react to separation as early as 2 hours after the introduction of the new stimulus, and that the maximum effect could take place in 24 hours. It is obvious that in the long continued contacts between mother and infant, stimuli are repeated hundreds of times and that the process of familiarization must therefore be carried on to an extreme degree.

Habituation. This may be defined as the tendency of an organism to respond less strongly when primary stimuli (those which elicit reactions in the absence of previous experience, including most reflex reactions) are repeated in the absence of reinforcement. An example is the repetition of sounds that elicit startle responses in an infant: the reactions die out after a few stimuli. Habituation is thus related to the well-known process of extinction, which also involves a tendency for responses to die out in the absence of reinforcement, although this latter process refers specifically to responses to secondary stimuli that have been previously reinforced. The mechanism by which habituation takes place is unknown but presumably consists of some neural phenomenon. It is well known that whereas habituation of responses to external stimuli take place readily and rapidly, habituation to internal stimulation of the emotional sort takes place very slowly, probably because emotional reactions themselves have reinforcing properties.

Habituation plays a part in familiarization, in that reactions to once novel stimuli die out quite rapidly. With respect to the emotional reaction to separation, however, the evidence is that habituation takes place very slowly. When an infant is separated, the distress vocalization reaction tends to build up in proportion to the duration of such separation, with pauses in vocalization only as the infant becomes exhausted. Habituation to the emotional reaction probably takes place only as separation experiences are repeated, which is usually possible only when short periods of separation occur. If such separation experiences occur in strange places or in the company of strange individuals, the effect will be confounded by the process of familiarization. In general, the effect of habituation should be to make possible longer periods of separation before the distress reaction occurs.

Attachment. The process of attachment is a general one, as indicated above. It includes the process of familiarization and depends upon the resulting emotional reaction of distress stimulated by the unfamiliar. The principal mechanism of attachment, however, is the latter response, which (as pointed out earlier) acts as an internal reinforcing agent, punishing either the infant when he separates himself or when he is separated from the familiar, and rewarding him when familiar stimuli are restored. The strength of the bond so created should depend on the well-known laws of reinforcement, principally that the strength of attachment should depend on the number of reinforcements and the magnitude of individual reinforcements (Cairns, 1966).

With respect to other processes involved, the distress reaction to separation should interfere with familiarization by interfering with investigatory behaviour. Thus a separated infant who is crying does not investigate new environments or individuals, but struggles to return to the familiar. Furthermore, the unpleasant distress reactions tend to become associated with the unfamiliar situation, with the result that the infant should experience the new situation as unpleasant, even after it becomes familiar.

Interaction of behavioural and emotional responses. There are three such basic reactions: the investigatory response to the novel or strange, the emotional distress reaction to separation from the familiar, and the emotional fear reaction to the strange. In the development of both human and canine infants, and apparently also in that of many birds, the fear response to the strange occurs later than separation distress and serves to limit the critical period in which the process of attachment can proceed rapidly Fear reactions inhibit familiarization by interfering with investigatory behaviour, but more definitely by preventing repetition of stimuli, since fear usually leads the individual to avoid future contact. Fear does not, however, interfere with the distress reaction to separation but actually adds to it, with the result that the relief of fear and relief of separation distress may be combined and thus have additive reinforcing properties. As indicated above, habituation to fear does not occur readily, in part because the escape response itself tends to prevent repetition of the stimulus. We may therefore conclude that the fear response to the strange plays an important, but later, part in the process of attachment. We can also state that any form of noxious stimulation, such as pain, will ordinarily not interfere with the process of primary attachment and the strengthening of an emotional bond, as has been experimentally demonstrated by the work of Fisher (1955) in dogs and

Hess (1964) in chickens, but that it will interfere with the formation of new attachments in later life. This provisional hypothesis should be reassuring to human parents, for punishment should not make a child stop loving his parents.

THEORETICAL PREDICTIONS

Normal development. During the socialization period, beginning at about 2 months or somewhat earlier, the human infant should become intensely familiar with its regular caretakers and the physical environment surrounding him, provided it is not changed. He should also become familiar to some degree with other individuals with whom he comes into repeated contact and also with a wider physical environment, depending on how much he is carried about. The extent to which familiarization occurs (and it can occur very rapidly at that age) will determine the circumstances under which the separation reaction takes place. During this time the infant will also experience repeated short separations, inducing a separation reaction which is relieved after a short time. (The usual interpretation of the mother is that the child is crying for attention.) This should have the effect of strengthening emotional attachments in proportion to the number of such experiences and the degree of emotional arousal experienced at each. It should also have the effect of partial habituation to such experiences, with the result that the infant can gradually tolerate longer periods of separation.

During the transition period, normally beginning at about 7 months, the infant becomes able to separate himself from the familiar and return to it, and at the same time able to investigate and become familiar with a larger environment and a wider circle of persons, all because of the development of his own locomotor abilities. He can thus control his own separation reaction. The result should be to reinforce attachment and to produce a greater degree of habituation to the distress reaction, thus permitting longer and longer periods of separation.

At the same time, the developing fear response to strangers, and probably also of strange objects, sets definite limits to the amount of wandering which the child will do, and definitely inhibits the formation of attachments which might result from casual contacts with strangers.

The environment and the number of individuals with whom an infant comes into contact during this time can be greatly restricted or considerably enlarged, thus circumstances will determine the number of individuals to whom some degree of emotional attachment can be formed.

Once an infant attains the power of locomotion, he attains some degree of choice concerning those individuals with whom contact is maintained. It can be predicted that an infant will tend to choose, under the influence of separation distress, those individuals with whom the greatest degree of attachment has already been formed. Thus, given a choice, a child would be expected to choose its mother rather than siblings, and, in an orphanage situation where multiple caretakers are available, to choose the one with whom the greatest degree of attachment had already been formed. This in turn would tend to intensify such attachments.

Variations in normal development. The chief variations which occur in early life are protection from separation experience by constant attention of the mother, and, at the opposite extreme, a change of caretakers, which, of course, involves prolonged separation from the original objects of attachment. With respect to protection from separation, which may occur with a mother who has an intense reaction to a baby and literally is never separated from it day or night, the result should be an intense emotional reaction on the part of the infant when separation eventually does occur, because of a lack of habituation. The result might well be an unusually strong fear of separation and hence greater dependency.

In most, if not all, of the nonhuman primates such an experience of no separation in the early months of life is normal, as the infant is constantly carried by the mother. The theory would predict an intense degree of familialization and a postponement of attachment reinforced by separation to a later date. Because of the difficulty involved in separating nonhuman primate infants from their mothers, there have been no attempts to measure the degree of attachment of the infant to its mother, and it could well be that most of the attachment in this early age is provided by the mother rather than the infant. (Incidentally, the development of the mother's attachment to the infant is a reciprocal part of the relationship, but has been relatively little studied and is as yet not well understood.)

Once an attachment has been formed, prolonged separation should result in an increased emotional reaction to separation, especially if it is continued over days or weeks. During this time it may have secondary effects such as interfering with normal eating or leading to depressed activity. The very strength of the reaction should result in a corresponding increase in the strength of the bond once separation has ended. There is some indication that this kind of experience may result in increased dependency. It is also possible, especially with older children, that a child may attempt to avoid re-establishment of the bond in order to avoid the anticipated effects of possible future separation. Since the emotional reaction to separation tends to interfere with familiarization, the formation of new attachments during the separation period becomes more difficult. The unpleasant emotion of separation should be associated with the new individuals. This is, of course, of practical importance in adoption. These predictions are in accord with the results obtained by Bowlby (1951) and his associates on the effects of prolonged separation due to hospitalization and other circumstances.

A third variation resulting from death, illegitimacy, etc. is a permanent change of caretakers. It is predicted that if such an event occurs during the neonatal period, the development of emotional attachments will proceed in a normal way. However, once the period of socialization has begun, at approximately 2 months, the child will suffer a separation reaction at the time of adoption. The degree of this reaction should be proportional to the amount of attachment, which in turn has increased in proportion to time. However, during the socialization period, which includes roughly the first 6 months, the formation of new relationships should not be inhibited by the fear response to strangers. Once the transition period is entered, the fear response to strangers becomes well developed. It can be predicted that if a child was suddenly adopted at this age it would suffer a massive distress reaction resulting both from breaking the old relationships and from fear of the new parents and the strange environment. This would mean that the new parents and the home would become associated with an intensely unpleasant experience, and while familiarization and attachment should gradually take place, there should always be conflicting emotional reactions associated with the adoptive parents.

Cairns' theory of attachment. Cairns (1966) has developed an explanatory theory of attachment based on associative learning theory. The theories independently developed in this paper do not conflict with Cairns's formulation, but rather extend it by defining some of the mechanisms which learning theory predicts. In any case, the propositions stated here are consistent with one of Cairns's major propositions, that attachment is proportional to the length of association. With respect to another problem with which Cairns was concerned, namely that attachment takes place more rapidly to animate than to inanimate objects, and which Cairns attributes to greater cue weight, I would only add that greater stimulation should also speed up the process of familiarization and thus operate to speed up the process of attachment.

SUMMARY OF THEORETICAL PROPOSITIONS

1. *The reaction of distress at the absence of the familiar acts as an internal reinforcing agent.* Nothing external has to be done to a puppy or a child to produce this effect except to remove him from the familiar, but the result is that he is automatically punished by this internal mechanism activated by separation from the familiar, and rewarded by the cessation of this internal punishment as soon as he returns to familiar object, and situations. This mechanism alone will account for the formation of an emotional attachment.

2. *On the basis of reinforcement theory, we can predict that the attachment of an infant should grow stronger in time because of repeated accidental and purposeful separations (reinforcement) day after day and week after week.* Such brief separations occur over and over again in the course of normal development as a mother leaves her child to attend to other affairs. Later, when the child becomes capable of locomotion, the child repeatedly leaves his mother and returns to her. We can also state a corollary from reinforcement theory: namely, that the degree of attachment should be proportional to the number of separations. A child who experiences more than the usual number of separations in a given length of time should form a stronger attachment than one who has experienced fewer separations.

3. *The greater the degree of change from one environment or from one set of individuals to another, the greater the degree of the emotional reaction.* We have relatively little quantitative experimental evidence on this point, but observationally the results seem to be quite consistent. We do know that in young puppies the combination of the absence from familiar places and familiar individuals produces several times as much distress vocalization as either one separately (Scott and Bronson, 1964). We also know that in an older puppy a developing fear of the strange intensifies the distress resulting from separation.

In a schoolchild one should, therefore, get a much stronger emotional reaction by sending him off to a distant boarding school than by sending him to a familiar school close by. In the case of a ghetto child, we could predict that being sent to school for the first time would produce a much stronger emotional reaction than one would see in the case of a middle-class child for whom the change would be not so great.

The most drastic example of such a change, and one which should be familiar to anyone who has travelled outside his own country, is that of "culture shock". This is a term applied by anthropologists to the emotional disturbance resulting when an investigator goes off by himself to study a primitive culture in some distant part of the world. The language, the people, the country, and the weather are all different from that which the individual has experienced for most of his early life. While most people seldom, if ever, experience anything so drastic, anyone can personally verify the existence of the strongly unpleasant emotions induced by the sudden removal of familiar stimuli, by walking alone along a strange country road at night.

4. *The longer the separation, the greater the reaction.* The emotional reaction to separation, as we have seen in puppies, is not a momentary affair, but continues over long periods of time. For example, one of the experimenters in our laboratory who first attempted this kind of experiment with a puppy took it home for adoption purposes at the age of 4 weeks and found that it vocalized almost continuously for 24 hours and eventually stopped only because it got so hoarse that it could not go on. Those of us who remember being sent away to summer camps as children may recall that similar emotions in human beings may go on for a week or more without any break except during the periods when we were actively stimulated or distracted.

A corollary that can be derived from this proposition is that, within reasonable limits, long periods of separation should produce greater degrees of attachment than short periods. Of course, the attachment is in part dependent on the relief of the emotion, and if the period of separation is permanent or semi-permanent it never becomes relieved. What happens in these latter cases has never been experimentally verified, although there is some evidence from human cases that children try to avoid resuming the old relationship as if to avoid the possibility of being hurt in the future (Bowlby, 1951). Working with more moderate periods of separation, we found that puppies which were regularly separated overnight from familiar places and individuals became attached to people much more rapidly than did puppies who suffered only brief separation. In human experience, the kind of separation which is most prolonged is, of course, the permanent separation that results from the death of close relatives or friends. This leads to a final proposition.

5. *The separation reaction is not merely an infantile reaction which disappears as the puppy or child grows older but is something which remains throughout life.* This implies that such a reaction is a major source of social motivation and hence one which has a great deal of

relevance to mental health and reasonably happy adjustments to new situations.

Because a separation reaction persists for long periods after separation begins, and because it may not, on account of habituation and other factors, appear immediately at separation, it may be very difficult for a child to realize the cause of this emotion. A child separated from its familiar environment may not realize that he is feeling bad because he is away from home. All that he will know is that he feels bad, and, of course, he will associate this feeling with whatever the strange environment may be. Here I think we have a phenomenon which may be very important with respect to school situations, even as late as college and university experience. I suggest that we are dealing here with a very serious and important reaction, and one which has to be considered in clinical experience along with the other strong emotions.

THE PROCESS OF ATTACHMENT IN OLDER INDIVIDUALS

The mechanisms contributing to the process of attachment described above do not account for the full complexity of social relationships developed in older individuals. Once an infant has formed an attachment to a particular individual, and vice versa, there is an opportunity for all sorts of other interactions to take place, certainly involving the care-giving and care-soliciting behavioural systems and also perhaps the more adult sexual system. Feeding and food rewards will modify behaviour and emotional reactions, although they do not account for primary attachment. Agonistic interaction and the painful stimulation accompanying it will also modify the behaviour of the two individuals included in a simple relationship.

Apart from this, we can make two assumptions, as yet not well founded on experimental evidence, but certainly consistent with everyday experience. The first of these is that the process of forming social attachments does not cease at the end of the critical period for forming the first attachments but takes place throughout life, slowed down by such developmental processes as the fear of strangers, and modified by previous experience and previous attachments. This implies, among other things, that the primary attachments will tend to become deeper and stronger, since the internal reinforcing mechanism is continued and will react with each separation and reunion. It also follows that older individuals will generally have stronger attachments than younger ones.

A second assumption is that individuals in later life will tend to generalize their earlier attachments, in accordance with the laws of learning. In addition, they will more quickly form new attachments to new individuals who seem familiar; in this case the process of familiarization has already taken place, at least in part. This may account for the occasional rapid attachments seen among adults, as for example, in the case of sexual attachments, the proverbial "falling in love at first sight".

Some general hypotheses regarding attachment behaviour in adult life. On the basis of the theory developed above, and the assumptions regarding the continuity of mechanisms in adult life, it is possible to make certain predictions.

1. Individuals will tend to form attachments to any persons and/or objects with whom or with which they come into prolonged contact. This contact may be voluntary or it may be the result of social institutions, as in the case of individuals brought together for work, or it may be the result of forced contact as in the case of imprisonment. In any case, the result will be the same. This principle will account for the odd collection of objects such as old clothes and old motor cars to which we become attached, as well as for the odd collections of individuals of whom we become fond, even though we might never have chosen them voluntarily.

2. Since pain or discomfort does not interfere with the process of attachment except that it may cause individuals to avoid each other, we predict that individuals who are forcibly or voluntarily held in contact for long periods will become attached to each other. Think of the odd assortment of individuals to whom each of us becomes attached because of accident of birth, many of whom we would never choose voluntarily as friends. Equally odd attachments may occur in marriage. There is more to marriage than sex, as everyone has been saying for years. The process of attachment that has been described should take place between married couples irrespective of whether sexual relations are successful or not, and it should develop whether or not the individuals actually hate each other, provided they have stayed together for long periods of time. All of us have known married couples of that kind, who cannot get along with each other but are unable to live without each other. Then there are other odd kinds of attachment that develop because of forced contact, as for example between jailers and prisoners, or masters and slaves, who may hate each other but who also become attached to each other. Thus, we have an explanation for the development of love–hate relationships.

3. Since attachments should grow stronger in time, permanent or

prolonged separation should result in even more profound emotional tractions in older people than in young ones. We predict, for example, heat the older an individual the more difficult it will be for him to move into a totally new life, as, for example, in attempting to emigrate to a new country, or even to change jobs or move into a new house. Adjustment is not impossible but simply more painful. This also raises the problem of the significance of these emotional reactions with respect to mental health and psychiatric practice. A great deal of attention has been paid to the emotional reactions of sex and anger as a cause of maladjusted behaviour but very little to the consequences of the emotional reactions connected with separation.

Preventive measures. All of us who have worked in this field have done so because we hope that understanding the phenomena of attachment and suffering will help to avoid some of the emotional maladjustment and suffering that is associated with such experiences. Here we can follow a basic principle of medicine, that prevention is always better than cure. Bowlby and his colleagues have already done a great deal to develop ways of avoiding traumatic separation experiences in early infancy. The theory which I have developed here does not lead to any striking differences in procedures, but rather strengthens the reasons for them.

To begin with, separation itself is not a bad thing, but is a necessary part of the process of attachment. The baby that cries when its mother leaves it for a few minutes is not suffering permanent damage but is learning to understand and cope with the emotions of separation, and is also experiencing one more reinforcement that strengthens the tie with its mother. The kind of experience which is harmful is prolonged separation once a strong attachment has been formed. In dealing with the problem of adoption, it is obviously better to do this at birth or as soon as possible thereafter, before primary attachments have been formed, and especially before the fear of the strange begins to develop in the second half of the first year. By this time the baby will not only suffer a painful separation reaction through being taken away from his old surroundings, but will also be afraid of the new. However, much can be done to alleviate these reactions, first by bringing the adoptive parents into the orphanage repeatedly so that they become familiar to the child, and then, when the actual adoption takes place, taking the child briefly to its new home and returning it to the orphanage several times before the final change is made. Even here it would be well to return the child on occasional visits so that his past is not completely dissociated from his future existence. It is well to remember the dual processes of familiarization and attachment, and that attachment cannot take place without separation.

Here it is interesting to compare human and puppy development. In the latter, adoption (in the sense of removing a puppy from its mother and litter-mates and taking it into a human family and a new home) is a normal part of dog development. In the case of dogs we recommend that this be done between 6 and 8 weeks of age, which is about the middle of the critical period for forming social attachments, and just before the fear of the strange begins to develop strongly. The puppy does suffer a strong separation reaction which is relieved by the foster parents as it becomes familiar with them. The result is a very quick and strong attachment and a great deal of dependency, much more dependency than would be desirable in a human being, where we hope that a child will eventually grow into a reasonably independent adult.

A second working rule is that the puppy should be introduced to the physical and social environment in which it will spend the rest of its life at some time between 8 and 12 weeks of age, the time when a puppy normally begins to explore the outside world. As yet, we lack the information which would lead to a similar rule for human infants. What the corresponding age in children might be is unknown, but one might guess that it begins some time between 1 and 2 years of age, when the child is first able to explore its world on its own. This and the following years are the time to take a child travelling so that he becomes familiar with a wide variety of places and individuals.

A great deal remains to be done. The theories I have suggested can and should be put to experimental test, both in human beings and appropriate animal subjects. Beyond this, there is the enormous practical problem of applying these theories so that a greater number of children and adults are enabled to lead satisfactory lives. The task is complex, but the eventual goal is clear, that of helping children to form emotional attachments that can be generalized to the entire human race.

REFERENCES

AMBROSE, J. A. 1960. The smiling response in early human infancy. Ph.D. thesis, University of London.

BAYLEY, N. 1932. A study of the crying of infants during physical and mental tests. *J. Genet. Psychol.* **40**, 306–329.

BOWLBY, J. 1951. *Maternal care and mental health.* World Health Organization, Geneva.

BRODBECK, A. J. 1954. An exploratory study of the acqusition of dependency behavior in puppies. *Bull. ecol. Soc. Am.* **35,** 73.

BRONSON, G. W. 1968. The development of fear in man and other animals. *Child Dev.* **39,** 409–431.

CAIRNS, R. B. 1966. Attachment behavior of mammals. *Psychol. Rev.* **73,** 409–426.

CAIRNS, R. B. and WERBOFF, J. 1967. Behavior development in the dog: an inter-specific analysis. *Science, N.Y.* **158,** 1070–1072.

FISHER, A. E. 1955. The effects of differential early treatment on the social and exploratory behavior of puppies. Doctoral dissertation, Pennsylvania State University.

FREEDMAN, D. G., KING, J. A., and ELLIOT, O. 1961. Critical period in the social development of dogs. *Science, N.Y.* **133,** 1016–1017.

HARLOW, H. 1958. The nature of love. *Am. Psychologist* **13,** 673–685.

HESS, E. H. 1959. Imprinting. *Science, N.Y.* **130,** 133–141.

HESS, E. H. 1964. Imprinting in birds. *Science, N.Y.* **146,** 1128–1139.

MORGAN, G. A. and RICCIUTI, H. N. 1969. Infants' responses to strangers during the first year. In B. M. Foss (Ed.), *Determinants of infant behaviour IV.* Methuen, London.

SCHAFFER, H. R. 1958. Objective observations of personality development in early infancy. *Brit. J. med. Psychol.* **31,** 174–183.

SCHAFFER, H. R. 1966. The onset of fear of strangers and the incongruity hypothesis. *J. child Psychol. Psychiat.* **7,** 95–106.

SCOTT, J. P. 1963. The process of primary socialization in canine and human infants. *Monogr. Soc. Res. Child Dev.* **28** (1), Serial No. 85.

SCOTT, J. P. 1967. The development of social motivation. In D. Levine (Ed.), *Nebraska symposium on motivation.* University of Nebraska Press, Lincoln. Pp. 111–132.

SCOTT, J. P. and BRONSON, F. H. 1964. Experimental exploration of the et-epimeletic or care-soliciting behavioral system. In P. H. Leiderman and D. Shapiro (Eds.), *Psychobiological approaches to social behaviour.* Stanford Press, Stanford, Calif.

SCOTT, J. P. and FULLER, J. L. 1965. *Genetics and the social behavior of the dog.* University of Chicago Press, Chicago, Ill.

Discussion

Mechanisms Underlying the Primary Social Emotions

KAGAN: I wonder if one could not combine your two primary social reactions into one process, but with differential phasing. The principle would be that the organism establishes representations of its experience—schemata, structures, call them what you will, and that the first representations are for the infant's initial ecology. Removal from this ecology provokes the first social emotion. Subsequently, as the infant matures perceptually and develops representations for more refined aspects of the environment he becomes capable of reacting to deviations from these events. So why not call on the same mechanism for both aspects?

SCOTT: We have done various experiments in order to discover precisely what it is that causes distress vocalizations following separation in the very young puppy, and the only thing we can find is the absence of the familiar. The crucial experiment is to leave the puppy alone in a familiar room, so that nothing is changed except that you have taken out some familiar objects, namely the other puppies with whom the animal has lived together. When that is done the puppy will start to vocalize. If you then take away the familiar room as well you get even more distress. This is a very different reaction, both in time of development and in the quality of the emotion expressed, from the fear response to the strange which comes in later. If, of course, you combine the absence of the familiar and the presence of the strange you get a much stronger reaction.

KAGAN: The absence of the familiar might then be regarded as a reaction to a change in something like a sensory adaptation level, and particular degrees of change may lead to distress. Considered in these terms, the mechanism involved may be very primitive and appear very early. This may account for what we found in Guatemala, where the infants in the villages are constantly on their mothers' backs. We could not do some of our experiments because of the distress involved in removing them. Presumably we were abruptly changing their adaptation level for postural, tactile, and olfactory sensations. This would not, however, be a cognitive mechanism, whereas the response to incongruity would be cognitive.

ROSENBLUM: It may be that the difference is one of sensory modality and not of cognitive meaning. In one case distress is evoked by things like loss of support and other primarily postural discrepancies, while in the other case discrepancies are conveyed by the distance receptors and take the form mainly of such visual experiences as seeing a stranger. Why then make a distinction in the mechanism?

KAGAN: For the second case you would have to know the history of the organism before you could predict which event will elicit distress. This does not apply to the first—everyone, for instance, will react to loss of support.

RICHARDS: So in terms of your distinction you would say that when all members of the species react in this way this does not involve cognitive functioning?

KAGAN: That is right. I would regard it as belonging to a different category, and I don't have a name for that.

Exploratory and Attachment Motives

Foss: You have drawn attention to one particular source of motivation involving the desire to restore the familiar. But the organism is also motivated to look for the unfamiliar, to show curiosity and exploration, and I suspect that one of the reasons for the appeal of the interacting person is that he can satisfy both sources at the same time.

Scott: It is possible that a number of motives may all be functioning at the same time. However, observations of young puppies show that when they are raised in a place that provides them with plenty of opportunity to move about they will not start to move away at all from the familiar kennel until they are about 12 weeks old. Up to that age their total range is about 20 feet although they may have a large field available to them. Only after that age will they start to explore, but even then they are likely to return from time to time.

Foss: Let us look at what happens when you have got more than one thing with which you are familiar. I was surprised that you said that a long period of separation produces a more intense attachment. Surely during the period of separation the individual is going to be exposed to a lot of stimuli that will in turn become familiar, as a result of which he will become attached to these too.

Scott: What happens as a result of separation is, of course, in part dependent on what happens during the period of separation. I attempted to simplify things by considering only separations during which the animal has no opportunity for contacts leading to other attachments. Under these circumstances you get a strong emotional reaction, which can only be fully alleviated by returning the animal to his former environment. Fuller and Clark (1966. *J. comp. physiol. Psychol.* **61,** 251), however, have done some experiments on alleviation of symptoms during separation and find that most methods are only partially successful. The most effective is stimulation by another playful young dog that has been normally socialized. Most of the experiments involve sudden and final separation from the previous environment, with exposure to what would be considered normally pleasant conditions for a kennel dog. Under these conditions the symptoms improve somewhat but the animal never becomes entirely normal.

Kagan: I was bothered by your suggestion that all that is required for an attachment to develop is the opportunity for contact with the object. If this were the case one would not be able to predict differential attachment: the infant would be as attached to his pillow as to his mother. Some sort of response is surely required, whether it is a motor response or one involving perceptual assimilation.

SCOTT: We have done a whole series of experiments on this problem. Let me describe one. We reared puppies in isolation and then introduced them to a room in which a human being sat. For half the puppies the human just sat there and did nothing. For the other half he interacted with them by playing, stroking, and so on. When we compared the two groups for objective evidence of attachment responses there was no difference. However, I agree that there is some evidence that interaction does make some difference. For instance, Cairns and Werboff (1967. *Science.* **158,** 1070) found that puppies reared with rabbits developed distress reactions to separation less rapidly if the rabbit was kept behind a glass window than if it was in the same rearing cage as the puppy. Interaction therefore does produce some effect. I maintain only that it is not necessary in order to produce attachment.

ROSENBLUM: I wonder if the question of interaction cannot be considered, as Cairns did, in terms of the general salience of any given stimulus in its particular environment. Clearly a stimulus, be it person or inanimate object, that is of variable appearance is more likely to stand out as figure from ground, and I am inclined to think that the more salient the figure the better its chances are of becoming an attachment object. But all this is part of a general process and not one that is confined to specifically social interaction. There is nothing special about animate objects as opposed to inanimate objects, except that the former tend to leap out from the environment to a much greater degree.

SCOTT: Yes, if the infant is to become familiar with something, he has to notice it is there, and this is much more likely to happen with an animate moving object.

Cognitive Structure and Early Social Behaviour

H. R. SCHAFFER
University of Strathclyde

INTRODUCTION

My purpose in this paper is to attempt to build some bridges between cognitive structure on the one hand and the manifestation of early sociability on the other hand. The nature of cognitive structure, in the sense of the total system of an individual's information processing strategies, differs with age and thus sets limits on the kinds of social behaviour that one can expect at various stages of development: the extent of memory span, for instance, will have implications for the infant's ability to differentiate one person from another, and in the absence of object conservation infants can hardly be expected to show any orientation towards the mother during her absence.

Cognitive structure also differs according to species; it is therefore necessary to take into account the nature of the whole sensori-motor organization before attempting to compare one species with another. One well-known characteristic of human development is, of course, its comparative slowness, as a result of which it is possible to watch in slow motion the development of processes that may be less easily discerned in lower species where growth proceeds at a faster rate. However, another feature which distinguishes early human development is less frequently mentioned, namely the disjunction that occurs initially between perceptual and motor functions. Long before he acquires any degree of motor competence the infant already possesses a well-developed perceptual apparatus, as a result of which he is capable of acquiring and processing information and yet is severely limited in the extent to which he can directly act upon the basis of such information. One may contrast this with the development of precocial birds, where sensory and motor functions appear contemporaneously and where early learned discriminations thus tend to be expressed immediately in overt, observable form.

THE NATURE OF EARLY PERCEPTUAL-MOTOR DISJUNCTION

We have recently been trying to understand the nature of this disjunction and its consequences for development during the second half of the first year. Our interest has focused in particular on the development of selective behaviour, i.e. the manner in which an infant becomes capable of directing his approach–avoidance responses in a discriminative manner towards stimuli differing in terms of the individual's past experience of them. Behaviour is initially indiscriminate in this respect; it may be guided by the sensory characteristics of particular experiences, but whether the event has been encountered before or not plays at first no part in determining the direction of behaviour. In time, however, the range of effective stimuli that will elicit particular responses becomes restricted: the chick no longer approaches every conspicuous stimulus in its environment; the monkey ceases to cling to all furry substances that it happens to contact, and the smile of the human infant becomes reserved for certain specific, familiar individuals instead of being manifested to every face-like configuration. The occurrence of selectivity is thus a widespread phenomenon with considerable implications for early development and in need of further study and explanation. That it is dependent on the availability of a fund of past impressions and on the ability to differentiate the known from the unknown is evident. But is this the only operative factor involved?

In one recent study (Schaffer and Parry, 1969) 6- and 12-month-old infants were familiarized on a nonsense object in a series of seven 30-second exposure periods, with 30-second inter-trial intervals. On the eighth trial a novel (differently coloured) object was introduced, and on the ninth trial the former object was brought back once again. A comparison of the visual and manipulative behaviour of the two age groups over trials makes two points apparent. In the first place, both groups showed similar visual behaviour to the changes in experimentally induced familiarity: a decrease occurred over the first seven trials in the length of the first visual fixation (see Fig. 1) as well as in the total length of fixation on the stimulus, while the number of fixations per trial increased. On the eighth trial, with the introduction of the novel object, visual attention increased once more, only to subside again

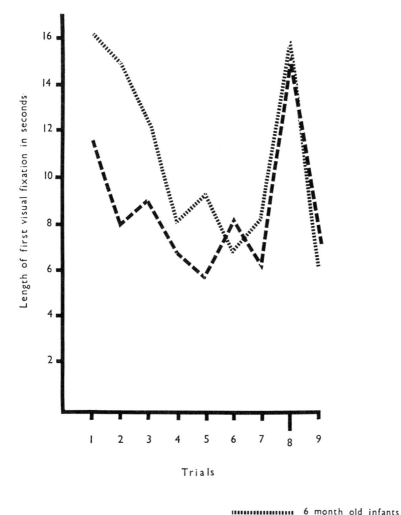

 6 month old infants
━ ━ ━ ━ ━ 12 month old infants

FIG. 1. Length of first visual fixation per trial for 6-month-old and 12-month-old infants.

on the ninth trial when the previous object was brought back. Such differential behaviour appears to indicate an ability perceptually to classify stimuli in terms of their familiarity that is as well developed at 6 months as at 12 months.

Manipulative measures, on the other hand, yielded a different picture. The older group behaved discriminatively in this respect too, and particularly so with regard to latency before making contact with the object (see Fig. 2): on its first appearance there was prolonged hesitation before the strange stimulus was touched, sometimes accompanied by a variety of avoidance responses, and only with increasing familiarity was contact made more and more readily at the beginning of each trial (though it is of interest to note that on the eighth trial, with the introduction of the novel object, manipulative latency for some reason did not significantly increase). The younger group, however, behaved differently in this respect, for from the very first trial onwards they showed quite indiscriminately an immediate approach response to the stimulus as soon as it appeared each time. In an almost reflex-like manner they reached for the object the moment it was seen, irrespective of whether it was recognized as familiar or strange. At this earlier age, therefore, discriminative behaviour could be observed to occur in the perceptual system yet not in the motor system—the ability to register information in terms of familiarity–unfamiliarity was thus not accompanied in this case by selective approach–avoidance behaviour, the integration between the two apparently occurring only in the second half of the first year.

A similar conclusion emerges from another study in which a simultaneous discrimination technique was employed (Schaffer and Parry, 1970). Three groups of infants, aged 5–7 months, 8–10 months, and 11–13 months, were given a 2-minute familiarization period with one stimulus object, followed by a $1\frac{1}{2}$-minute discrimination test involving the familiar and a novel (differently coloured) object. Again visual indices show that there are no age differences in the extent to which selective *visual* attention is paid at the beginning of the discrimination test to the novel as opposed to the familiar stimulus, the youngest group being as capable as the oldest of discriminating between them (Table I). In the two older groups this is accompanied by selective *manipulative* behaviour: the infant is not only observing but also touching the novel stimulus to a significantly greater extent than the familiar stimulus. In the youngest group, on the other hand, this does not occur, manipulation there being distributed indiscriminately between the two stimuli. Once more we find that the ability to make the distinction perceptually is no guarantee for the occurrence of selective motor behaviour.

Some kind of disjunction between observing behaviour on the one hand and approach–avoidance behaviour on the other is thus made apparent. However, these findings do not mean that the 6-month-old infant is incapable of making selective manipulative responses under any circumstances. The point is made by the results of a study in which

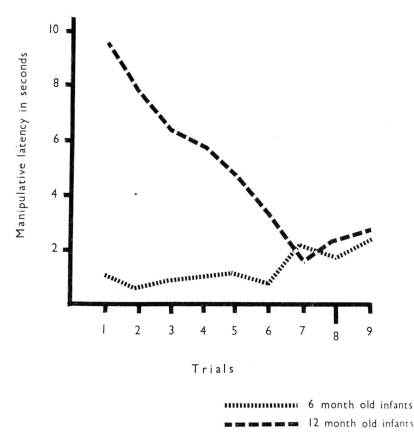

FIG. 2. Manipulative latency per trial for 6-month-old and 12-month-old infants.

we attempted to induce a conflict between the attractions of perceptual salience on the one hand and of novelty on the other, in order to ascertain the manner in which infants of different ages resolve such a conflict. Two stimuli, a plain disk and a multi-coloured disk, were first shown to infants in the relevant age range in order to establish that the latter was indeed of greater perceptual salience and that it elicited more attention than the plain disk. Three age groups (5–7 months, 8–10 months, and 11–13 months) were then given a short-term (2-minute) familiarization period on the multi-coloured stimulus, and immediately afterwards were simultaneously exposed to this inherently more interesting but now familiar stimulus and to the novel but perceptually less salient stimulus (the plain disk). Two relevant points emerge from the

TABLE I. AMOUNT OF VISUAL AND MANIPULATIVE ATTENTION TO NOVEL AND FAMILIAR OBJECTS DURING FIRST HALF-MINUTE OF SIMULTANEOUS DISCRIMINATION TEST

	Age groups					
	5–7 months		8–10 months		11–13 months	
	Novel	Familiar	Novel	Familiar	Novel	Familiar
Visual fixation	16·3	9·7	13·8	10·0	15·2	9·9
Manipulation	12·0	12·1	16·1	11·5	16·7	12·4

results of the experimental group who received this treatment (see Table II).

In the first place, the conflict, it appears, is resolved in different ways at different ages. The youngest infants paid more attention during the discrimination period to the high-salient stimulus, even though it was familiar; the oldest infants, on the other hand, paid more attention to the novel stimulus, even though it was of low perceptual salience. As

TABLE II. AMOUNT OF VISUAL AND MANIPULATIVE ATTENTION DURING 30-SECOND DISCRIMINATION TEST TO TWO OBJECTS VARYING IN DEGREE OF PERCEPTUAL SALIENCE AND FAMILIARITY. A. EXPERIMENTAL GROUP (FAMILIARIZED ON HIGH-SALIENT OBJECT). B. CONTROL GROUP (FAMILIARIZED ON LOW-SALIENT OBJECT)

A. *Experimental Group*

	Age groups					
Object characteristics:	5–7 months		8–10 months		11–13 months	
Perceptual salience	High	Low	High	Low	High	Low
Familiarity	Familiar	Novel	Familiar	Novel	Familiar	Novel
Visual fixation	15·4	10·3	13·3	10·9	7·4	11·2
Manipulation	12·9	8·6	15·9	14·8	7·9	9·7

B. *Control Group*

	Age groups					
Object characteristics:	5–7 months		8–10 months		11–13 months	
Perceptual salience	Low	High	Low	High	Low	High
Familiarity	Familiar	Novel	Familiar	Novel	Familiar	Novel
Visual fixation	9·1	14·0	8·9	13·7	4·1	9·9
Manipulation	8·3	12·5	11·1	14·3	4·4	9·3

we also ran a control group who were familiarized initially on the low-salient stimulus, and as here, too, the youngest infants preferred the multi-coloured disk in the discrimination test, we may conclude that their choice was dictated by the perceptual attributes of the stimulus irrespective of experience, whereas the choice of the older infants was each time based on past experience, with the attractions of novelty overriding the stimulus attributes. We thus have a shift with age from "outer-directedness" to "inner-directedness"—a topic to which I shall return later on.

The second point of interest refers to the finding that in this situation the data indicate a concordance of visual and manipulative functions even for the youngest group. In other words, in a situation where the choice is made on the basis of perceptual attributes even the 6-month-old infant is capable of behaving selectively with regard to manipulative responses.

These data clarify the nature of the disjunction under discussion, and the point may be most easily illustrated by reference to what is admittedly an over-simplified model of the discrimination process (see

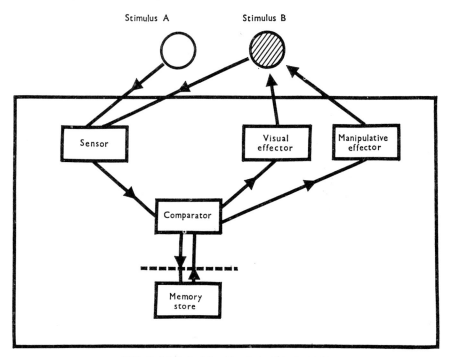

FIG. 3. Model of the discrimination process.

Fig. 3). If an infant is confronted by two stimuli which differ in terms of perceptual salience, so that their comparison involves merely the sensory impressions received from them, then even the 6-month-old infant can behave discriminatively not only with regard to visual but also with regard to manipulative effectors. Not just his eyes but also his hands are guided towards the more "interesting" stimulus. If, however, the stimuli differ in terms of familiarity, so that the process of comparison must draw on a memory store, only infants later on in the second half-year can show co-ordination between the two effector systems; around 6 months of age, on the other hand, the disjunctive phenomenon is observed, in that visual behaviour shows the effects of familiarization but not simultaneously occurring manipulative behaviour. It is thus past experience, not present sensory input, that fails to act as a guiding influence on manipulation: despite the fact that representations of the previously encountered stimulus are centrally available, they play no part in controlling approach–avoidance responses.

These findings suggest that we are confronted here with an early form of *mediational deficiency*. So far this term has generally been used (e.g. by Reese, 1962) to refer to the fact that the pre-school child may have verbal labels available which he can apply correctly to particular stimuli but which he is unable to use as mediators in order to guide choice behaviour in a discrimination situation. As Kendler and Kendler (1962) observed, children of this age will frequently verbalize the correct solution in a discrimination learning task while simultaneously making the incorrect choice. The mediational process and the motor process are thus running in parallel but not interacting, and it is only later on in childhood that they come to be integrated so that the one may regulate the other.

The mediators with which we are concerned here are, of course, of a different nature. We may think of them as stored images rather than as responses and as being ikonic rather than symbolic in content. We assume their presence because of the differential perceptual behaviour to novel as opposed to familiar stimuli: habituation of visual fixation to a repeatedly exposed stimulus, for instance, is explicable in terms of the impressions retained from preceding trials. In the 12-month-old infant it appears that these stored impressions can act as mediators not only within the perceptual system but also in guiding motor responses; in the 6-month-old infant, on the other hand, they fail in the latter respect. They are potentially available, yet the manipulative system remains shielded from their influence. Thus, while central representations of features of the external environment eventually come to play a vital role in the control of behaviour, their presence in the young infant is no guarantee that they can already play this part.

TWO PROCESSES, NOT ONE

It is apparent that the occurrence of discrimination in one system of behaviour is not necessarily accompanied by its occurrence in other systems. Thus the advantage of the disjunctive nature of human development lies in its demonstration that the ability to make perceptual differentiations in terms of familiarity is insufficient to explain the appearance of selective approach–avoidance behaviour. Yet in precocial birds, where no perceptual-motor disjunction is found, the perceptual discrimination alone is often taken as the sufficient cause of both imprinted preferences and fear of strangers. Imprinting, for instance, has been characterized as a "learning of the characteristics of the parent-object" (Baer and Gray, 1960), as an acquired ability to discriminate the object to which an animal was first exposed at the critical period (Gray and Howard, 1957) and as development "from seeing gross differences to the seeing of fine differences" (Thorpe, 1956). No wonder Gibson (1969) reviews the topic as a "type of perceptual phenomenon". Similarly fear has been described as a consequence of having become familiar with something (Bateson, 1966) and regarded as a consequence of the establishment of neuronal models brought into being by perceptual exposure (Salzen, 1962). For both phenomena a template-matching hypothesis is advanced, their onset being related to the growth of the ability to form central representations and thus to categorize experiences in terms of their familiarity.

These explanations are based on a one-process account. The human data, however, indicate that two processes must be hypothesized, the onset of which may well coincide in precocial animals but which, in human development at least, appear in sequential order. The first of these refers to a *perceptual learning mechanism* and involves the acquisition by the organism of central representations, as a result of which differential attention to stimuli varying in degree of familiarity will occur. There is evidence that in the human infant it is possible to detect such an ability from about 3 months of age (Fantz, 1964), though naturally much depends on the particular parameters of the procedure employed. The second process sets in later and is concerned with a *response selection mechanism*. This is linked to the preceding perceptual learning, in that the appropriateness of the response is determined in the light of past experience. Previously any stimulus automatically elicited the primary approach response irrespective of recognition; now, however, the appraisal which relates the stimulus to previous encounters must first run its course before a motor response is emitted. Whether the individual then takes approach or avoidance action will be determined by the outcome of such appraisal. The first process in thus a necessary but not a sufficient condition for the occurrence of selectivity: the development of a link with motor functions must also be hypothesized.

Perceptual-motor integration may, of course, take many different forms. Thus Bortner and Birch (1962), working with brain-injured children, found that the ability to discriminate among block designs may be intact even though the ability to reproduce them is impaired, and concluded that the latter difficulty is not due to any fault at a recognition level but to an inability to translate a perceptual organization into an appropriate action pattern. Two functionally autonomous systems were therefore said to exist: a recognition–discrimination system which appears earlier in the course of ontogenetic development and a perceptual-motor or more complex integrative system which develops later and may also be more vulnerable to brain damage. Again the disjunctive nature of human development makes its mark.

The perceptual-motor integration studied by us, however, is of a very specific nature, for it revolves around the mediating role of the individual's memory store. Our remarks, moreover, stem from the observation of just two behaviour systems, the visual and the manipulative. How far it is possible to generalize beyond them to other sensory and motor systems remains to be established.

THE ROLE OF CENTRAL REPRESENTATIONS IN EARLY SOCIAL BEHAVIOUR

The development of selectivity, particularly in social behaviour, is often indexed by the onset of fear of the strange. Let us therefore examine the beginnings of this phenomenon more closely.

There are two types of explanation that have been offered for the onset of fear, stressing maturational and experiential factors respectively. As to the former, it is difficult to find positive evidence for the role of maturation (Bronson, 1968), and in any case it is not at all clear what it is that is supposed to mature—certainly both the required sensory and motor equipment are generally in existence long before the age when fear first appears.

The other type of explanation, that based on experience, is embodied in the theories of Hebb (1946) and Hunt (1963) and considers that fear arises from perceived incongruity between sensory input and some central standard within the organism representing information already stored within the brain as a result of previous encounters with the category of circumstances concerned. As usually formulated, this account suggests that exposure to a structured environment is all that is required to explain the onset of fear, and the ability perceptually to differentiate familiar from unfamiliar is thus regarded as a sufficient condition for the emergence of avoidance behaviour. Such one-process explanations have already been called into question; moreover, observations of social behaviour in the human infant indicate quite clearly that the discrimination of strangers from the mother generally occurs several months before fear of strangers sets in (Schaffer, 1966).

In fact, the Hebb–Hunt position makes an assumption which must be challenged. The assumption is that as soon as the infant has acquired a central representation as a result of experience, he has, even in the early months of life, free and spontaneous access to it, that he can readily retrieve it in order to compare it with various sensory experiences, and that he can act selectively under its guidance—in brief, that from the beginning such representations function as in the mature individual. However, what evidence there is suggests that, quite on the contrary, infants in the first half-year are severely limited in the extent to which they can make use of centrally stored as opposed to peripherally available stimulation, that they can only gradually free themselves from exclusive dominance by the latter, and that representations influence behaviour only under certain quite limited conditions.

An incidental observation made by us in the course of a recent study can serve as an illustration of this early handicap. During a comparison of the responses of 6- and 12-month-old infants to a visual stimulus array it became apparent that some of the subjects were somewhat ill at ease in the experimental situation. We therefore asked the mother of each subject to sit just behind him in order to deal with any difficulties that arose, but with strict instructions not otherwise to interfere or in any way draw attention to herself. At first we regarded this arrangement as just an evil necessity, but it soon became apparent that in fact it provided us with the opportunity to observe something rather interesting—the "turning-to-mother" phenomenon, as we came to call it. Quite simply, we recorded the number of times that each infant looked away from the stimulus placed by the experimenters in his perceptual field and turned to that other stimulus, the mother, behind him. The results are clear-cut. The younger infants hardly ever turned—they tended to behave in a "stimulus-bound" fashion and acted towards the mother in an "out of sight out of mind" manner. The older infants, on the other hand, frequently turned in the course of the experimental session from one stimulus to the other, apparently well able to keep in mind the perceptually absent object, integrating it with other activities, and so showing a much more flexible type of behaviour.

We have here a simple example of the shift from "outer-directedness" to "inner-directedness" already referred to, from domination by the immediate sensory environment to the ability to make *spontaneous* use of centrally recalled information. The importance of this shift may be appreciated by referring to a number of other examples indicating the same development and also taking place in the second half-year:

1. As his operational definition for the establishment of the object concept, Piaget used the appearance of search behaviour. Here too the ability to remain oriented towards a perceptually absent object is involved: in the early months the object exists only as long as it is perceived, for once it is out of the immediate perceptual field the infant no longer shows any sign of being aware of its existence. Only in the second half-year can one observe the beginnings of an orientation towards a missing object and only then can the infant initiate activities involving stimuli experienced in the past rather than perceived in the present.

2. The same applies to separation upset, which also first becomes apparent after the age of 6 months (Schaffer, 1958). Yet some form of central representation of the mother is already in existence several months earlier, judging by the various indications of recognition that can be found from at least 3 months on (Ainsworth, 1967; Fitzgerald, 1968). The existence of such representations, however, becomes evident only in the perceptual presence of the mother (by, for instance, greater or more easily induced responsiveness to her than to unfamiliar individuals), whereas in her absence there is no sign of orientation towards her. It is as though the central representation can function only when confronted by the corresponding sensory input, for however excited and responsive the infant may be on each encounter with the mother, in the intervening periods the representation remains dormant. In brief, *the infant is capable of recognition but not yet of recall.* Only from about 7 months onwards can he remain oriented towards the mother long after her disappearance and initiate proximity-seeking activities directed

towards her in her absence. Spontaneous access to the central representation is indicated from this point, but not before.

3. Our third example takes us back to fear of strangers. Following the incongruity hypothesis, this phenomenon also involves the retrieval of stored information, though this time for purposes of comparing sensory input from an unfamiliar stimulus with the familiar standard. Fear of strangers is often discussed as though it arises quite suddenly at about the age of 8 months in its fully fashioned form. However, a number of intriguing suggestions seem to indicate, albeit tentatively, that under certain conditions fear may be observed rather earlier: (a) in a longitudinal study of early social behaviour (Schaffer and Emerson, 1964) we found that fear of strangers would initially appear only if the mother was present at the same time as the stranger (unlike our findings for older infants, in whom fear was much more likely to occur when the mother was absent). The infants, it was observed, would look to and fro as though comparing the stranger with the familiar person and only then show avoidance responses to the former. If, however, the mother was not present the infants merely stared, unsmiling but also without any sign of fear. It seems that the standard of comparison had to be simultaneously present in the perceptual field before the one individual could be related to the other. In the absence of the standard the infant could not use it, its spontaneous retrieval being a later development. (b) Wolff (1969) observed a 5-month-old infant to cry whenever his mother put on a bathing cap that covered her hair and obscured her hairline, yet the same infant smiled in the usual manner when a stranger appeared in the bathing cap. We may assume that in the former case enough of the familiar standard of comparison was perceptually present to make the infant realize the incongruity, whereas in the latter case that same standard of comparison would have had to be retrieved from its central storage. (c) In a study by Bühler (1928) the responses of infants aged 2 to 8 months to familiar and unfamiliar stimuli were recorded. The familiar stimuli used were human faces and voices, and for the unfamiliar stimuli masks, growls, and falsetto voices were presented. When the unfamiliar stimuli were shown on their own, Bühler found no indication of fear; when, however, the infants observed one stimulus changing into another (the experimenter, for instance putting a mask over his face or the auditory stimulus changing from a speaking voice to a falsetto voice), fear responses occurred.

It appears from these three sets of observations that fear of the strange can be found rather earlier than is normally stated if the infant's task is made easier by providing him with the standard of comparison either simultaneously or (as in Bühler's experiment) in immediate succession to the unfamiliar stimulus with which it has to be matched. This explanation may well account for the incidents of "early fears" that a number of writers (Benjamin, 1963; Morgan and Ricciuti, 1969; Schaffer, 1966) have reported as occurring even in the first half-year and which generally refer to the response elicited by a familiar person assuming a "distorted" appearance (such as the mother putting on a pair of spectacles not previously worn). If, however, the standard of comparison is not present in the perceptual field and has to be retrieved from the infant's memory store, a much more sophisticated cognitive operation is demanded which does not become evident till rather later. In view of what has already been said, it appears that the third quarter of the first year is the period when one can generally expect this more mature ability first to manifest itself.

CONCLUSION

In his *Principles of Psychology* William James (1891) reports an observation on his own son to whom he gave a live frog once, at the age of 6 to 8 months, and again when he was a year and a half old. "The first time he seized it promptly, and holding it, in spite of its struggling, at last got its head into his mouth. He then let it crawl up his breast, and get upon his face, without showing alarm. But the second time, although he had seen no frog and heard no story about a frog between whiles, it was almost impossible to induce him to touch it." The child, in other words, was no longer responding indiscriminately with approach behaviour to whatever object appeared in front of him; he had, instead, developed the ability to respond selectively. This development, apparent in both social and non-social contexts, requires explanation.

Although avoidance behaviour would appear to be the most obvious indication that an infant has become capable of acting selectively, it is probably more accurate to view this development in terms of the onset of "not-approach"—that is, the ability to check a primary tendency to make approach responses to every stimulus confronting the individual and replace it by an appraisal process involving the infant's memory store that will then exercise a controlling and guiding influence on ensuing motor responses. These may, under certain conditions, take the form of avoidance behaviour; on the other hand, under different conditions they may take the form of approach behaviour in that the infant decides to investigate and explore the stimulus further. In either case, however, the nature of the response is now under central control instead of being, reflex-like, a function of sensory stimulation alone.

The growth of selectivity is, we believe, intimately linked to the manner in which central representations function in infancy. When first acquired in the early months of life, representations affect behaviour under only rather limited circumstances. They are evoked when the corresponding sensory stimulus appears, as a result of which a variety of behaviour patterns is elicited that enables us to conclude that the infant has "recognized" the stimulus. When a novel stimulus is perceived, the infant may show differential behaviour (longer visual fixations, cardiac deceleration, etc.) but it should be stressed that such behaviour alone does not necessarily signify that the infant is comparing the unfamiliar stimulus with a central standard. A more economical interpretation is that the infant merely finds it impossible to assimilate the stimulus to his existing schemata—that it is regarded as strange only in the sense of being not familiar and therefore puzzling, not that it is seen as unfamiliar in the sense of being different from the familiar as a result of an active process of comparison. It is only subsequently that the infant becomes capable of the latter, much more sophisticated accomplishment, when each stimulus is no longer merely treated in isolation but events become related to one another and experiences are inserted into total systems. The components of these systems must at first also be perceptually present, but, starting in the second half-year, need not be so any more and can instead be drawn from the much more freely available fund of central data. Thus, once an infant can relate to more than one stimulus at a time and can treat several in juxtaposition (first in a physical, then in a mental sense), his natural impulsiveness will be blocked as he becomes aware of the simultaneous existence of several alternative courses of action. Selectivity then becomes possible.

REFERENCES

AINSWORTH, M. D. S. 1967. *Infancy in Uganda.* Johns Hopkins Press, Baltimore, Md.

BAER, D. M. and GRAY, P. H. 1960. Imprinting to a different species without overt following. *Percept. Mot. Skills* **10**, 171–174.

BATESON, P. P. G. 1966. The characteristics and contexts of imprinting. *Biol. Rev.* **41**, 177–220.

BENJAMIN, J. D. 1963. Further comments on some developmental aspects of anxiety. In H. Gaskill (Ed.), *Counterpoint*, International Universities Press, New York.

BORTNER, M. and BIRCH, H. G. 1962. Perceptual and perceptual-motor dissociation in cerebral palsied children. *J. nerv. ment. Dis.* **134**, 103–108.

BRONSON, G. 1968. The fear of novelty. *Psychol. Bull.* **69**, 350–358.

BÜHLER, C. 1928. Die Affektwirkung von Fremdheitseindrücken im ersten Lebensjahr. *Zeitschr. f. Psychol.* **107**, 30–61.

FANTZ, R. L. 1964. Visual experience in infants: decreased attention to familiar patterns relative to novel ones. *Science* **146**, 668–670.

FITZGERALD, H. E. 1968. Autonomic pupillary reflex activity during early infancy and its relation to social and nonsocial visual stimuli. *J. exper. child Psychol.* **6**, 470–482.

GIBSON, E. E. 1969. *Principles of perceptual learning and development.* Appleton-Century-Crofts, New York.

GRAY, P. H. and HOWARD, K. I. 1957. Specific recognition of humans in imprinted chicks. *Percept. Mot. Skills* **7**, 301–304.

HEBB, D. O. 1946. On the nature of fear. *Psychol. Rev.* **53**, 259–276.

HUNT, J. McV. 1963. Motivation inherent in information processing and action. In O. J. Harvey (Ed.), *Motivation and social interaction.* Ronald Press, New York.

JAMES, W. 1891. *Principles of psychology*, Vol. 2. Macmillan, London.

KENDLER, H. H. and KENDLER, T. S. 1962. Vertical and horizontal processes in problem solving. *Psychol. Rev.* **69**, 1–16.

MORGAN, G. A. and RICCIUTI, H. N. 1969. Infants' responses to strangers during the first year. In B. M. Foss (Ed.), *Determinants of infant behaviour IV.* Methuen, London.

REESE, H. W. 1962. Verbal mediation as a function of age level. *Psychol. Bull.* **59**, 502–509.

SALZEN, E. A. 1962. Imprinting and fear. *Symp. zool. Soc. Lond.* **8**, 199–217.

SCHAFFER, H. R. 1958. Objective observations of personality development in early infancy. *Brit. J. Psychol.* **31**, 174–184.

SCHAFFER, H. R. 1966. The onset of fear of strangers and the incongruity hypothesis. *J. child Psychol. Psychiat.* **7**, 95–106.

SCHAFFER, H. R. and EMERSON, P. E. 1964. The development of social attachments in infancy. *Monogr. Soc. Res. Child Dev.* **29**, no. 3, Serial no. 94.

SCHAFFER, H. R. and PARRY, M. H. 1969. Perceptual-motor behaviour in infancy as a function of age and stimulus familiarity. *Brit. J. Psychol.* **60**, 1–9.

SCHAFFER, H. R. and PARRY, M. H. 1970. The effects of short-term familiarization on infants' perceptual-motor coordination in a simultaneous discrimination situation. *Brit. J. Psychol.* **61**, 559–569.

THORPE, W. H. 1956. *Learning and instinct in animals.* Methuen, London.

WOLFF, P. H. 1969. The natural history of crying and other vocalizations in early infancy. In B. M. Foss (Ed.), *Determinants of infant behaviour IV.* Methuen, London.

Discussion

Experimental Analysis of Early Social Behaviour

AXELRAD: In what way do you think experiments with inanimate objects throw light on social development?

SCHAFFER: Let me say first of all that I do not believe in the existence of two quite separate categories of processes related, respectively, to social and non-social behaviour patterns. These patterns are based on the same mechanisms, and behaviour towards a social object is every bit as much dependent on such cognitive functions as attention, perception, and learning as is behaviour towards an inanimate stimulus. Obviously certain differences have to be taken into account: social objects are generally very much more salient and, being important for survival, are so constructed that maximum interaction with them is ensured. Moreover, the relationship with inanimate objects tends to be a one-way affair while with social objects it is two-way, thus making it possible to set in motion interaction sequences. Nevertheless, as the ethologists in particular have shown, it is both feasible and legitimate to isolate certain aspects of social behaviour and transfer them to an experimental context containing non-social objects. This is especially so in the earliest stages of development, when the distinction between social and non-social stimuli is merely one that the observer makes rather than the infant. Yet it also applies later on: the development of selectivity, for instance, is common to early behaviour in general, and it is therefore useful to lift it out of its normal context and study it in relation to inanimate objects, with all their advantages of greater experimental control, rather than in relation to mothers and strangers.

AXELRAD: The mother may be a stimulus, but she also gratifies certain needs in the infant that your stimuli can hardly gratify.

SCHAFFER: That is right, but gratification involves stimulation that is related to particular requirements of the infant, as a result of which the mother will become more salient and evoke certain responses sooner than inanimate objects. This does not mean, however, that behaviour towards her is based on qualitatively different mechanisms, and it is the mechanisms after all that we are attempting to study.

Impulsiveness and its Inhibition

FOSS: The inability to inhibit which you observed is paralleled by what Luria described in rather older children. He too found that stimuli (verbal, in his case) could at first initiate motor responses but could not stop them, and that the impulsiveness of the child's behaviour was brought under verbal control only later on in the course of development.

SCHAFFER: The analogy is a good one, for in Luria's case too the eliciting function of stimuli took developmental precedence over their inhibitory function. What is more, here too the inhibition of impulsiveness was said to become possible only when the child was able to consider two things simultaneously and so generate a conflict of intentions. One can take the similarity even further, for Luria also stressed that the conflict had in the first place to involve *external* sources, namely two conflicting verbal commands given to the child by the experimenter, and that it was only later, when behaviour became fully regulated by speech, that the conflict could be initiated by *internally* generated self-commands. Thus the formal developmental properties are very similar, though they are to be found at different age levels and with different contents.

TIZARD: How general is the phenomenon of immediate approach to unfamiliar objects which you described for the younger infants? Does one find it with all stimuli?

SCHAFFER: We have found it to occur with a very wide range of objects and have so far failed to find any conditions under which prolonged manipulative latency occurs in these younger infants. The only exception is when the mode of presentation is so sudden or intense that it elicits a startle response. On the other hand, the extent to which older infants show inhibition of manipulative approach appears to be very much affected by a number of conditions related to the nature of the object, the environment in which it is presented, and various organismic factors responsible for producing quite considerable individual differences in this respect.

KAGAN: One condition affecting impulsiveness appears to be social class. The middle-class infants we have been observing showed more vacillation when confronted by a new and an old toy than lower-class children before making their choice. Then too there are reports which indicate that macaques subjected to mild anoxia at birth showed no inhibition towards strange objects, whereas normal animals did.

Conditions Eliciting Approach and Avoidance Responses

AMBROSE: It may be useful to stress that the unfamiliar does not inevitably elicit fear and that, under certain conditions, positive responses connected with exploration and curiosity appear instead. It would be interesting to devise an experiment in which the infant, having been taught instrumentally to vary a stimulus so as to make it more or less like a familiar standard, could be tested to see if he would in fact show a preference for some degree of discrepancy.

SCHAFFER: That is indeed why I feel the emphasis should be on the onset of "not-approach" behaviour rather than on the onset of avoidance. There are two quite separate problems to be explained here: the first concerns the ability to inhibit an immediate approach response and the consequent development of selective behaviour, and the second involves the nature of the response which the infant can then select. As far as the second is concerned, the imprinting literature has on the whole tended to stress avoidance of the unfamiliar (and a corresponding seeking of the familiar), whereas the curiosity literature has emphasized rather the tendency to approach the unfamiliar.

AMBROSE: It is clearly important to isolate the conditions under which one rather than the other response occurs. There are several possible explanations, of which the degree of unfamiliarity is perhaps the most often mentioned. Another is age: there are various suggestions that during the phase when schemata are being built up, the corresponding familiar object is preferred, but that subsequently the infant is more interested in discrepancies.

FOSS: Another and perhaps even more important condition is the state of the organism. Studies of imprinting have shown that, if the animal is anxious, it will seek the imprinted object; if it is secure, it will explore.

AMBROSE: Semantically it would be a help if we were to differentiate the novel from the strange. Both are the opposite of familiar but, especially when we consider infant perception, their meaning is not necessarily identical. A strange object could be regarded as having reference to something that is already familiar and with which it can be compared; a novel object, on the other hand, could be regarded as having no reference to anything because it is utterly outside the infant's sphere of knowledge.

The Role of Motor Responses in Perceptual Learning

ROSENBLUM: I wonder if you would comment a little further on the likely interaction of proximal and distance receptors. Work with various primate species indicates that, given a difficult discrimination, the opportunity to handle the stimulus objects seems to facilitate the discrimination. What part do vision and touch play in the human infant?

SCHAFFER: That has been a controversial issue for a long time: is touch the mother of the senses, or does vision play a more important part initially in acquainting the infant with his surroundings? Tactile exploration has generally been emphasized because younger children benefit more from handling objects than do older children; that, however, does not justify the conclusion that touch is in any sense primary to vision. Let me illustrate: in our second experiment which I described in the paper we compared two kinds of familiarization conditions, namely a visual-tactile and a visual-only condition. In the former the infants were able to handle as well as observe the stimulus, but in the latter they sat just out of reach and could observe only. The visual-tactile condition gave us very much better discriminations between the familiar and a novel object, but particularly so among the youngest (6-month-old) infants. In other words, the older child benefits less from additional information available via another sensory modality, whereas at earlier ages tactile sensations are required to a greater degree to supplement visual sensations. Yet our results also indicate the extent to which vision is already a well-functioning system capable of fairly sophisticated cognitive operations long before there is any appreciable manipulative involvement.

LEWIS: Why is there such a curious insistence, even among cognitive psychologists, on the introduction of motor responses into every act of learning? Why must we assume that internal representations or schemata are always developed through action? Is it not possible that rather more passive modes of behaviour—such as attention—are sufficient for their development? Infants obviously lack motor abilities, but to arrive at conclusions about their intellectual ability from observation of their motor behaviour can be very misleading. As more research is conducted using less overt behavioural manifestations we have discovered that the mind of the infant is far more developed than we imagined. Action at this early age, in other words, is not an appropriate construct for learning or knowing.

The Beginnings of Retrieval

KAGAN: The recall–recognition distinction as applied to early behaviour is a useful one, but I am inclined not to put too much weight on one particular age as representing the beginnings of the retrieval ability. Under your conditions it may be 7 or 8 months, but we have data suggesting its existence already at 4 months. What is particularly crucial here is the length of the interval during which the infant has to hold the impression, and this, it appears, becomes progressively longer with age. So I see it not as a discrete stage but as a gradual development.

LEWIS: We must also consider the possibility that differences in retrieval may be a function of differences in familiarization. Younger infants are less able to acquire internal representations and for this reason may have less that can be retrieved.

SCHAFFER: Within the age range we investigated there were no obvious indications of differences in familiarization measures. I agree, of course, that we must take into account the various parameters defining this operation and that retrieval may, for instance, appear earlier in relation to social than to non-social objects. Nevertheless, we ought not to be afraid of postulating developmental discontinuities and we must acknowledge the possibility that a radical restructuring takes place from time to time in psychological functioning. Piaget has described many such realignments, and there is considerable evidence to suggest that one of these steps takes place in the third quarter of the first year. Both the material on object permanence and that on separation upset suggest this, and although these developments depend on processes that take place in earlier months, it does seem that their appearance in overt behaviour given, the conventional tests, is relatively sudden.

The Growth of Competence: Issues of Conceptualization and Measurement

WANDA C. BRONSON

University of California

INTRODUCTION

STANDING BY THE side of a low table the 12-month-old girl bangs on a pegboard with a block she has been holding; at the far end of the table the lid of an improperly closed coffee pot produces a loud rattle. The little girl freezes; her eyes explore the table top. She hits the pegboard again, and the small movements of the lid attract her attention. She moves over, picks up the lid, and rattles it against the pot; then back to her pegboard and block. She bangs: the lid rattles. The little girl gurgles, a wide smile appears on her face. A glance at her mother—still with that enormous smile—and on with her banging and the pot's rattling, to an accompaniment of gurgles, babblings, and small bounces of delight.

The behaviour of this little girl—its nature, function, antecedents, and consequences—is the subject matter of the research I am about to undertake. I have no data to offer as yet; all I can share is the conceptual framework within which I propose to study the growth of competence in the second year of life.

THE CONSTRUCTS: EFFECTANCE AND AN ORIENTATION OF COMPETENCE

The little girl in my anecdote is self-directed; she is producing changes in her environment; she is delighted. She shares her delight with her mother, but her mother's response is neither the source of her pleasure nor the impetus for her behaviour. The motivational system directing her behaviour has been called "effectance" by White (1959). Retaining

269

the name for the time being, I want to delimit the construct, suggest its origins and examine some facets of the developmental route that links it with the achievement of an "orientation of competence" in later life. Orientation—a concept I have found useful in studying continuities in personality development (W. C. Bronson, 1968)—I take to mean a generalized, characteristic mode of approach and response to transactions with the environment. An orientation of competence, the end result of the processes with which I am now concerned, is evidenced in an individual's approach to his milieu and characterized by the expectation of being an effective doer, capable of actualizing his goals and of finding gratification in his own potency. Used in this sense, the term competence is purposely stripped of many of its common valuative connotations: a belief in one's capacity for self direction and the ability to seek pleasure in acts resulting in mastery or control over one's environment are the definitive characteristics of the orientation.

To start with the construct of effectance. I want to limit the term effectant behaviour to mean *behaviour which has as its goal the attainment of an effect upon the environment that is contingent upon the organism's own action*. The child engages in exploration, manipulation, locomotion. Since such activities are ideally suited to achieving the goal of effectant behaviour, they frequently—though not necessarily always—will be used in the service of effectance. However, many other activities can be effectant behaviour and the environmental field for action may be social as well as physical. Whatever the activity, it is only when the child's overall plan—that is, the hierarchical process which controls the sequence of operations he performs (Miller *et al.*, 1960)—contains as one of its controlling goals the achievement of some effect contingent upon his own actions that his behaviour should be properly called effectant. I make the point for more reasons than semantic fussiness. The distinction between exploratory behaviour and effectant behaviour is difficult to make operationally and so has often been blurred, to the detriment of understanding the nature and consequences of either. I follow Hunt (1965) in thinking of exploratory behaviour as resulting from an intrinsic motivation" inherent in data processing and action", and derived from the incongruity between the organism's level of adaptation and the input available to its receptors. But I submit that another and distinct characteristic, also intrinsic to the structure of the human organism, is to be motivated towards achieving effects that are contingent upon its own actions. It is true that the effect brought about by the organism will nearly always result in a change in the environment and thus produce new input; however, the continued repetition by the little girl in my anecdote of the contingent effect she had achieved—and her continued delight in it—suggest that her behaviour should not be understood in terms of Hunt's "intrinsic motivation" alone.

Lewis and Goldberg (1969) took the position that, if he has sufficient experience of consistent reinforcements with short latencies, the infant learns in the course of his interactions with the mother "a generalized expectancy that his behaviour has consequence in affecting his environment". I agree that the behaviour of the mother is an enormously significant factor but I see it as affecting rather than determining the development of her child's effectant behaviour. Some time ago I was privileged to read Mary Ainsworth's original observations of the home behaviour of a normal group of infants throughout the first year of life and of their subsequent performance in the "strange situation" at age 1 year. This material made it apparent that a few of the more insensitively mothered infants, that is, infants whose experience had lacked consistent, quick, and appropriate responses on the part of the mother, became very deeply engaged in controlling their environment during the laboratory observation. The behaviour of these infants suggested that an "escape" into effectant behaviour was required of them as a coping device, precisely *because* the mothering they had experienced was not geared to follow the sequence of their needs quickly enough. While we await collection of sufficient data to settle our differences I prefer to postulate that the impetus for achieving contingent effects is intrinsic to the structure of the human organism. Experience merely determines the degree to which this impetus is developed and the way in which it becomes integrated with other motivational systems.

In common with some others, I find no embarrassment in postulating characteristics that are inherent in the structure of the organism as long as these characteristics can be seen to be fundamentally adaptive for the species. In this instance, not to be intrinsically motivated to attain effects that are contingent upon one's own actions in a species whose members go out to meet life equipped with little but a neocortex and an opposable thumb would seem to be the height of maladaptiveness.

I find some welcome evidence for the position I espouse in Watson's (1967) work on what he calls "contingency awareness". In advancing the concept, Watson proposes that the infant arrives predirected to scan his memory of stimulus input and response output under "the guidance of a 'learning instruction' reading: 'Find and repeat the response which preceded the reception of the rewarding stimulus'." The infant is thus ready to become aware of effects that are contingent upon his own actions; however, if he is to make use of this potential, his experience must be properly timed. The pre-directed process of memory scanning (what Watson calls "contingency analysis") takes some time. If the response which preceded the rewarding stimulus recurs too soon— before this process is completed and the infant had the time to "find" the memory of the response-reward—the child cannot learn that a particular behaviour which he has emitted was responsible for the given effect. And since the infant's memory span is limited, too long a delay in the recurrence of the rewarding response will also be ineffective since now the child no longer has the relevant memory to be retrieved.

Watson's empirical results, obtained in two studies of learned visual fixations in infants 9–10 and 13–14 weeks old, fit beautifully the theoretical learning curve derived from this proposition. Of particular interest to me is the initial portion of this curve. Re-emission of the rewarding response within less than 3 seconds from the original response-reward event did not increase the probability of learning: the claim that some internal process must be completed before contingency learning can occur is shown to be tenable. The hypothesis that this process is some pre-direction which alerts the individual to experiences of contingent events and which is inherent in the structure of the human organism because of its high adaptive value is extremely congenial to my thinking.

From contingency awareness, through effectant behaviour, to an orientation of competence: that is the postulated chain of development whose one segment I propose to study. I focus my research on the child's experiences in the second year of life since I see it as particularly relevant in the developmental sequence that concerns me. It seems inevitable that the functional maturation of perceptual and motor skills at the beginning of this period should steeply increase the infant's capacity and impetus for self-direction. New mutual adaptations between the caretakers and one who is now more a doer than a passive recipient become mandatory. Interactional patterns centring on the direction and limits of control are evolved, expectations are established, and the child's image—the term used by Miller and associates (1960) for "all the accumulated, organized knowledge that the organism has about itself and its world"—expands to accumulate increasing information of the consequences of his effectant behaviour.

FOUR MOTIVATIONAL SYSTEMS

How are we to approach the study of the infant's experience in the second year of life and of its effects on the subsequent development of an orientation of competence?

Bowlby's control theory of attachment behaviour (1969) provided me with the model I want to use. I shall allude here only to what is most immediately relevant to my presentation. Bowlby is concerned with behavioural systems that mediate the child's attachment behaviour and that have as their "set-goal" the maintenance of a certain proximity to the mother. As long as that goal is maintained—as long as the infant remains within a radius of the mother that fulfils the requirements of his particular "setting"—on-going behaviour can be directed towards the satisfaction of other current needs. However, if the conditions change and the proximity requirements are no longer fulfilled, attachment behaviour is activated and maintained until the right psychological distance is once again regained.

Stimulated by this and by many other aspects of Bowlby's thought, I propose to view the 1-year-old's behaviour as always directed towards four goals: (1) to maintain a certain proximity to the mother; (2) to approach the novel; (3) to avoid the too unfamiliar; and (4) to attain effects that are contingent on his own actions. Whether curiosity, fear and effectance should be properly conceived as hierarchical patterns of behaviour systems that evolve in a similar fashion, and are characterized by a "set-goal" in the same sense as Bowlby uses the term in discussing attachment, I am by no means yet sure. There is certainly an immediate difficulty in fitting effectance into this scheme. The qualities of the object or classes of objects that serve to activate the goals of attachment, curiosity, and fear can be specified in some detail; the infant's behaviour can then be seen as a movement towards or away from these objects, the direction of movement varying as a function of such factors as the intensity, the proximity, and the coexistence of different objects in the same field. The qualities of objects that would serve to activate the goals of effectant behaviour are difficult to specify precisely at the present time; and it is a certain dynamic pattern of action–effect sequences, rather than the achievement of a given distance, that most clearly fulfils its requirements.

Despite these conceptual difficulties, I find a heuristic value in provisionally viewing the four systems as fundamentally alike. The framework I adopt postulates that the capacity for attachment, fear, curiosity, and effectance are intrinsic to the structure of the human organism: the research question is not how the organism comes to learn behaviour appropriate to these goals but how individual behaviours within the child's repertoire come to be organized into co-ordinated hierarchical behavioural systems and what experiential factors serve to enhance or interfere with their development. It also dictates that to study the development of effectant behaviour, and to determine its role in the growth of an orientation of competence, I must concern myself with attachment, curiosity, and fear as well. I say "must" advisedly since I consider the interplay among these four systems to be one of the critical factors to affect the development of each.

Descriptions of how some infants behave when left by the mother in a strange situation (Ainsworth and Wittig, 1969; Cox and Campbell, 1968)—how, in an attempt to regain proximity to the mother and avoid the too unfamiliar, their attachment and fear behaviours become activated to the near exclusion of effectant or exploratory behaviour— are a clear example of one aspect of such interplay. Most, perhaps all, events that occur within the infant's phenomenological field affect the balance he is maintaining among his four goals and thus, directly or indirectly, are of consequence for the development of each of the behavioural systems. For a different facet of this interplay, consider Watson's report (1969) that some 2-month-old infants respond to a mobile whose actions are under their direct control with the kind of smiling and greeting behaviour we have come to associate with attachment. Here the object instrumental in achieving satisfactions required by one of the systems appears to become the goal of another system. And for an example of still another type of the same interplay, this time between fear and effectant behaviour, note that working with somewhat older children Gilmore (1966) finds that anxiety can either increase, or decrease the child's preference for toys relevant to the source of his anxiety. At a certain level of intensity, fear will preclude the activation of effectant behaviour, but opportunity for the exercise of effectance may prevent it from rising to such disruptive levels.

We shall eventually have to systematize some of the rules of this interplay which is so critical to my research. Let me add one further point. It is obvious that the mother plays an important and very direct role in the development of each of the four behavioural systems I have examined. Since she is the normal object of the infant's attachment she necessarily plays a large part in determining the qualities of that system (Ainsworth, 1969); by timing her responses to her baby's signals the mother allows him opportunities for being effectant (Lewis and Goldberg, 1969); if a comfortable attachment has been developed, she fulfils the role of a "secure base" which acts to extend her infant's exploratory behaviour (Ainsworth and Wittig, 1969); her presence in the child's vicinity generally helps to allay his fear of the unfamiliar (G. W. Bronson, 1968).

Since I try to encompass an extended developmental span in my thinking, my concerns include some of the more indirect effects of maternal behaviour as well. Let me remind you of the little girl of my opening anecdote who was sharing her delight at her own effectance with her mother, and contrast this with the 1-year-olds observed by Mary Ainsworth who, I suggested, were "escaping" into effectant behaviour under the pressures of the "strange situation". I assume that all these infants will grow up into children who value effectant behaviour and who believe in their own effectance. But I also suggest that somewhat different conditions may come to activate or terminate their effectant behaviour, and that the qualities of the orientation of competence they eventually develop will differ. Whether the effectant behaviour is directed towards people or towards objects is one dimension of the distinction I am drawing; whether the orientation of competence becomes structured to include a regard for other people's plans or not is another. I see the behaviour of the mother as highly relevant to these differences, yet I wonder whether it may not have been her responses to the infant's attachment behaviour rather than to his effectant behaviour that lie at the heart of the matter.

Let me conclude by alluding briefly to only two of the problems which occur in the research strategy required by the position I have adopted. If the focus of study is on the interplay among four co-ordinated behavioural systems, the first and most obvious requirement is that behavioural assessments be structured so as to allow this interplay to occur. Breadth of observation as well as sampling across situations becomes mandatory, and the knotty issue of situational specificity versus generality of behaviour becomes an immediate concern. How do we handle the inevitable variability in infants' and mothers' behaviour? By selecting a particular situation—say feeding—*a priori* as the paradigm of interactions relevant to developments under study? By describing the individual's "average expected environment" across all daily situations, irrespective of their nature? By invoking state variables and treating them either as error or as meaningful independent variables? Secondly, the assumption of co-ordinated behavioural systems whose components remain interchangeable will remain no more than an assumption (and a potential source of confused and contradictory findings) unless the co-ordination within the system is described, its behavioural components specified, and the limits of their interchangeability defined. The problem may be tackled by severely limiting each system and allowing it to be represented by only a very few "pure" indices of that particular class of behaviours. If possible, such an approach would have the virtues of methodological elegance but would hardly do justice to the human ability to use identical means in somewhat different configurations to achieve a variety of different ends. Since each behavioural system is directed towards a certain goal there is the danger of falling into unsound analysis and classifying some particular behaviour on the basis of *post hoc ergo propter hoc*: in any given instance a particular behaviour is considered to have been directed towards that goal whose achievement was sufficient for its termination. To use the infant's plans as units for the description of his behaviour entails obvious empirical difficulties but is conceptually very attractive.

In the absence of data, problems of research strategy may lead to no more than programmatic statements of intent. Nevertheless, they must be considered seriously if we are to ensure that the methods of our inquiries are adequate to resolve the questions we pose.

REFERENCES

AINSWORTH, M. D. S. 1969. Object relations, dependency and attachment: a theoretical review of the infant–mother relationship. *Child Dev.* **40,** 969–1025.

AINSWORTH, M. D. S. and WITTIG, B. A. 1969. Attachment and exploratory behavior of 1-year-olds in a strange situation. In B. M. Foss (Ed.), *Determinants of infant behaviour IV.* Methuen, London: Wiley, New York.

BOWLBY, J. 1969. *Attachment and loss, Vol. 1. Attachment.* Hogarth Press, London; Basic Books, New York.

BRONSON, G. W. 1968. The development of fear in man and other animals. *Child Dev.* **39,** 409–431.

BRONSON, W. C. 1968. Stable patterns of behavior: the significance of enduring orientation for personality development. In J. P. Hill (Ed.), *Minnesota symposia on child psychology*, Vol. II. University of Minnesota Press, Minneapolis.

COX, F. N. and CAMPBELL, D. 1968. Young children in a new situation with and without their mothers. *Child Dev.* **39,** 123–131.

GILMORE, J. B. 1966. The role of anxiety and cognitive factors in children's play behavior. *Child Dev.* **37,** 397–416.

HUNT, J. McV. 1965. Intrinsic motivation and its role in psychological development. In David Levine (Ed.), *Nebraska symposium on motivation*, University of Nebraska Press, Lincoln. Pp. 189–282.

LEWIS, M. and GOLDBERG, S. 1969. Perceptual-cognitive development in infancy: a generalized expectancy model as a function of the mother–infant interaction. *Merrill-Palmer Q.* **15,** 81–100.

MILLER, G. A., GALANTER, E. and PRIBRAM, K. H. 1960. *Plans and the structure of behavior.* Holt, New York.

WATSON, J. S. 1969. "Infant attention to response-contingent stimuli". A paper delivered at the meeting of the Society for Research in Child Development, March 1969. Santa Monica, Calif.

WATSON, J. S. 1967. Memory and "contingency analysis" in infant learning. *Merrill-Palmer Q.* **13**, 55–76.
WHITE, R. W. 1959. Motivation reconsidered: the concept of competence. *Psychol Rev.* **66**, 297–333.

Discussion

Development of Effectance

KAGAN: There seem to be at least three different conditions for effectance, each emerging at a different time in development. Initially the child is trying to make sense of his environment by, for instance, turning to a stranger and examining him. Some time later the child acquires internal representations of events, and tries to match his behaviour to these internalized standards. The third basis for effectance behaviour is related to anxiety and the reduction of uncertainty. If one creates a situation that makes a child anxious a great many of the resulting activities, including autoerotic ones, can be regarded as ways of putting the system into harmony again. These are three dynamically different mechanisms for effectance, though I suspect that the observer will find it difficult to tell which one is mediating the behaviour.

W. BRONSON: What you are describing is a developmental progression in one type of condition which may serve to activate effectant behaviour. However, I think it is important to remember that incoherence or incongruity is not the only type of condition that activates such behaviour, and that recurrence of a contingent effect will be sought even in the absence of any extrinsic motivation, simply for the gratification inherent in achieving such an effect. It is the distinction between what serves to activate a system and what defines the system that is at issue here. As long as the observer is alert to this distinction he will maintain the definition of what constitutes effectant behaviour irrespective of circumstances, and focus on describing the configurations of conditions required to activate it. The generality of such conditions across individuals and their change over time should describe what kinds of developmental progressions do occur without confounding the meaning of the motivational system to which they apply.

Contingency Learning in Social Contexts

ROSENBLUM: The development of effectance is in some respects rather like the growth of learning sets, for in both cases one can see extrapolation from a series of discrete events to a more general set or motive. Being reared in a particular kind of social environment will therefore foster a particular kind of learning set about the impact of the individual's behaviour on the environment, and the learning will be of a general nature with respect to his effectiveness rather than referring to a series of specific outcomes. He learns, for example, that some of the things he can do have no impact on the environment; that other things he can do have certain perfectly predictable outcomes; and then he also learns that there is another class of behaviours that will sample from a specifiable group of events but will not tell him precisely which ohe of them he will get in return, and it is this third category that is most prevalent in normal social interaction. The animal raised in isolation may develop the first two contingent learning sets: if he is a caged animal, for example, he learns that there is nothing he can do to his steel box; on the other hand, he learns to produce 100 per cent predictable outcomes by, say, biting his arm. What he does not learn is the third class of outcome, i.e. if he does A it may result in B or C or D, but not in E or F or G. It seems to me that it is the development of these kinds of contingencies that are most critical to the development of social interaction. And it may well be that if an animal reared in isolation is given the opportunity to develop this kind of abstract learning set it will subsequently adapt socially quite readily and become a quite competent social individual.

G. BRONSON: It may become a competent social individual, but it might lack other characteristics that define our notion of attachment. Institutionalized infants could be exposed to mobiles which are partially under their control and in this way be given sufficient contingent experience; but that might give rise to a person who is oriented towards achieving competence with objects but who treats people as objects too.

ROSENBLUM: What is most important here is the acquisition during early development of the potential or capacity for ultimately achieving social competence. Unquestionably one would find important differences in foci of behaviour and in the specific behaviour elements initially utilized; nevertheless, I suggest that infants sufficiently experienced with these partially predictable contingent relationships between particular responses and their outcomes might well retain the capacity for relatively normal levels of social competence. Those infants whose early experience was devoid of such opportunities may well be those who become permanently deficient in this respect.

AINSWORTH: Provence and Lipton (1962. *Infants in Institutions.* International Universities Press, New York) have described how institutionalized infants, whose contingent experiences must have been minimal, did not play with toys even when they were available. This suggests that before a child can manipulate inanimate objects and gain some feeling of efficacy from the feedback he receives from his manipulations, he may first have to experience something as contingent upon his actions at a time when he is too immature to bring about this effect himself, and must therefore depend on others to give him such feedback or arrange that he receives it. One of the most fundamental things a mother can do to encourage a baby's effectiveness in relation to non-social objects is to set the stage for him to gain appropriate access to such objects. Once locomotion begins to develop, the amount of floor freedom permitted to a baby is a factor of significance in his development of competence. The children who develop great interest in the control of the physical environment seem, more than others, to have substantial opportunity to explore. The mother is important, in other words, because she monitors so much of the baby's experience, and so to a significant extent sets up his phenomenological world for him.

LEWIS: I agree that the mother—at least in the opening months—is an important, if not the most important, source of contingency behaviour and therefore of efficacy development. This is not only because of her continuous involvement with the child but because her involvement concerns the reduction of important needs as well as the production of pleasurable experiences. Thus although the child may independently reinforce itself (such as opening and closing its eyes in order to see and not see), these self-contingent experiences may not have the same impact as, for example, the mother's feeding the infant in response to his cry. The infant's self-contingent behaviour may not be as powerful or as frequent as the mother's contingent behaviour and will consequently be less effective in producing a generalized expectancy. It is thus the mother's contingent behaviour which is primary and upon which the infant's self-contingent actions will eventually rest.

W. BRONSON: The promptness and sensitivity of the mother's reactions will of course be an important source of relevant experience, but I am not convinced that the infant's experience with non-maternal contingencies is not of equal importance. Indeed, one may argue that it is easier for the infant to realize his effectance in interaction with simple elements of the inanimate environment than with the mother.

Individual Differences in Effectiveness

LEWIS: Some of our work has indicated that individual differences in infant competence, at least as reflected in exploratory and attentive behaviours, bear some relation to the nature of the mother's contingent behaviour. I wonder how you would account for such differences in the feeling of effectiveness?

W. BRONSON: Through experience, essentially. The readiness to be alert to experiences of contingency and to seek their recurrence is part of the inherent structure; but the extent to which this readiness continues to be maintained, and the form it eventually takes, depend on what opportunities and feedback are provided by the environment. An infant living in a totally chaotic milieu will have little opportunity to achieve an effect contingent upon his own actions, let alone to seek its recurrence. A toddler who is consistently punished for effectant behaviour, or whose gratification at his own effectance is consistently distorted as he is overwhelmed by rewards focused solely on the particular effect he has achieved, is unlikely to come to value effectiveness for its own sake. The point of suggesting that the attaining of contingent effects is a universal goal is not to deny the role of experience in determining how strongly this goal will be maintained or how its achievement will come to be sought. It is simply to assume an active seeking on the part of the infant for the relevant experience: the contingently responding mother fulfils and enhances the development of effectant goals but does not create them.

AMBROSE: If we are to employ these concepts to guide empirical work, operational definitions will be required. I wonder if you can make any suggestions in this respect.

W. BRONSON: It is not so very hard to differentiate behaviour which is merely repetitive from that which is goal-directed—at least within the second year of life, the age which I have observed most, although I admit I am far from having formalized the cues I use. There is a quality of focused attention and expectancy, expressed via posture, facial expression, visual orientation, and frequently vocalization, that is very characteristic of goal-directed behaviour. Often it is the temporal sequence of actions that indicates whether a particular behaviour is directed at attaining a specific effect, or whether it is accidental or automatic. Video-tape records of play-group behaviour which I am collecting in the course of my research should allow me eventually to pinpoint and describe these cues in a systematic fashion.

Mother–Infant Interaction: Characteristics and Dynamics

GENERAL DISCUSSION

Synchronization of Maternal and Infant Responses

ROSENBLUM: It is clear that the successful mother–infant relationship involves synchronization of the activities of both partners and that it is characterized by "smoothness". This term describes it with great aptness; I used it in my own work on monkeys, and it has also been used in some human studies, especially by Ainsworth. Can we define its meaning more precisely?

AINSWORTH: In the strange situation we found that an infant classified as having a smooth relationship, when placed on the floor, usually turns away from the mother immediately in order to explore and play; from time to time he will drift back on his own initiative to make brief contact with the mother. She, on her part, tends not to interfere with the play until the baby is seeking some sort of interaction with her. If, for instance, the baby attracts her attention from across the room to show a toy the mother at once responds. If the baby comes to her and seems to want to be picked up she picks him up; she does not, however, pick him up if that involves interrupting his play. So the shift from exploration to proximity seeking proceeds quite readily on the initiative of the baby, the mother being responsive to his initiative.

LAWICK-GOODALL: If the mother then makes a demand on the baby how does he respond?

AINSWORTH: We coded the mothers' verbal commands to see how the babies responded. There was considerable difference in the frequency of their commands, but there was no doubt that infants classified as having a smooth relationship heeded the mother's commands significantly more often than the other infants.

BOWLBY: So you might say that this was reciprocal: when the baby takes the initiative the mother responds, and when the mother takes the initiative the baby responds. From what you say, however, it seems that the mother does not often take the initiative.

AINSWORTH: Yes, and some of these mothers were really extraordinary in the extent to which they respected the baby's activities. And if they had to interrupt him for purposes of feeding or changing they would not just grab the baby—they would time their intervention carefully and then first talk to or play with him to get him into the right mood before going on to the next activity.

ROSENBLUM: A mutual pacing of activities is one of the ways by which smoothness comes about. Some of my data on monkeys indicate that much of an infant's behaviour is paced to the mother's behaviour, in the sense that when a mother is highly active it is likely that there is some eliciting of high activity on the part of the infant. If, in other words, the mother is running to and fro in a state of agitation one would not expect the infant to be sitting quietly in the corner. Or at times when the mother becomes quiescent, as when she is about to have a nap, it is likely that the infant will return to her and perhaps go to sleep also. I have some film shots of mothers who have been given an anaesthetic, and as the mother is about to go out there is the baby going out with her. Are any equivalent data on human infants available?

BRODY: There are clinical data which indicate that kind of synchrony between mother and baby from a very early age onwards. However, by no means all couples show it: one also finds a polar reaction, such as a hyperactive mother and an apathetic baby, or vice versa.

AINSWORTH: Louis Sander has some useful observations on this point. He hired nurses to room-in with newborn infants, and found that the baby's activity cycle was very quickly modified by the type of intervention he experienced from his particular nurse.

BRODY: It looks as though a baby is capable of responding very early on to tiny cues from the mother, and it is therefore desirable to try to specify these cues and the ways in which they affect babies at different ages. We might find, for example, that a mother who tends to move more rapidly than an infant can visually follow is not reinforcing visual following in the same way as a mother who moves at a speed at which the infant can remain in smooth visual contact with her. The former infant would be more likely to be discouraged from visual or social responsiveness.

ROSENBLUM: One way of investigating the interlocking of responses of mother and infant is experimentally to change the behaviour of one of the partners. I have some filmed observations of the responses of monkey mothers to babies that we had made drunk on sodium penta-thol, and these provide a most dramatic illustration of the fact that maternal behaviour is very much influenced by particular infant characteristics. One normally protective mother, for example, was presented with her drugged infant who was active but ataxic and disoriented. She not only failed to move towards it but actively avoided the infant each time it crawled or clumsily lurched and fell in her direction. We also carried out a study on mothers' responses to anaesthetized babies, and found that under these circumstances the mother tends to compensate fully for the fact that the baby cannot do anything on his own initiative. The mother therefore takes over, so that, for example, the relative distance between the members of the dyad is almost identical when the baby is unconscious as when it is moving about. When it is conscious it is primarily the infant who regulates the distance from the mother; after it has been given the anaesthetic the mother undertakes this function and it is she who now ensures that proximity is retained. One sees the same sort of thing when the baby dies. If it is a newborn, and particularly if it is a pigtail rather than a bonnet, it may be eaten. But if it is an older baby, one who is presumably differentially recognized, the mother will carry it about with her, protect it, and cherish it until it is so decomposed as to be lost.

LAWICK-GOODALL: Some of our observations on chimpanzees in the wild indicate the same sort of thing. We have had several deaths of babies, ranging in age from 1 month to $1\frac{1}{2}$ years. A primiparous mother continued to carry the body of her dead infant for about 3 days in the normal ventral position, remaining very close to it whenever she put it down—to groom or "feed"—and picking it up when she moved off again. On the other hand, multiparous mothers carried dead infants for a comparable time but no longer treated them as though they were babies. The bodies were placed rather carelessly over the shoulders during locomotion, and when the mothers sat down they often pushed the bodies into their groins or held them idly by a leg or arm. One particularly interesting case concerned a fairly old female whose 1-month-old infant got a paralytic disease—almost certainly human poliomyelitis. The baby became more and more helpless during his last few hours until, eventually, he was unable to move any of his limbs. Every time his mother moved the baby screamed. She was very solicitous, holding him carefully, cradling him every time he cried out, and also taking care to arrange his legs and arms so that they would not be squashed when she sat down. Then the infant either died or lost consciousness, and the sudden change in the mother's behaviour was fantastic. She simply got up, threw the body over her shoulder, and walked off. It was as though the sudden cessation of his crying was responsible for the change—for even before his death he had not been able to cling. The mother, it seemed, no longer recognized the baby as such and was no longer stimulated by it to act in a maternal manner.

Negative Aspects of the Mother–Infant Relationship

BOWLBY: The role of punishment and rejection in the relationship between mother and child is of considerable interest to those studying human development. I wonder if the comparative material can throw any light on this problem. It seems to me in particular that Rosenblum's description of the pigtail mothers' behaviour contained a strong element of aggression to the infant.

ROSENBLUM: The adjective I feel most appropriate to pigtail maternal behaviour is coercive. That is to say it is at each stage most intrusive on the infant's own propensities: early on, the mother prevents the infant from leaving when he wants to go, later she throws him out when he wants to stay. It is my own view, however, that punishment, at least in pigtail monkeys, enhances infant attachment and does not deter or destroy it. Far from immunizing the infant against loss of the mother the maternal rejective behaviour seems to make him all the more vulnerable. Every time she shakes him off, bites or punishes him, he just makes all the more strenuous efforts to get on her back again.

BOWLBY: Clinical observations also indicate that the more a child is rejected the more clinging he becomes. On the other hand there is probably a limit to this relationship, so that punitive behaviour beyond a certain level is no longer associated with attachment responses.

ROSENBLUM: It is probably also a matter of chronology. That is, rejection very early in life, prior to the establishment of real attachments, is likely to deter attachment. Similarly, rejection experienced after the attachment has begun to wane may encourage its dissolution. On the other hand, when the rejection occurs right in the middle of an intense attachment relationship it is most likely to enhance it. So we have a U-shaped relationship between punishment and attachment in terms of the chronology of the infant's development. However, it is worth emphasizing that, at least in monkeys, one rarely sees pure rejection—it is always mixed with positive responses. Pigtail mothers at their own feeding time will treat their infants in the most heartless fashion and be utterly undisturbed by their screams while they eat. Yet when the mother has finished she will come back to the baby, take it up, allow it to suckle, groom it, and so on. So there is no clear-cut pattern but rather an oscillating set of responses.

SCHAFFER: Aggression between mother and offspring is an interesting phenomenon, for in accounts of the developing relationship we tend to concentrate so much on the positive side by studying phenomena like care giving, affection, and proximity seeking that we overlook the part that negative responses such as aggression play. We have just mentioned maternal aggression; are there also statements that can be made about infants' aggressive behaviour towards the mother?

AINSWORTH: The situation where one most frequently sees this is on reunion after a separation. Even in the brief separation episodes which we studied as part of behaviour in a strange situation, aggression could be found. This was more evident with some children than with others and appeared to be a function of the previous interaction with the mother. Certainly in longer separations there is very apt to be an ambivalent response, in which rejection of mother by child is mixed up with contact seeking.

SCOTT: One explanation of such behaviour might be that the child considers the mother to be responsible for the distress he experienced. One of the universal conditions that brings about fighting among animals is a situation in which two individuals are in close proximity and one of them suffers, say, from being given electric shock. Under these circumstances it will attack the other animal—as though it was he who had hurt him. I am wondering if the child is similarly punishing the mother for having brought about his distress.

AINSWORTH: Whether this is the right interpretation I do not know. But some of the infants we observed certainly did attempt to hit the mother when she tried to pick them up after the separation episode, although they may have simultaneously been seeking to be picked up too.

ROSENBLUM: There appear to be species differences here, for neither in our own studies nor in those by Harlow and by Hinde has overt aggression by the infant ever been reported for monkeys' behaviour under these circumstances. However, one of the factors that might inhibit it is that by the time these separations took place social dominance had become an important factor in organizing infant behaviour. Mother is not only mother but also an adult female, and one does not readily threaten or attack an adult female. Thus she has characteristics which are, in a sense, ambivalent in what they elicit. Some years ago, when I was working on mother-surrogate reared infants, I did a study on "doll play" in order to find out why aggression was not directed towards the mother. I was working on rejecting mother-surrogates that administered air blasts to the infants. Despite this treatment the infants never showed any aggression to the mothers, and I wanted to see whether, given small replicas of the surrogates, the infants would redirect their aggressive drive to these. I did get many of the positive responses that are shown to real mother-surrogates, but I never saw any aggression displayed towards them.

BOWLBY: These findings show very clearly how different species may react in different ways to the same situation—for example, separation from the mother. This is further illustrated by the failure in non-human primate studies to find another response that is very commonly observed in human children after reunion, namely the pattern of non-recognition, unresponsiveness, or detachment vis-à-vis the mother. This can be seen briefly after quite a short period of separation, but may develop into an established pattern of reacting to the mother after more prolonged separations. It is a very curious phenomenon that, could we explain it, might throw fascinating light on the child's intrapsychic mechanisms. So far no one has been able to account for it; the fact that it seems to occur only in humans suggests, however, that considerable cognitive sophistication may be required for it.

Culturally Determined Differences in Early Behaviour

RICHARDS: Species differences are clearly important, but even when we confine ourselves to human beings we must be aware of the possibility of cultural differences in our data. I am sure, for instance, that if Ainsworth were to repeat her study in Cambridge, England, she would get a very different kind of distribution in her sample.

AINSWORTH: I did look at babies in Uganda, and there are differences. For example, my American infants were very used to the mother coming in and out of the room and, before floor-freedom was given to them, would watch her frequent disappearances from a play-pen. Most of the Ganda infants, on the other hand, were kept in more continuous proximity to the mother: if she went out of the room the baby was usually taken as well. And so disturbance when the mother disappears is very much less conspicuous in the American sample than it is among Ganda infants. I do not know how the African babies would have behaved in a strange situation, but my guess is that they would have been quite undone by it. They would have explored while the mother was present, but her departure would probably have completely stopped all play and subsequently they would have just clung.

ROSENBLUM: The important point here is not so much the numerical distribution and how this might show cultural variation, but whether the relationships among the different sets of variables referring to things like home conditions, rearing circumstances, and the test situation will still hold up in different samples. From this point of view the existence of cultural differences is a challenge to the generality of our hypotheses about such relationships, and it is with these that we should be primarily concerned rather than with the frequency with which particular groupings occur.

Author Index

Numbers in italics refer to pages where References are listed at the end of each article.

Subject Index

A

Adoption, 236 *et seq.*
  in chimpanzees, 121
  in monkeys, 99
Aggression, 284
  and male hormone, 71
  in monkeys, 87, 88, 285
Ambivalence,
  in infant's attitude to mother, 25 *et seq.*, 55
Anxiety, 113
  and fear, 113, 217, 220
  and social class, 179
Apathy, 163. *See also* Distress.
Approach, 18 *et seq.*
  and avoidance, 248, 250, 251
  and fear, 217, 220
  to novelty, 273
Arousal, 197
Attachment(s), 14, 18 *et seq.*, 234 *et seq.*, 273, 274, 277, 284
  and detachment, 48, 75, 77, 81–82
  and distress, 230, 231, 233
  and exploration, 18, 33–40, 51, 55, 245–246
  and learning theory, 236
  and separation in dog and man, 227–246
  and social class, 186
  determinants of, 146, 230–231
  conditioning of, 48
  in chimpanzees, 128
  in dogs, 145, 227–246
  in older individuals, 239–241
  intensity of, 50, 94, 154
  multiple, 139
  of home and nursery children, 150–151, 153–154, 157 *et seq.*, 161 *et seq.*

Attachment(s)–*continued*
  of polymatrically reared infants, 137–146
  specific, 141, 142
  substitute, 161–162, 246
  theory of, 230–231, 236
  variables of, 86–87
Attention, 266, 280
  manipulative, 250, 252
  maternal, 42, 44, 47
  visual, 250, 252
"Aunting", 86, 105, 106, 107
Avoidance, 19, 23, 46, 104, 249 *et seq.*, 264–265. *See also* Approach.
  and fear, 217, 220
  of the unfamiliar, 273

B

Behaviour
  and emotion, 233–234
  causal and functional analysis of, 132–133
  goal-directed, 280
  interpretation of, 129–132
  manipulative, 249 *et seq.*
  patterns of, 218–221
  protective,
    of monkey mothers, 91
  searching, 29–33, 50, 258
  visual, 249 *et seq.*
Berkeley Growth Study, 59 *et seq.*
Bird studies, 131, 213, 214, 230, 231, 234, 247

C

Caretakers. *See also* Mother, Maternal.
  attitudes of, 145, 146, 165–186